P9-CFU-461

HITLER'S SPY CHIEF

HITLER'S SPY CHIEF

Richard Bassett

PEGASUS BOOKS
NEW YORK

HITLER'S SPY CHIEF

Pegasus Books LLC
80 Broad Street, 5th Floor
New York, NY 10004

Copyright © 2011 by Richard Bassett

First Pegasus Books hardcover edition 2012

All rights reserved. No part of this book may be reproduced in whole or in part without written permission from the publisher, except by reviewers who may quote brief excerpts in connection with a review in a newspaper, magazine, or electronic publication; nor may any part of this book be reproduced, stored in a retrieval system, or transmitted in any form or by any means electronic, mechanical, photocopying, recording, or other, without written permission from the publisher.

ISBN: 978-1-60598-370-7

10 9 8 7 8 6 5 4 3 2 1

Printed in the United States of America
Distributed by W. W. Norton & Company, Inc.

IN MEMORY OF

Julian, Alan and Nicholas whose world this was.

AND FOR

Beatrice and Edmund whose world this may, with luck, never be.

Contents

Acknowledgements

Writing must be one of the most selfish of all creative pursuits. While the writer loses himself in the seductive labyrinth of mental creativity, his wife, children, friends and colleagues are subject to the company of someone who is in an unsatisfying state of near permanent self-absorption. I must therefore thank, first and foremost, my wife Emma-Louise, my children Edmund and Beatrice, my mother, parents-in-law and other relatives who have had to put up with the demands of 'the admiral'. I should also like to take this opportunity to thank my agent, Kate Hordern, without whose tireless encouragement none of this would have been possible.

The riddle of Admiral Canaris first impinged on my mind several years ago when, on leaving journalism, I had the privilege to work quite closely for a few years with the late Julian Amery, the late Alan Hare and the late Nicholas Elliot. For the benefit of their insights, kindness and camaraderie, I shall always be immensely grateful. In many ways the story of Canaris is also the story of the challenges and choices these men faced. In some cases, as this book shows, they played more than just walk-on parts. I am also grateful for the wisdom and kindness of the late Ihsan Bey Toptani, whose knowledge of Anglo-German wartime intelligence relations was profound.

This book would also never have been possible without the kindness

3

and support of many friends in many different countries. In Spain, I am indebted to the hospitality and company, among others, of Boojum, Peebles and Dorry Friesen in whose Mallorquin library I first chanced upon the story of the Abwehr. Also in Spain, I am grateful to members of the Spanish Diplomatic Service including Carmen Fontes and Alfonso La Palata. In Portugal, I have also enjoyed the help and hospitality of Anthony Allfrey and Frances Beveridge.

In Germany, the staff of the Institut für Zeitgeschichte in Munich, surely the most comprehensive archives on the Second World War in Europe, were unfailingly helpful. I am especially grateful to Mrs Grossman and Mr Bockner who, over many weeks, guided me through what seemed, at times, to be miles of microfilm. I have also been helped by Anton Graf Wengersky, Dr Nina Bushart, Dr Christine Pfeiffer, Fr. Christoph Martin, Frau Claudia Eiles, Karl-Christian Jacobi and my ever patient colleagues in the Koeniginstrasse. I should also like to thank my many friends in Kronberg, notably Andreas and Gabriela von Erdmann, and Donatus von Hessen in whose tower at the Friedrichshof part of this book was written. I should like also to extend my thanks to the staff of the German Military Archives at Freiburg in Breisgau, and to the Canaris family.

Also in Germany, I am especially grateful to Erich Vermehren, whose defection to the Allies had such dramatic consequences for the Abwehr and Admiral Canaris. His sharing of memories and thoughts with me has illuminated the extraordinary events of early 1943. In Berlin, I have been helped immensely by the kindness of Gabi and Daniel von Scheven. I am also particularly indebted to Diemut Köstlin who enabled me, after some days of fruitless research, finally to identify Canaris' house in Schlachtensee. I am also grateful to David Blow and Andrew Clegg Littler for consistent advice, especially on some details of the 1940 Finnish campaign.

In Italy, I am grateful to Luciana Frassati, perhaps the last person alive to have known Heydrich in Prague. I am also indebted to Tiziana

Frescobaldi, Francesca Galli, Wanda Gawronska, Fr Anthony Barrett S.J., Alessio Altichieri, Piero Kern and Paolo Rumiz. I should also like to record my thanks to the staff of the Vatican library and Don Vincenzo Paglia. In Trieste, I am grateful for the insights and kindness of the late Baron Gottfried von Banfield, who served with Canaris in Pola during the Great War.

In Salzburg, I have been helped by Elizabeth Waldedorf, Cornelia Meran, and above all, Reinhold Gayer of the Paracelsus Bookshop, which together with that oasis of civilisation, Gilbert's Bookshop in Düsseldorf, has been largely responsible for securing many of the German secondary sources for me. In Vienna, I am grateful to John Nicholson, Charlotte Szapary, and the late Georg Eisler. In Prague, I was helped by Marian and Lisa Schweda and Daniel and Victoria Spicka. In Warsaw, I am indebted to Igor Witkowski and his friends in Polish Military Intelligence. I am also grateful to Mikolaj Radziwill and Eva Dzeduszinska.

In London, I am indebted to the sterling efforts of my two researchers in Kew, El'vis Beytullayev and Beytulla Destani. Documents held at the Public Record Office are Crown copyright and are reproduced by permission of the controller of H.M.Stationery Office. In Chile, Crispin Sadler generously shared his archive of eyewitness accounts of the aftermath of the sinking of the *Dresden* after the Battle of the Falkland Islands.

I have also been helped by Inge Haag, one of Canaris' secretaries, Francesca Scoones, Andrew Gimson, Gina Thomas, Joachim von Halasz, Giles MacDonough and Desmond and Tina MacCarthy, whose library at Wiveton offered the calm necessary to prepare the early stages of this manuscript. Mary and Johnny James' Aldeburgh Bookshop was one incomparable source of elusive books, the London Library another. I am also grateful for the insights and company of the late Justin Crawford, whose interest and enthusiasm for obscure but important footnotes to twentieth-century history was always an inspiration.

I should also like to thank Mrs Ian Colvin, Neal Ascherson, David

Smiley, Jill Hare, Elizabeth Elliot, Penelope Tay, Leo Amery, Professor Norman Stone, Mark Almond, John Stevens, Katharina Kelton and Brendan Donnelly. I should like to record my thanks to the Imperial War Museum for allowing me access to the diaries of my wife's cousin, Captain Troubridge R.N., who was naval attaché in Berlin before the war. My former colleagues at Janes, notably Clifford Beale, Nic Cook and Chris Aaron, all helped significantly in different ways.

In Ridge, where much of this book was written, I must extend my thanks to my Wiltshire neighbours, notably Charles Elwell, Robin and Iona Carnegie, Daphne Lamb and Gordon Etherington Smith, the last surviving member of the senior staff of our embassy in pre-war Berlin. Clare and Julian Thomas, James and Sarah Rundell, Rosemary Macdonald, Joe Cant and Michael and Henrietta Dillon helped sustain the creative process.

In the United States, I should like to record my thanks to Cran Montgomery III and the late Ted Shackley, whose insights into historic trends in intelligence matters I was briefly privileged to share.

Finally, I should like to thank all those serving members of various intelligence services whom it would be invidious to name but who have offered, in that true spirit of fraternity which Canaris would have certainly recognised, support and direction for this modest enterprise.

Ridge 2004

Preface

The would-be biographer of Canaris could hardly choose a more difficult subject. Notwithstanding several excellent biographies on him, notably by André Brissaud and Heinz Hoehne, the mystery of the German admiral who somehow helped Britain win the war remains, even more than fifty years after his death. Despite the thousands of words devoted to the admiral after the war, the riddle of his links with Britain continue to cast shadows over almost every chapter of the war's history. It is therefore with some trepidation that I have attempted to shine my torch into the already much visited and, by now, quite Stygian cellars of the Abwehr.

The hazards of working with material related to secret operations are immense. Long-standing friendships with this or that member of a particular service are only a disadvantage, as events still covered by the Official Secrets Act and therefore subject to archival embargo obviously cannot be discussed. The consistency with which the most modest and oblique of enquiries have been met with a wall of dignified and amicable silence in certain quarters, usually quite voluble on other topics, is an impressive testament to the oaths of loyalty that servants of the Crown, distinguished and undistinguished, embrace. If there is one great lesson to be learnt by those who research the more obscure dealings of the British secret services during the war, it is that the officers of those services cannot, on the whole, be persuaded to break their vows. For those who believe that a country without an efficient and loyal intelligence force is automatically doomed, this is reassuring.

It is, however, always a pleasure to be able to talk to men who took part in what Lewis Namier called, albeit in a less capitalist age, the 'transactions' of contemporary history. Moreover, as he pointed out, a great many profound secrets are always somewhere in print and easily detected when one knows what to seek. Previous knowledge is a marvellous stimulant to cogent reasoning and astute deductions. However, the published literature is pitted with inaccuracies and false trails, and the unpublished archives are occasionally contradictory.

To illustrate this point, Namier recalled a story related by Sir Arthur Conan Doyle on how, when crossing Paris from the Gare de Lyon to the Gare du Nord on his way back from the Riviera, the taxi-driver acknowledged his generous tip with the words, 'Thank you, Sir Conan Doyle'. The author of the greatest detective stories of his time was astounded. 'How do you know who I am?', he asked, to which the driver replied, 'I saw in the papers that you were coming from Cannes by way of Marseilles and I see that your hair is cut in the Cannes style and that on your boots is the mud of Marseilles.'

'Is this all you recognise me by?', the bewildered writer asked.

'No,' came the reply, 'on your luggage is your name, printed in very large letters.'

There is much in print to help those wishing to focus on links between Canaris and his opposite number in the British secret service, Sir Stewart Menzies, and there can be no doubt that both men worked together for an understanding between Britain and Germany, with Churchill's tacit encouragement, which could, by 1943, have led to the war ending far sooner than it did.

As to whether Menzies and Canaris ever met, the reader must draw his own conclusions. The circumstantial evidence appears to be against Menzies' post-war and oft repeated mantra to journalists that the meeting never took place, though unsurprisingly, no documentation for such an encounter exists in the public domain.

The criteria for decisions taken by those in power are rarely easily understood, even when those decisions are taken in the full glare of modern democratic transparency. This is especially the case in time of war. However, it is not the purpose of this book – nor would it, in my view, be appropriate for those of my generation, however well informed – to pass judgement on those statesmen and servants of the Crown whose decisions vitally affected the duration of the Second World War. As Leo Amery once noted, it requires practical experience of great affairs to judge the conduct of public men fairly. In the intelligence world there is the added problem of facing confusing and different sets of choices, a situation which most people not in that world would have difficulty in understanding.

The story of Canaris illuminates in sharp relief the alternatives which faced those in power at the twentieth century's moment of supreme crisis. The reader must decide for himself whether the very tangible chances of ending the conflict two years earlier with the consequent saving of life, certainly many millions, can be weighed successfully against the durable balance of power hammered out by the victors in 1945, which kept the peace of the world for half a century – more or less – though at a high price for the countries of central and eastern Europe.

One of the consequences of Canaris' failure to achieve an understanding in 1943 is that the Germany that has emerged to take its place in the twenty-first century, after the total destruction of the twentieth, is without any shadow of a doubt a democratic, largely Christian country, committed to cooperation, consensus and values that are the exact opposite of those espoused by the Nazi regime. The Federal Republic, whatever its faults, has proved a stable and moderate cornerstone of peace in Europe for two generations.

Such a conversion may well have been possible without the near-annihilation of Germany that took place between 1943 and 1945. The desperate and often painful experiences of those families in post-war Germany who had been actively against the regime, and their often very difficult attempts at reintegration into post-war German society in the 1950s, suggest on the other hand that the virus of Nazism, with its powerful pagan hatreds, might have survived all but the most comprehensive of inoculation programmes.

The Germany that has entered the twenty-first century would have been recognisable to Canaris as a country more or less conforming to the Germany 'within the fold of Western civilisation', to quote Keynes, which he and his fellow conspirators strove for and which ultimately they and the little admiral died for.

Author's Note

This biography of Admiral Canaris, the first to appear in English for nearly thirty years, caused some controversy among those historians who reviewed it in England on its arrival early in 2005. I am grateful to them for focusing, mostly to the exclusion of anything else, on points which bore often little relation or relevance to the basic narrative.

Certainly, with only limited knowledge of German, it is difficult for those historians and critics to grasp perhaps the main themes of the German spy chief's career. I have found German sources often as enlightening as British ones which on the whole are rather dismissive of the German resistance and Canaris. Such are human affairs that even when they are most deserving of praise, they are often the subject of sinister interpretation by those who sit in judgement on the interior state of others.

More than fifty years after the end of the war, the enigma of Admiral Canaris, like that of the man with the dark lantern of the 'Powder Treason' or that other man of mystery in the iron mask, continues to baffle and perplex. The false but oft-repeated mantra that the German opposition could have removed Hitler whenever they wanted continues to cast a shadow over Canaris' integrity. One great advantage of generally accepted theory is that it is generally accepted. But repetition, however endless, does not make truth and, as has been pointed out in another context, where truth rests on evidence which is incomplete, it must be subject to challenge and revision even at the expense of national mythology.[5]

This story of Canaris does not illuminate some great unrevealed truth about the Second World War. Intuition and imagination suggest that is still to come. But there are shafts of lightness in between patches of obscurity. Whether, once the Moscow archives on the war are opened beyond 1941, there will be clarity, remains to be seen. In London, the archives subjected as they are to intense pruning on such delicate matters are of limited assistance and, as has been showed recently, capable of mischief. In America, where the papers are more complete, the recent changes in the intellectual climate there suggests access will become in time less generous than hitherto. The least that can be said is that this book is a reasonable interpretation of such evidence as survives. The most one could say is that it is more plausible than any other.

The present received wisdom is that Britain and Germany fought each other for six years without thought of compromise. Canaris' career reveals, perhaps all too clearly for some, that this thesis merits an alternative. There is another related widespread misunderstanding concerning the role of Pius XII whose actions highlighted here show not only how he personally intervened to save Rome's Jewish population but also how he saw his mission was to bring about that compromise peace which this book shows was far from unthinkable even in 1943. Only in this way could the factory slaughter of the innocents and the unique bestiality of the holocaust be brought to an end.

This book cannot attempt to give all the evidence, solve all the problems or comment on all the documents but it is offered tentatively as a spotlight on a career of one of the most fascinating figures of the twentieth century and one whose story has been far too long neglected by historians in this country.

Richard Bassett, London

---

[5] Francis Edwards, S.J., *The Real Story of the Gunpowder Plot*, London, 1969

Preface to the American Edition

A book which challenges some of the basic assumptions concerning the 1939-1945 war is clearly offering a hostage to fortune, and several reviewers differed with my assessment of Admiral Canaris.

It was therefore doubly pleasing to receive letters from those few survivors of the Abwehr and wartime Germany who recalled the Admiral in a more sympathetic light. Of those, some were living proof that the Admiral had risked his position and intervened directly to rescue people.

In a letter to me, Dr Stefan Heyden[1] remembered the Admiral visiting his father, who was the local vicar in Zehlendorf, the smart suburb of Berlin where the Admiral lived. The Admiral's fine uniform with its naval 'dirk' and black trimmed hat always impressed them. As Dr Heyden recalled:

> The Admiral was instrumental in rescuing my father on at least four occasions. The most notable of these was when he intervened after an incident relating to the horrendous *Kristallnacht*. My parents, listening on the radio and feeling shocked but helpless, told us what was happening and in a desperate show of solidarity took us to a Jewish paediatrician. Then, the following Sunday, my father gave this sermon:
>
> > What a terrible harbinger of events to come for our Germany, the land of the Reformation, that the synagogues of our fellow human beings should be ignited and burned down with deliberate criminal intent.

---

[1] 3 November 2008

At this moment our housekeeper noticed about five people getting up to leave the church. One of them denounced my father and he was summoned to the local police station the following day. Under intense questioning he bravely said they should ask Admiral Canaris, who was one of his parishioners, what he had said. They did go and ask the Admiral, who simply replied: 'The Reverend Hayden would never say such a thing,' upon which all charges were dropped.

Dr. Heyden further recalled:

During the early 1940s, thirteen Jewish men who had married non-Jewish women and had been living in our Zehlendorf community were deported to different camps. Fortunately, their wives knew their whereabouts and these they communicated to my father, who compiled a list and handed it to Admiral Canaris. All of them were released, thanks to the combined efforts of Canaris and his staff. My father told us that the Admiral succeeded in organising their transport in a closed train compartment to Madrid, where they came under Franco's protection. Canaris used his connections to put up the thirteen in private homes in Madrid before some of them were flown to England. Most of these men joined the British military.

A friend of the author Dorothee Fliess described a similar scenario with a life-saving train ride from Berlin to Basel in Switzerland around 29 September 1942:

Some fourteen passengers were under great threat, and one lady among them was awaiting deportation to a concentration camp. Two of those present were half-Jewish girls who were schoolfriends of the Admiral's daughter, Brigitte. In a complex operation the Admiral persuaded the Gestapo that the passengers were part of an important group of informers for Nazi Germany.[2]

Nor were these the only examples. 'Numerous Jews or half-Jews were dressed in army uniforms on Canaris' instigation, carrying official military intelligence ID cards,'[3] wrote another eyewitness.

My attention was also drawn to Operation Aquilar (described by Winifried Meyer in her book Unternehmen Sieben) in which 'after

---

[2] Dorothee Fliess: Geschichte einer Rettung, extract sent to author 14 April 2009
[3] Letter S.H., 3 November 2008

tedious negotiations, six train transports of Jews numbering about five hundred were taken via Belgium and Holland into Spain and Portugal'. These were to work as 'spies for Germany in Latin America.'

Most interesting of all was a message via a third party from some of the close friends of the last descendants of the Admiral: 'I think that almost no writer – including no German – has managed better to recognise Canaris and his work in the Abwehr and in the military resistance as you did.'[4]

For those who still believe Canaris was a 'shadowy figure', these eyewitness comments and the pages which follow should leave the reader in no doubt as to the Admiral's convictions once the battle was joined.

Richard Bassett, Hampshire

---

[4] Letter H.S., 18 September 2009

INTRODUCTION

Damned brave and ... damned unlucky.

SIR STEWART MENZIES ON CANARIS [1]

'Sergeant Soltikow!' The official barked out the command as the heavy iron doors of the dark cell in the vaults of the Gestapo headquarters were thrown open. The prisoner stood up with the alertness that only imminent physical danger invests. A bucket and brush were deposited on the floor with a loud clatter. A few steps ahead of the Gestapo man, a dishevelled white-haired figure in a grey suit shuffled into the room. A brief glance of recognition passed across Soltikow's countenance. He had worked very closely with this old man for four years, since 1940. Admiral Wilhelm Canaris was no longer a prestigious naval officer in command of Hitler's intelligence machine. It was hard to recognize him now.

'Sergeant Soltikow,' the command rang out, 'order your fellow prisoner to clean this place up.' With that the door slammed shut and both prisoners fell to their knees. [2]

The events of 20 July 1944 – Stauffenberg's failed assassination attempt against Hitler – had not directly implicated Canaris but had renewed suspicion towards the admiral, long perceived to be politically unreliable. Arrest and interrogation had followed. Now in the late summer of 1944, Canaris was granted a brief respite from the proceedings against him. Canaris, in any event, knew far too much to be allowed even the strictly controlled publicity of the People's Court. But the Gestapo were getting nowhere in pinning complicity with the July attack on the admiral. Perhaps the naval officer would betray himself in conversation with his old colleague, Count Soltikow. The two men had known each other for four years. Canaris had always considered Soltikow a 'born intelligence agent'. As the two prisoners talked, the three Gestapo microphones in the cell were activated.

Canaris was under no illusions as to what his fate would be. Even if Allied bombing would soon kill the hated People's Court Judge, Freisler, the machinery of Nazi 'justice' had the admiral well in its sights. 'We will end up on the gallows', had after all, as Soltikow well knew, been one of his favourite phrases throughout the war. But if he appeared a broken man, the admiral remained as alert as ever. As Soltikow talked, Canaris pointed discreetly to the walls and made a circular movement with his finger and thumb around his ear.

Two conversations ensued, one loud and stiff for the benefit of the eavesdroppers, the other *sotto voce* and intimate for the benefit of each other.

Soltikow was a cousin of the resistance lawyer Dohnanyi, a principal conspirator in the Abwehr ring around Hitler. Canaris had made him responsible for gathering intelligence from the neutral diplomats *en poste* at Berlin, a role which Soltikow had performed with tremendous élan. Much of this intelligence had been of significant value to the Abwehr in gauging, amongst other things, the progress of the Americans in their nuclear weapons programme. Soltikow was a confirmed anti-Nazi and had a long record in the files of the Gestapo. Perhaps for that reason alone Canaris was prepared to be expansive. In any event, after a long formal discourse as to how the Gestapo must be mistaken to imagine either of them could be connected with the bomb plot, he articulated thoughts which, even if some senior members of the Abwehr had been prepared to consider, they had never before openly ventilated. 'Imagine, Count Soltikow,' the admiral whispered, 'that the English contemplated breaking with the Russians and that Winston Churchill had said fight with us against the East, against the Bolsheviks. Imagine further that the first feelers in this direction came carefully via the Abwehr.'

'If Germany had ever wanted to make peace with England it would have needed an organisation which London would have trusted.' Only the Abwehr, under Canaris, could have acted as such an 'instrument', he continued, 'precisely because Churchill knew he had nothing to fear from me and that I would never betray such a proposal to the Russians'.[3] At that stage, the irony of such comments, as British bombs rained down on Berlin over their heads, was not lost on either Soltikow or Canaris, but the older man knew that in any event history would now run its course. In a few months the war would be over; Canaris, within the sound of approaching Allied artillery, would be hanged.

The passing of the twentieth century has made the events of the 1939-45 war no less fascinating. Every month sees the publication of books that try to cast new light on the grand strategy, dramatic campaigns and increasingly, if still somewhat tentatively, the experiences of the vanquished Germans.

Despite these developments the name of Admiral Wilhelm Canaris is still surprisingly unknown. Notwithstanding a steady stream of books about Hitler's chief of intelligence up to the 1970s, the significance of Canaris' contribution to the Allied cause has seemingly not impinged on the consciousness of a later generation of historians.

Meanwhile, the generation which was in contact with Canaris both on the British and German side has all but passed away, and the name is now so obscure that a recently published and otherwise excellent study of Churchill's relationship with the intelligence world mentions Canaris only twice, and then in the most fleeting of ways.[4]

Churchill himself might have approved of this development, as he was brilliantly adept at disguising intelligence and could at times even distance himself from any facts that might, even slightly, smudge the shining, seamless coat in which the story of our 'finest hour' was dressed. In private, however, there is ample evidence that he fully acknowledged the debt England owed Canaris and that the admiral was indeed at the centre of a possible peace deal between Germany and Britain, not only in 1940 but also in 1943.

Shortly after the war, Churchill received Count Soltikow at Chartwell.[5] The discussion ranged over many topics before coming to rest on Hitler's failure to invade England in 1940. Soltikow asked if Churchill ever could be sure that Hitler would not pursue 'Operation Sea Lion'. The statesman quietly got up, went to a bookshelf in the library and took down a copy of an early biography of Canaris. Referring to the Abwehr's significant and, from London's point of view, helpful over-estimate of the British divisions stationed in the Home Counties to repel the German invaders, Churchill left Soltikow with the impression that, as we shall see, Britain had benefited from Canaris' long-term pessimistic assessment of Nazi Germany's chances.

That Churchill might have been in touch with Canaris during the war is also underlined by his own chief of intelligence, 'C', Sir Stewart Menzies, who after the war admitted that the possibility of a meeting with his 'opposite number' had been discussed, though he would always say such a meeting had been 'blocked by the Foreign Office' for fear of offending the Russians.[6]

Menzies would have appreciated Canaris as they were both 'terrific anti-Bolsheviks'. The incomparable Soviet section of the Abwehr was the best informed intelligence department in the world on the activities of Soviet Russia. Several times, even when Britain and Russia were allied, as we shall see, Menzies would gratefully receive Abwehr intelligence on the Soviet forces and the Abwehr would receive appreciations of Churchill's political intelligence from SIS.[7] In one case, Menzies – sensationally –

even supplied the Abwehr, via Finnish signals intelligence, with the latest wireless intercept equipment to compile a list of the Soviet order of battle days ahead of the German invasion.

Soviet Russia was by no means the only sphere for cooperation between the two services. It was with some relief that the admiral's remark to General Franco's intelligence chief – ' You can tell General Franco that no German soldier will ever set foot in England' [8] – was received by 'C' at the height of British fears of a German invasion of England. According to accounts in the Institut für Zeitgeschichte in Munich, this message was intended for export to London. Moreover, as would also have become apparent in 1940, Canaris was keen to help prevent Spain becoming embroiled in an attack on Gibraltar, the key to the Mediterranean and a potential dagger pointed at England's imperial jugular. On Churchill's orders, 'C' had authorized no less than £13 million in gold bullion to be delivered to Franco and a group of his officers to 'persuade them of the sweets of neutrality'.[9] The go-between was Juan March, a Mallorquin banker and old contact of Canaris from long before the war.[10]

It was Canaris, however, who supplied General Franco with the key arguments he needed to outwit Hitler when the two men met at Hendaye, at the foot of the Pyrenees, for what Hitler thought would be a relatively straightforward negotiation on the merits of a joint Hispanic-German invasion of Gibraltar; after all, Germany had conquered most of Europe. But Hitler later famously described the event as comparable to having teeth pulled, so intractable and 'surprisingly well briefed'[11] was the *Caudillo* in his unwillingness to concede the Germans any right of passage over Spanish territory. Years later, Goering would tell Ivone Kirkpatrick that Germany's 'gravest mistake'[12] in the war had been Hitler's failure to seize Spain in 1940.

On New Year's Eve 1940, shortly after this event, Menzies had summoned the Abwehr double agent Dushko Popov, alias 'Tricycle', to his study in the country. 'I want to know much more about everyone who is intimately connected with Canaris,' he said as they drank brandy in the book-lined room in front of a crackling but 'miraculously steady' fire.[13]

Warming to his subject, 'C' continued: 'We know that Canaris, Dohnanyi and Oster are not dyed-in-the-wool Nazis. They are what might be termed loyal officers or patriotic Germans. In 1938 Churchill had a conversation with Canaris ... eventually I may want to resume the conversation Churchill initiated.' As if to underline the unconventional nature of this request, Menzies continued: 'I am handling this matter myself. All information you pick up is to come directly to me with no intermediary.' Popov, though a volatile Slav, clearly thought this encounter the climax of his career and was careful to get it right.

Such vignettes suggest that there was more than just the usual professional interest in acquiring whatever information was necessary in order to neutralize an enemy service and its leaders. Moreover, it begs the question as to how Churchill had been in contact with Canaris in the first place. In 1938, Churchill was still out of office, enjoying the coda of his wilderness years. It is not immediately apparent how he could have met even an intermediary of the head of German intelligence. Above all, the suggestion by Soltikow that London, at some later stage during the war, might have contemplated breaking with Moscow and allying herself with a non-Nazi Germany is also not easily explained, although it was nearly always at the forefront of Stalin's suspicious mind.[14]

It is perhaps not completely a coincidence that along with the late Professor Hugh Trevor-Roper, the second of the two SIS officers detailed to evaluate information from Canaris was Kim Philby, the KGB's man in SIS whose priority would have been not only to gather all sensitive material on Anglo-German peace-feelers but also to do his best to derail them.

Both men played down the significance of the intelligence they received and Trevor-Roper appears to have found the Abwehr curiously disappointing. He was seemingly far more impressed by the violence and terrorism of Schellenberg's SS organisation. In an article published in the *Cornhill Magazine*,[15] shortly after the war, Trevor-Roper attempted a less than generous critique of Canaris and the Abwehr. He described the former as a 'Catholic mystic', (a phrase skilfully chosen to appeal to two fashionable prejudices of the British establishment) and accused the latter of being little more than a 'pretty incompetent outfit', even though by 1941 the Germans had penetrated so many British and American ciphers that Goebbels could record in his confidential diary: 'If the British know in detail about us everything we know about them it will have grave consequences.'[16]

Moreover, as is now widely archived, Philby regarded his crowning achievement as the disruption of attempts at a rapprochement between Germany and Britain through the Abwehr: a disruption which culminated in the defection of the relatively junior, but not insignificant, Erich Vermehren from the Abwehr's Istanbul station. Philby, though an unreliable source to be treated with extreme reserve, later noted in 1988, shortly before his death: 'I had a personal interest in this work. I was directly responsible for the deaths of a considerable number of Germans.'[17] After the Vermehrens had been spirited away to safety in London they had been billeted in Philby's mother's flat. Charmed as many were by Philby's charismatic intellect, the Vermehrens gave Philby a list of all their contacts in the Catholic underground in Germany, and the role they could play in a post-war democratic and Christian Germany. When Allied officers tried to link up with them at the end of the war, it was found that they all had been deported or liquidated.

Vermehren's defection with his wife, Countess Plettenberg, had other more immediate effects. It was ruthlessly exploited by Himmler to provoke Hitler into closing the Abwehr down and retiring Canaris.[18] At a stroke, the 'instrument' described by Canaris to Soltikow was at an end.

Yet if Philby and others worked hard to undermine Canaris from the British side, there is also some evidence to suggest that earlier, when Canaris was in danger of being outmanoeuvred by his rivals in the snakepit of competing intelligence agencies that characterized the Third Reich, others in England were prepared to resort to drastic measures to protect his authority. To this day the assassination of Reinhard Heydrich, head of the RHSA – Canaris' deadliest rival in the intelligence world of Nazi Germany – on the outskirts of Prague in May 1942, barely days after he had more or less bullied Canaris into surrendering some of the Abwehr's authority, is a mystery. Bitterly opposed, as we shall see, by the Czech underground both in Prague and London, the assassination was carried out in February 1942 by SOE agents acting with the knowledge and support of 'C', despite the sure conviction that reprisals would be brutal. Indeed they were: the village of Lidice was razed to the ground and the entire adult male population executed.

Yet 'C', by liquidating Heydrich, had preserved Canaris' pre-eminence in the German intelligence world for a few more months to come. Long enough, it would seem, for renewed peace-feelers to have been advanced in the early months of the following year.[19] These feelers took many forms, but there can be little doubt that beneath the surface a great deal of clandestine diplomatic and intelligence activity was being directed to this end. In some cases they were often quite public. As the later executed diplomat von Hassell would note in his diaries in March 1943: 'Yesterday, an outright offer was made to England to join with Germany in guaranteeing the freedom and security of the "West".'[20]

The story of Canaris, therefore, deserves a wider audience. His organisation and officers were not only part of the machinery of war, they were at the centre of clandestine wartime Anglo-German relations and the many attempts between what Hitler's interpreter, Paul Schmidt, called men of *'bon volonté* [good intentions]'[21] to reach an understanding against the background of increasing violence and the dynamics of global conflict.

At the same time the organisation was legitimately and, until well into the war, successfully waging the intelligence war against the Allies: sowing considerable disinformation and confusion among the British, especially in the run-up to the attack on France, but most devastatingly against Moscow in the run-up to Barbarossa. Hitler would gleefully recount that his attack on Russia in 1941 was so effective in its initial phases partly because the High Command knew every detail of the entire order of battle of the Soviet forces by the day Barbarossa was launched. This was entirely due to the Abwehr.

If this were not enough, the Abwehr also took on the role of protecting anti-Nazi conspirators and, as an organisation which was, uniquely, exempt from the crude restraint of the Aryanisation laws of the Third Reich, saved many Jews. Moreover, as will be seen, Canaris also intervened to save many others from the SS execution squads following the front line, and elsewhere.

However, the temptation to beatify the admiral must be resisted. He was, in his own way, a ruthless exponent of all the techniques of deception, disinformation and other patterns of subterfuge without which no successful secret intelligence agency can exist. He was also for far too long a 'believer'. It took Canaris slightly longer than many others to see the Nazis for what they really were. But once he became convinced that they were leading his country to ruin, both physical and moral, he never wavered from a policy of systematically undermining the regime from within, and seeking an understanding with the West. To do this, he inevitably pursued a course of engagement with Hitler, believing that his influence and power could only be sustained by the avoidance of open conflict with his Nazi masters.

Only a man of formidable courage and nerve could have played such a hand in the face of so many dangers and so many disappointments. Unlike his opposite number, 'C', on whom opinion is more or less consistent, Canaris is unsurprisingly a more controversial figure with a fair share of detractors as well as devotees. Even those who knew him well were cautious in their assessments of him. Like every competent spy chief he was quick to read other personalities, while being slow in revealing his own. That he was a born leader is beyond doubt, as the organisation he assembled in the Abwehr was both effective by its own standards and even until the very end a hundred per cent loyal to the values he had instilled into it. Unlike other services both in and outside of Germany, political assassination was not tolerated in the Abwehr.

Whether Canaris was the deeply spiritual officer of almost pathological sensitivity, as some maintain, is less clear, but of one thing we can be sure: he was, to the tips of his fingers, the embodiment of the old naval intelligence tradition, a tradition where intellect, discipline, strong ethics and a knowledge of the world were inseparable.

As General Reinhard Gehlen, a former German intelligence officer who later created the German Federal intelligence service, noted, Canaris had that rare gift among intelligence officers of following historical trends and projecting them into the future:

> Blessed with broad intellectual interests far in excess of those normally expected in senior officers, he was endowed with traits not seen in officers since the first half of the nineteenth century - traits which had led officers like Roon, von der Goltz, Yorck von Wartenburg as well as Clausewitz and Moltke, to spectacular achievements in knowledge other than the purely military ... Canaris knew how to think in global terms: this was how he was often able to predict the future course of world affairs with uncanny accuracy. [22]

Nothing could have been more distant from the world of the Prussian generals, with their monocles and boots and their relatively limited horizons, restricted to the battlefields of Europe.

For Canaris, like every naval officer of his generation irrespective of his country, the navy was the supreme calling of armed service. Only the navy offered its officers the greatest of martial challenges against the backdrop of the ever physical threat of the elements.[23] He himself was a veteran of two out of the three major naval engagements of the 1914–18 war.

It is therefore impossible to understand Canaris without exploring his naval career, and in this respect he is akin to that legendary chief of naval intelligence in the First World War, Admiral 'Blinker' Hall, whom Canaris admired and almost certainly met, albeit briefly, as a naval cadet at Kiel in 1908.[24] Both men enjoyed fierce loyalty from their subordinates. Both men built their departments more or less from scratch and both men displayed a subtlety in their game not usually encountered among more straightforward military officers.

For the young Canaris, as for all naval officers of the world, the Royal Navy, undefeated in its five-hundred-year history, was the textbook model, setting the tone for behaviour, dress and of course aggressive engagement. As one English expert on the German navy wrote before the war: 'As is only right and proper we in this country have set the fashion for naval service for the rest of the world and Germany like everyone else has followed our lead.' [25]

Such a service was never for the faint-hearted. 'The purest test of any officer's courage, skill and discipline',[26] naval service presented to an officer the greatest challenge and the greatest rewards, uncomplicated by the civilian casualties of military campaigns.

Unsurprisingly, it would be the Royal Navy before any other organ of the British state which would first register Canaris' intelligence skills. Moreover, no less a person than Winston Churchill would be the recipient of the first reports.

CHAPTER ONE

A NAVAL TRADITION

I wish to record my admiration of the very gallant and
determined manner in which the Imperial German
Navy fought. The courage and discipline of officers and
men who put up such a good fight is unquestionable.
CAPTAIN J.D. ALLEN, HMS *KENT* , REPORT ON THE
BATTLE OF THE FALKLAND ISLANDS 1914[1]

The guns of the British cruiser opened fire. With the cool, almost non-chalant, delivery of a battle-hardened veteran, the fire control officer gave the range and watched for the fall of shot as the grey projectiles hurtled through the air towards their prey.

The German ship, lying icily calm in the sharp cold light, showed no sign of movement. Its profile cast a shadow on the rocks of the Chilean inlet that had afforded a welcome, if temporary, refuge from the vengeful determination of the most powerful navy in the world.

On the morning of 14 March 1915, the captain of HMS *Glasgow* could be forgiven for allowing himself a grim smile. As the precipitous bleak cliffs of Más-a-Tierra came into view, Captain Luce could make out the four funnels of the German light cruiser *Dresden* which he and many others had wasted months searching for, since the Battle of the Falkland Islands the previous December had sealed the fate of the rest of the German battle squadron in the South Atlantic.

As *Glasgow*'s fire straddled the *Dresden*, the fact that the ship was in neutral Chilean waters offered no refuge; such legal niceties could, in Luce's memorable phrase, be 'left to the diplomats'. Here was, if not the closing of an important chapter in British naval history, at least a very long overdue removal of an irksome footnote.

And yet here, half a world away from the life-and-death struggle between Germany's and England's armies, this footnote had inflamed the tempers of politicians and admirals, including Winston Churchill. This drama, involving as it did a disproportionate amount of senior naval officer and political time, had, like a large stone cast into a calm pond, ripple effects that went far beyond events in the South Atlantic.

The *Dresden* had eluded the Royal Navy thanks to the brilliance of its intelligence officer. It was he who outfoxed his ship's pursuers and it was he who would, that crisp March day, deprive Luce of his prize. Lieutenant Wilhelm Canaris, later head of Hitler's intelligence organisation, young and fair-haired but otherwise untypically German, was about to make his debut as a formidable opponent of British interests.

But to understand how such a seemingly insignificant event could be invested with such resonant echoes, it is important to delve a little more deeply into Canaris' background and the tradition that nurtured him – the Imperial German navy – and above all that force's duel with the Royal Navy in the South Atlantic.

It is one of the great ironies of the beginning of the twentieth century that the Anglo-German naval race, so often correctly described as one of the celebrated 'causes' of the First World War, actually contributed, at one level, to a tremendous mutual esteem between the two countries.

Notwithstanding the huge difference in traditions, pitting one service with five hundred years of virtually unbroken victory against a parvenu arm of barely a generation, the formal relationship between veteran and upstart was always cordial and respectful.

Nevertheless, elements of both sides saw a showdown as inevitable, especially after 1903 when plans drawn up in secret for the German navy to bombard Manhattan and land forces in New York failed to tempt London into any close alliance.* London chose to develop ties with Russia and France and to encircle Germany, preferring to deal with the nearer threat to her imperial interests. As an American officer remarked to a Royal Naval officer at the time: 'Make no mistake, we shall be fighting Germany in the next war.'[2] But even those officers who were convinced that the next war would be between England and Germany found themselves united by the brotherhood of the sea and naval tradition. The Royal Navy set the *ton* for all navies of the world but especially for a service as ambitious as the new Imperial German navy.

A certain chivalry was an essential feature of the relationship and was never far from the surface, even when both navies fought each other as determined opponents from the first weeks of the war.

The opening sequence of events saw the tremendous engagements of the Coronel and the Falklands Islands: the first a devastating blow to the Royal Navy's pride, the second, a swift and decisive revenge. At the Coronel, a German squadron had destroyed a British force under Admiral Cradock in a humiliating action, all the more painful for it being so unexpected. At the Falklands, six weeks later, the Royal Navy pursued her revenge, sinking all but one of the German ships.

Both battles were, however, punctuated by fulsome respect on the part of both sides for their opponents' courage. These were, after all, old style engagements between worthy foes where gunfire and seamanship, unaided by aircraft, unencumbered by civilians, counted for everything in waters still free at that stage from mines and submarines. In these battles, effective gunnery killed hundreds in seconds. Broadsides fired at close range played havoc among crowded groups of men as they were mown down in heaps

---

*These plans, recently published in Germany (see F.A.Z. Archive), cast some light on the growing awareness of potential rivalry between Europe and the United States at the start of the twentieth century.

by shell splinters. Those who might have contemplated jumping overboard knew the water would numb them in seconds. Only the strongest mixture imaginable of courage, discipline and skill could enable such embattled humanity to fight on. Yet time and again the officers and men of a navy that had barely existed thirty years earlier showed that they were as capable of 'fighting and dying like Englishmen' as their opponents.

The reports of the engagement by British officers repeatedly testify to the courage of the enemy, while the Germans were no less chivalrous in their turn.

Thus, after Graf von Spee's squadron had destroyed Admiral Cradock's cruiser squadron at the Coronel, with the deaths of several hundred sailors including Cradock himself, a German consul who proposed a toast to 'the damnation of the British Navy' found himself suddenly frozen by the glare of his German naval guests.

Von Spee's response cut the cheerful victory celebration atmosphere with the skill of the surgeon's knife. 'I drink', he said, 'to the memory of a gallant and honourable foe.' [3] Von Spee had known Cradock well before the war and both men enjoyed each other's company.[4] Coincidentally, both men had premonitions of their deaths: Cradock, talking to the Governor at the Falklands, Von Spee* accepting a bouquet at Valparaiso. It should not be forgotten that both navies had cooperated on a number of occasions in the run-up to 1914, especially in South American waters when gunboats and showing the flag were an essential part of the old powers' economic and political influence in the new world. As Commander Pochhammer, the senior surviving German officer after the Falklands battle, wrote to Admiral Sturdee: 'We regret, as you do, the course of the war, as we have personally learned to know well during peacetime the English navy and her officers.'[5]

Sturdee replied to Pochhammer : 'We so much admire the good

---

*In von Spee's case he went down with his two sons, both serving naval officers.

gunnery of your ships. Unfortunately the two countries are at war; the officers of both navies who can count friends in the other navy, have to carry out their country's duties which your Admiral, Captain and officers worthily maintained to the end.' [6]

In his official report, which was censored, as the face of the foe in wartime must show no humanity, Sturdee went even further: referring to the battered and blazing *Gneisenau* which though under a hail of fire from three ships on different bearings continued firing with what armament was still in action, even scoring a last hit on Sturdee's flagship *Invincible* as Sturdee gave orders to his ships to cease fire. He wrote: 'They fought magnificently and their discipline must have been superb ... we were all good friends after the fight and both agreed we did not want to fight at all but had to.' [7]

These remarks alone testify to an intimacy and mutual admiration between German and British naval officers that transcended the variables of conflict and underline the strength of an already well-established relationship which had no counterpart at a military level between the two countries.

From the carnage of the Falkland Islands, one German ship, however, had made its escape: the cruiser *Dresden*, pursued doggedly but ineffectively by HMS *Glasgow*. Aided by darkness, mist and above all speed, this light cruiser managed by her survival to just take a bit of the icing off Admiral Sturdee's victory. For the next four months the *Dresden* was to become the focus of tremendous Royal Naval activity. It was to be many weeks before the full victory of the Falkland Islands could be enjoyed by any of its protagonists, whose mutual jealousies the *Dresden* seemed destined to exacerbate at every turn.

The chase that followed saw rather less generous exchanges of views between the Admiralty and Sturdee than those reserved for a gallant enemy. Rarely had such a search resulted in such a fraying of tempers at all levels of the Admiralty executive.

Captain Luce, commanding HMS *Glasgow*, had correctly noted that only the 'swiftest of actions could wipe the stain of dishonour from the Royal Navy's record' which the Coronel had inflicted. But there was more to it than that. Cradock's orders from the Admiralty, whose First Lord was Winston Churchill, had been so ineptly worded that the defeat of his inferior force by Admiral Graf von Spee was as much the result of a breakdown in Royal Naval staff machinery as superior German gunnery.

Churchill, who as First Lord left little conduct of naval operations to the First Sea Lord, is to this day largely held to blame.* The naval staff set up by him and Battenberg in 1913 had broken down miserably in the opening weeks of the campaign. Cradock was so ambivalently instructed that he felt compelled to give action even though his forces were unequal to achieving any decisive success. The subsequent victory at the Falkland Islands, six weeks later, only partly washed away the memory of this disastrous miscalculation.

Churchill's reputation had suffered. At an only slightly less exalted level, Admiral 'Jackie' Fisher, First Sea Lord, was also under tremendous pressure. The successful action of the Falklands did little to ease this. The sudden glory of his rival, Vice Admiral Sturdee, and his brilliant seamanship at the Falklands, threw Fisher's earlier staff ineptitude into sharp relief.

The escape of the *Dresden* from the Falklands engagement was thus a thorny issue. For Churchill, as long as the *Dresden* survived there was an ugly reminder of the defeat at the Coronel and an untidy blemish on the victory of the Falklands. For Fisher these considerations were mixed however with a degree of vindictive *schadenfreude* towards Sturdee, whose failure to find the *Dresden* could be used untiringly to detract from his earlier success. As long as Fisher could play up Sturdee's lack of success in finding the *Dresden*, the greater the chance that his own earlier technical shortcomings would not be explored in further detail.

As a result, an unusual amount of traffic, much of it heated, was

*This is, at least, the leading authority Bennett's conclusion.

generated by the failure – for more than three months – of the Royal Navy to track down the *Dresden*. Thus Fisher could signal Jellicoe, commander of the main battle fleet, of Sturdee: 'His criminal ineptitude in not sending a vessel to Punta Arenas has disastrously kept from you light cruisers now hunting the Dresden.'

This tone was reinforced in Fisher's signals to Sturdee, which kept up a veritable barrage of complaints about the failure to find the *Dresden*. Yet Sturdee gave as good as he got. Long explanations of his movements, justifying his failure to find the quarry, were signalled to the Admiralty, culminating in a memorably impertinent signal from a subordinate to a superior officer which even the usual terseness of encrypted correspondence failed to disguise:

'I submit,' signalled Sturdee, 'my being called upon in three separate telegrams to give reasons for my subsequent action is unexpected.'

Fisher responded with equal brevity: 'The last paragraph of your signal is improper and such observations must not be repeated.' Nor did Sturdee's difficulties with Fisher end with his re-posting to England. On his return to London, Fisher kept him waiting for two hours and then saw the 'hero of the Falklands' for a mere five minutes, during which he made no mention of the battle but dwelt only on the failure to catch the *Dresden*. Upon hearing later that day that Sturdee had been invited to Buckingham Palace by the King to give an account of the battle, Fisher promptly ordered Sturdee to depart for Scapa Flow immediately with the clear intention of preventing the audience. Regrettably of such bitter and ungenerous rivalries are great sea lords sometimes made.

Whether Captain Luce on the *Glasgow* was aware of this unedifying exchange is not known. He had his own reasons for settling scores with the *Dresden*. At the Coronel, Luce had had to flee from von Spee and during the subsequent Falklands battle, he had been detailed to pursue the *Dresden* when she broke off the engagement, but had lost her. He had thus been involved in every part of the humiliating saga.

It had been this failure which had tied up ships desperately needed elsewhere, because the *Dresden*, through a series of brilliant deceptions and counter deceptions, had always managed to outwit the Royal Navy. As Fisher acidly noted: 'If the *Dresden* gets to the Bay of Bengal, we shall owe a lot to Sturdee.'

In a sequence of dazzling false trails, the intelligence officer of the *Dresden* had not only refuelled and resupplied his ship, he had drawn off significant enemy forces, including HMS *Inflexible*, *Glasgow* and *Bristol*, all needed by the Grand Fleet in the North Sea. Moreover, he had bamboozled Royal Naval intelligence officers throughout Latin America and led a clutch of British agents, informers and consular officers a merry paper dance which had only served to highlight the shortcomings of naval intelligence as conducted by the Admiralty in London and its ships in the South Atlantic.

The intelligence officer on the *Dresden* responsible for this, from the Royal Navy's point of view, increasingly humiliating game of hide and seek, was barely into his twenties. Lieutenant Canaris was gifted linguistically – fluent in six languages – and comfortable in the ways of Spanish America, where he had served in the years before 1914 on the completion of his training as a cadet at Kiel in 1911.

Bribing local officials one day, sending false signals the next, Canaris was already making his first, admittedly cameo, but irritating appearance in the sights of the Royal Navy even before Luce's HMS *Glasgow* found the long sought-after silhouette of the *Dresden* that chilly March day in Cumberland Bay. Canaris' feints and counter-feints had already left a score of misleading and inaccurate signals referring to the movements of the *Dresden*.

Following the defeat at the Falklands, Berlin had suggested the *Dresden* try to return to Europe via the Atlantic, an option which her captain,

Lüdecke, understandably saw as tantamount to suicide. Briefed by Canaris, however, Captain Lüdecke decided instead to put a different plan into action, which involved setting course in a northerly direction 200 miles off the Chilean coast. The *Dresden* would intercept what enemy merchant-men she could before finding refuge in the neutral waters of Chile.

Canaris' immediate need was coal, but the German supply ships would not answer his signals. By 12 December the light cruiser had reached Punta Arenas. Here Canaris was able to persuade the local authorities to allow her to remain for as long as it took to fill her empty bunkers. By a happy chance, the signal of the Chilean government which, under British pressure, denied the *Dresden* the right of coaling at all did not reach the authorities at Punta Arenas until the following day; not the last stroke of luck to assist Canaris.*

In any event, Canaris was not keen to stay any longer than absolutely necessary. He knew that the ship's presence would be reported by the British consul, Captain Milward, and indeed it was: no fewer than five warships were sent to trap her.

As soon as the Admiralty learnt of Lüdecke's escape from Punta Arenas, Sturdee was signalled to 'Press your chase' and, should Sturdee have entertained any other alternatives to finding and sinking the *Dresden*, the signal noted that the 'Object is destruction not internment.'

But while the Royal Navy searched up and down the waters off Patagonia, the *Dresden* sought refuge in the lonely Hewett Bay and then the even more remote Christmas Bay. In Punta Arenas the intrepid Milward received news of the German ship's presence but his signal was discounted by both the Admiralty and Stoddart, who had taken over from Sturdee on the latter's return to England. In both cases Canaris had, by planting false information on local British agents, 'persuaded' his pursuers that he was somewhere else.

*Banfield notes that the signal did arrive in time, but was not distributed until after the ship had departed, a result of some financial *douceur* administered by Canaris from the *Dresden*'s treasury.

On 14 February the pursuit calmed down for the *Dresden* as she encountered a violent snowstorm, but by 19 February she was able to carry on cruiser warfare and sink the *Conway Castle* and its cargo of 2,400 tons of barley destined for Australia, predictably provoking another harsh encrypted reprimand for Stoddart from Fisher.

By this time there had been many reported sightings of the *Dresden*, including one by HMS *Kent*. But once again she slipped the net, causing yet another senior naval officer, this time the captain of the *Kent*, J. D. Allen, considerable anger and frustration. A few days later, after receiving news of his C.B. for his part in the Falklands Battle, Allen would write: 'I felt no pleasure, as our failure to catch the *Dresden* was too recent. I should rather have sunk her than have every honour there is.' [8]

But by now Stoddart was a baffled, if not to say harassed, man. Conscious of the importance London attached to his achieving the *Dresden*'s destruction, and no less aware of the difficulties which the failure to do so had inflicted on his predecessor's relations with the Admiralty, he determined to take up the intelligence chase personally. Meeting with Milward, he received a persuasive report that the *Dresden* was still in the area. Unfortunately, the Admiralty was getting reports, carefully spread by Canaris via Patagonia, that the ship was in the Vast Hope Inlet, the remotest recess of that maze of fiords that spreads northwards from Smyth's Channel. Churchill at the Admiralty, and consequently Stoddart, fell for this ruse. In vain did the hapless Milward cable that it was only a feint. HMS *Glasgow*, *Kent*, *Orama* and *Bristol* all set off on the wild-goose chase. And yet another cross signal from Fisher reminded Stoddart that these ships were needed in the North Sea. This sporting ruse not only drew off the only four British ships in the area, allowing the *Dresden* to set sail for the Pacific, it also resulted in one of the ships, the *Bristol*, seriously damaging her rudder on an uncharted coral, so putting her into dry dock.

By now half a dozen British cruisers had been playing hide and seek with the *Dresden* for three months. But yet again, the Admiralty was hoodwinked by a Canaris deception, to the effect that the *Dresden* was back at Good Hope. The hapless Luce was again ordered to change course and search this unlikely place.

But this time, the legendary Room 40 of the Naval Intelligence Division under the able direction of Admiral 'Blinker' Hall and staffed largely by Cambridge-educated code breakers and the odd naval officer of German extraction, intervened to bring Canaris' run of luck to an end.

Hall, who was on this occasion to act as Canaris' nemesis, had visited Kiel in 1908 where, according to Banfield, he had met the young Canaris. As Hall had been on a covert intelligence gathering mission, he would no doubt have made notes on all the officers he met, especially the promising cadets who spoke excellent English, as Canaris did long before his tutor at Kiel, Hughes, praised his written English.

Hall, whose gaze was described as 'seeing the very muscular movements of your immortal soul,' was perhaps the most appropriate opponent for the *Dresden* and her wily intelligence officer. Years later, during the second 'German War', Canaris would betray his own respect for Hall when, on hearing the news of a new chief of naval intelligence in London, he noted: 'The Naval Intelligence Division is not as circumspect as it was in Admiral Hall's day.' [9]

In the words of the signal officer on HMS *Glasgow*, 'Our luck turned.' Hall's team decoded a simple signal sent by Canaris to a collier. It read 'Am proceeding Juan Fernandez. Meet me there March 9th. Very short of coal.'

This was all Luce needed. Together with *Kent* and *Orama*, a course was plotted to intercept the *Dresden*. Lüdecke, meanwhile, received a telegram from the Kaiser allowing him absolute discretion to accept internment. On receipt of this, Lüdecke informed the Chilean authorities that he would await the dispatch of a Chilean warship to oversee internment in Cumberland Bay.

This time, Canaris' strategems had far reaching repercussions in London, for it was this exchange, intercepted again by Hall, which ignited Churchill. On hearing the news that *Glasgow* had the *Dresden* more or less in its sights, Churchill ordered an immediate attack. Hall, however, tipped off Maurice Hankey, the cabinet secretary, in a not untypical example of a senior intelligence officer working internal lines of communication to restrain a politician. Hankey, however, did not need to be told that there were implications, as Chile was a neutral power, and Churchill's order had serious political ramifications.[10]

A full scale row now ensued at a hastily convened meeting between Asquith, Churchill and Grey in which Asquith, who had been understandably kept in the dark about the entire affair, is reported to have been highly unamused, emerging from the encounter looking 'heated'. Indeed, everyone appears to have left this encounter the worse for wear, save for the ever-serene and impassive Grey. But Luce was not countermanded and on 14 March the long delayed final act of a pursuit that had consumed a totally disproportionate amount of naval and political energy finally now took place.

Only as the sun rose on 14 March 1915 could the captain of *Glasgow* be sure this was not another alarum or excursion. As the precipitous bleak cliffs of Cumberland Bay, in Chilean waters, came into view, there was the *Dresden*, which had eluded him for so long.

While *Glasgow* and *Orama* approached from the west, *Kent* took up position from the east. Luce, who had had to flee von Spee at the Coronel and had lost the *Dresden* at the Falklands, spending months chasing Canaris' false trails as a result, was in no mood for diplomacy. In the absence of any Chilean warships to enforce neutral waters, Luce noted that the *Dresden* was still flying the German ensign and so opened fire at 8,400 yards, straddling her with his second salvo.

At this point, the *Dresden* , facing imminent destruction, could have surrendered, but as the *Gneisenau* and the other German ships at the

Battle of the Falkland Islands had vividly shown, this was not the German tradition. As the *Kent* joined the action, Lüdecke returned fire but being anchored was at a serious tactical disadvantage, so that he soon hoisted a parley flag.* Seeing this, Luce ordered a cease fire and awaited the arrival of a launch which, despite the falling shot, had been lowered from the *Dresden* and was calmly proceeding with a small but dapper Lieutenant Canaris towards the *Glasgow*.

The heavy naval binoculars of the Royal Naval officers trained onto the slight figure, who, with a studied air of insouciance, but as someone later remarked a rather serious expression, continued on his way to the British ship. Shells had fallen perilously close to the launch but the German officer stood impassively, determined to give no sign of flinching from the danger every naval officer of those times was trained for.

Saluting as he boarded *Glasgow*, he was taken to Luce, who received him coolly but correctly. The German pointed out, in the clear and confident English that his Cambridge-educated tutor at Kiel had taught him, that the *Dresden* was in neutral waters, the point which had so exercised Churchill, Asquith and Grey a few days before.

Canaris made, if contemporary reports are to be believed, a good impression. His bearing was confident but not arrogant. He exuded little evidence that he was the representative of a unit that was about to be wiped off the face of the map.

As another German officer would write after a later war: 'It is the function of bluff to redress the balance between one's own inadequacy and the other man's superiority and as this cannot be done in actual fact but only by psychological means, which are independent of tangible resources, it is a weapon peculiarly suited to a man on the run.'[11]

Canaris spoke excellent English, as those who had followed his false trails over the last few months knew to their cost. Luce would not have

*The archived photographs distinctly show a white flag, though the German naval ensign has not been lowered.

been true to that international brotherhood which has always bound together naval officers of whatever nationality if he had not felt some professional admiration for his enemy's evasion tactics of the last few months. But there was now no question of showing any sign of such sympathy. The formalities were brief and stiff.

Luce asked Canaris bluntly if his ship had struck its flag. To which Canaris replied 'You will see it still flies to the fore,' whereupon Luce told the German sharply that his orders were very clear: he was to destroy the enemy wherever he found her. The niceties of international law could be left to the diplomats.*

Irrespective of the precise details of the exchange, Canaris' mission had only one objective, which was to prevent his ship falling into British hands while avoiding further loss of life among the *Dresden* crew. No German naval officer could honourably allow his ship to surrender. Canaris had to gain the time needed to prepare her for scuttling. The ship was in the shallow waters of the bay and in order for scuttling to be effective and give no chance of salvage, ten sea cocks, condensers and torpedo tube doors would have to be opened while charges were laid in the magazines.

Canaris returned, agreeing to report Luce's words to his Captain, but in a last ruse he persuaded the Chilean authorities to send a boat to *Glasgow* protesting at Luce firing, no doubt inadvertently, on the Chilean governor's launch. This again played for time. As Luce apologized to the Chileans, offering to pay full compensation for any damage to local property, Lüdecke followed the last of his men and officers ashore. Five minutes later, at 10.45 a.m., a huge explosion ripped open the *Dresden*'s forward magazine, echoing round the cliffs and shattering all conversation on board the *Glasgow*.

The company of the *Dresden* were fallen in on shore, cheering as

*The Admiralty version, which understandably did not wish to underline the contempt of the Senior Service for the Foreign Office, states that on hearing from Canaris that the *Dresden* had already been interned, Luce had required, in a phrase which would haunt Anglo-German relations in a later war, 'unconditional surrender'. See the introduction to Ian Colvin's *Chief of Intelligence*, London 1951.

their ship, still flying the black and white German ensign, listed over and sank. The British crews also cheered, and Luce chivalrously offered to convey the sixteen wounded of the *Dresden* to the nearest hospital. Canaris and the rest of the crew were interned though many later escaped. Unsurprisingly, Canaris, with the permission of his commanding officer, was the first.

As a fluent Spanish speaker – he spoke Chilean Spanish with no trace of a foreign accent – he found he could easily pass in a South American crowd. With linguistic skills was combined resourcefulness. Sofia Krause, whose elder sister Olga received Canaris and some of the other officers a few times at her villa recalled: 'He had dark hair and skin and was well educated and mannered. He did not look German. Neither was he good-looking, but he had an attractive personality.'

Señora Krause witnessed the first stage of Canaris' escape, which was clearly well planned and may have involved several people: 'My brother-in-law as a German descendant gave him money and a false passport. One morning Canaris arrived from the island. There was a tense atmosphere. I was not allowed to leave my room but I saw everything from my window. Canaris was wearing his usual clothes, a formal suit, and carried a suitcase. He was here for a while; then he left dressed as a pedlar wearing clothes and a cap which seemed to cover his face almost entirely. He had exchanged his heavy German suitcase for a canvas bag.' [12]

He then crossed the Andes, partly on foot and partly on horseback. By Christmas he had reached Buenos Aires, it having taken him eight months to cross from the Pacific to the Atlantic coast. And there, exhausted, dishevelled and weak he found a cousin of the German ambassador in Rome, von Bülow, to take him in and assist his next move.

The von Bülows were wealthy, well-connected and patriotic. They had the means and the will to help and, in a city dominated in those days by British commercial and political interests, they were discreet and subtle.

The identity of the dashing lieutenant Canaris was obliterated and in his place there emerged the mournful Chilean widower, Reed Rosas, who would return to Europe to inherit property in the Netherlands. Setting sail on the Dutch Lloyd steamer *Frisia*, Canaris ingratiated himself with his fellow English passengers, boasting of an English mother and cannily using the long weeks to absorb English habits, customs and language. He was a popular travelling companion and able bridge player.

By the time the *Frisia* reached Plymouth, he was sufficiently plausible and confident to assist the English naval officers in their inquiries about fellow passengers. The ship, with Canaris still aboard, was allowed to proceed to Rotterdam from where, armed with a Chilean passport, Canaris found no difficulty slipping back into Germany. A few months later, in Germany, a silver medal would be struck commemorating the 'honourable sinking' of the *Dresden* – appropriately perhaps, given later events, the only known copy of the medal is in the possession of the Maritime Museum in Greenwich.

Thus ended the first wartime encounter between Hitler's future intelligence chief and the Royal Navy. Early accounts of Canaris dwell on the impact Captain Luce and his officers had on the clearly Anglophile German but, as is clear from this account, Canaris also left an impression; and those, including Churchill, Admiral Hall and 'Jackie' Fisher who had followed the irritatingly elusive *Dresden* so closely, might have been forgiven the sigh of relief which no doubt greeted the news of her long awaited destruction and the internment (though not for long) of her formidable intelligence officer.

For Canaris, this incident made his name in the highest circles of the German Admiralty. Meanwhile, in London, for the first but by no means last time, the name of Canaris was to be passed across the desk of the Admiralty, perhaps to lodge in some deep elephantine recess of the sophisticated memory of Winston Churchill.

CHAPTER TWO

THE LEAGUE OF GENTLEMEN

Secret Work must always be the preserve of gentlemen.
When this ceases to be the case, all is doomed to failure.
COLONEL NICOLAI, FIRST CHIEF OF THE IMPERIAL
GERMAN INTELLIGENCE SERVICE [1]

The young Canaris, by his epic journey and his well-documented outwitting of the Royal Navy, returned to Germany something of a minor hero in naval circles and also decidedly someone with a flair for intelligence work. But in 1915 what kind of opportunities existed in Germany for such talents?

Nicolai's oft-quoted words have long comforted intelligence officers from all countries with the implication that, when all is said and done, after foreign nationals have been suborned, agents blackmailed, sources bribed and spies liquidated, espionage is an honourable profession. But in Germany, as opposed to England, Russia, France or even Austria, the need for this newly emerging power to have an intelligence service opened many neuroses.

How could upright Prussian officers, educated daily by the chimes of the garrison church in Potsdam to practice 'immer treu und redlichkeit' (eternal loyalty and probity) and to be direct, sincere and loyal, involve themselves with spying and double-dealing?

In England the long centuries of internal scheming by powerful opposing interests had made espionage a fact of life and a crucial dimension of statecraft in the island's struggle to remain independent and prevent Europe uniting to its disadvantage; though even in England some military circles took a dim view of intelligence work. In Russia, harsh methods of internal repression created the dreaded Cheka long before the NKVD was conjured up by Felix Dzerzhinsky. Even easy-going Austria had developed spying into a fine art under Metternich, where famously, at the Congress of Vienna in 1815, the contents of the wastepaper baskets of monarchs were exactingly scrutinised by one of the most feared secret police organisations in Europe.

In Germany, the early years of the nineteenth century offered nothing so ambitious. True, the principalities and dukedoms had their agents but it was not until Bismarck that anything remotely coherent was established. In 1866, during the brief campaign against Austria and then later during the Franco-Prussian War, the earlier primitive and often improvised spying techniques were replaced by a Prussian military intelligence service working closely with the field police under Wilhelm Stieber. But here, even after the German Empire was created, the general staff proved most reluctant to sanction the creation of a secret intelligence service.

'I am most concerned,' wrote a war minister shortly afterwards, 'that young officers must year after year engage in regular contact with people of dubious reputation.'[2]

When, eventually, Kaiser Wilhelm II allowed such an organisation to come into being it was with a modest budget of 300,000 marks and a cadre of no more than a dozen officers with support staff. This could not compete with France or England, whose imperial traditions required a global network and vast secret budgets. Even Austria's imperial and royal Evidenzbüro, reorganized after the treachery of Colonel Redl under the capable leadership of Feldmarshalleutnant Urbanski von Ostrymicz, was, with its vast network of agents spun throughout the Balkans, a first division service compared to anything imperial Germany had to offer.

The German service was strictly limited to military information in other 'potentially hostile' countries and expressly forbidden to research economic or political developments. German military officers were not expected or trained to apply their minds to political problems and police methods or lower themselves by becoming involved in political machinations. These dubious activities offended the strict code of honour with which every German officer was imbued.

Another brake on developing a credible military intelligence capability was the jealousy of the German Foreign Ministry's own intelligence service and the informal intelligence gathering operations of the various German political parties who were more than happy to see the new military intelligence apparatus limited to conventional military targets.

As a result, the German Empire may have enjoyed the most formidable military machine in the world, but it possessed no centralised political intelligence capability under a unified command. Diplomats gathered intelligence with scant regard for the military implications. Soldiers evaluated intelligence in a political vacuum. There was thus no relationship between military intelligence and political intelligence.

Unsurprisingly, in 1914, the German High Command possessed neither reliable information on the political objectives of France, England, Russia and Serbia nor indeed any solid data on the reactions of its enemies to its projected planning. Had it had any inkling of what the reaction in London would be to the German violation of Belgian neutrality, it is tempting to think that this act, in Asquith's words, of 'almost Austrian crassness',[3] together with the other parts of the attendant and infamous Schlieffen strategy, might have been consigned to the Chief of the General Staff's equivalent of the shredder.

True, a start was made in 1912, when the relatively junior Oberleutnant Nicolai was entrusted by the then Colonel Ludendorff with the task of reforming military intelligence and creating a new department known by its organisational shorthand as IIIB. Walther Nicolai was himself the embodiment of the old Prussian officer caste. The product of generations of Brunswick pastors and officers, he differed perhaps only in one respect from his peers: for Nicolai, it was not only the destiny of the German officer class to defend the country's future, it was his personal duty to employ all means at his disposal. Ultra-conservative, monarchist, Nicolai had no scruples about expanding his intelligence department into previously uncharted territory.

Ludendorff encouraged him. Unlike most of his contemporaries, Ludendorff was fascinated by intelligence and saw that a secret intelligence service was essential for the 'total war' that Ludendorff envisaged in the future. Such an instrument was no less necessary for the authoritarian regime that would wage such a war.[4]

But even in these early days, there arose a problem that would daunt German intelligence a generation later in the Second World War. Nicolai's intelligence officers, in the organisational chart of command known by their staff shorthand as IC, were never quite sure whether they should answer to the High Command or the General Staff. The line of reporting was kept deliberately vague by Ludendorff in an attempt to concentrate the service, via Nicolai, in his own hands. Needless to say civilian supervision was of course anathema to both men.

Consequently, few spy chiefs took up the reins of office as confidently as did Nicolai in 1913. By this time he was a major, and barely forty years old, a spectacularly young age in Wilhelmine (and indeed later) Germany for an appointment of such sensitivity. In common with most Prussian officers, he saw war as the highest destiny of mankind, without which it would lapse, as Moltke had warned, into materialism, atheism and sloth. For Nicolai wars were 'the days of reckoning'.

However, when war came, in addition to the shortcomings in intelligence evaluation described above, on an operational level the early months were an utter fiasco. Nicolai's agents were rolled up in France and Russia with astonishing ease, while at the same time, the general staff, suddenly aware of the tactical advantages to be gleaned from sound intelligence, overwhelmed Nicolai with demands for information his small organisation could in no way meet.

The dearth of information from France even forced Nicolai to re-activate a seventy-three-year-old agent by the name of Schluga in Paris, someone who had last seen active service in the Franco-Prussian War forty years earlier. In addition, there was a strict demarcation between operations and evaluation with the result that, in a relatively small organisation, neither part knew what the other was doing, a common and recurring theme in twentieth-century intelligence operations by no means exclusive to Germany.

Nicolai set to work to improve this in every way he could and by the end of 1916, with Ludendorff all but dictator of Germany, he had the chance he had always prized of expanding his organisation into the political sphere. Press censorship, domestic intelligence and the support of propaganda in favour of a war climate all became the work of IIIB. Republicans were smeared or suborned. Nationalist parties were established to promote conquest in Eastern Europe and stimulate German minorities to promote war aims. Supported by the dynamic of war, Nicolai's section IIIB was becoming a powerful instrument of state. Promotion to Colonel and a vastly increased budget enabled Nicolai to consolidate his position, increase his network of agents and stamp his authority over the internal police counter-intelligence organs. By 1917, hardly any Allied offensives were not communicated in advance by Nicolai's agents to the High Command and in the Middle East the level of penetration of British forces was remarkable. If Schellenberg is to be believed, it was Nicolai who suggested the idea to Ludendorff of sending Lenin in a sealed train back to Russia via Germany, after the Habsburg Emperor Charles, sensitive to what a revolution in Russia would mean for his empire, refused to allow the Communist to reach Russia the more direct way from Switzerland via Austria.[5]

Thanks to Nicolai, once Canaris had recovered from his exertions, there was indeed work for him: work that would exploit his resourcefulness and knowledge of Anglo-Saxon methods. For Canaris had come to know and admire the Anglo-Saxon world. The first love of his life was an American, Edith Hill, daughter of a wealthy businessman, to whom he had more less become engaged in the last months of 1913. The affair soon ended, but not before Canaris had come to learn much of Anglo-Saxon customs and business habits.[6]

Promoted to *kapitänleutnant*, Canaris, despite being troubled by a recurrence of malaria he had picked up in the tropics before the war, was initially posted to Kiel to take eventual command of a torpedo boat. But the German naval intelligence department of Nicolai's organisation was reluctant to see such a gifted officer wasted on conventional naval duties. Canaris, they knew, had already proved that he could deceive the enemy, operate effectively in hostile territory and use agents to organise not only his supplies but also to weave a web of carefully orchestrated deceit to make fools of the Royal Navy.

In the spring of 1915, Italy, in an act the Austrian Emperor Franz-Josef described as 'a breach of loyalty whose equivalent is unknown in history' had denounced the Triple Alliance and declared war on Austria and Germany. Bribed by the British and French with promises of colonies in the Adriatic, to the consternation of the Russians who had their own Pan-Slav ambitions in the Adriatic, the Italians went to war on the promise of Trieste, tracts of Dalmatia and the South Tyrol enshrined in the secret Treaty of London. [7]

The Mediterranean, key to the lines of communications of the British Empire, was now an important theatre of war and, as every naval staff knew, a happy hunting ground for submarine warfare. But neither Austria nor Turkey had effective submarines, though the former possessed a significant force of Dreadnoughts. The German fleet of U-boats was 4,000 miles away from the principal Austrian naval base of operations at Cattaro.

The distance for submarines was enormous: typically, U-21 took more than a month to reach the port from the North Sea. The alternative of sending smaller submarines in parts by rail down to Pola and reconstructing them was not of much strategic value, though in practice this saved two weeks. But the smaller submarines were not as effective.

At the same time, with increasing American hostility to submarine activity in the North Sea, the pressure to deploy the U-boats around the Mediterranean increased, not least as they were an ideal way of supplying subversive elements in British and French-controlled North Africa. By the end of the year, a number of U-boats had travelled south to spread psychological warfare and sink a number of Allied ships in Funchal on the island of Madeira. The success of such operations, however, depended entirely on the submarines being able to refuel and resupply, somewhere nearer to home than Cattaro on the other side of the Mediterranean.

In particular, the tribesmen who were prepared to raise the flag of revolt in North Africa against the French and Italians needed modern weapons and money on a regular basis, from somewhere nearer than the Eastern Adriatic. Only one country in the western Mediterranean offered the benefits of neutrality to the Germans, and that was Spain. Only Spain could act as a suitable port of call for the U-boats, though obviously in order to maintain Spain's neutrality such replenishments of supplies would need to be handled with the greatest delicacy. Spain, therefore, was critical to the German war effort, but at this stage of the war, much underestimated by many in Nicolai's organisation.

Nicolai's representative in Madrid was Major Kalle, the military attaché. Kalle, however, appears to have found Spain, miles away from the fronts where titanic armies were locked in battle, to be very dull and asked Berlin to be posted elsewhere. 'There is,' he wrote, 'little intelligence of importance here.'

The naval intelligence officer in the embassy in Madrid, *Korvettenkapitän* Hans von Krohn, was well connected with Portuguese businessmen thanks to his marriage to a daughter of a wealthy Portuguese industrialist. But he also was rather unenthused by Spain. British intelligence noted that he had a French mistress. He lacked energy and imagination in the eyes of his superiors in Berlin, who felt that Canaris, with his fluent Spanish and Latin American experience, was the right man to inject some ginger into the Madrid operation. Spanish society was pro-German and then, as now, appreciative of excellent manners. After all, the mother of the queen was an Austrian princess.

Thus, by the spring of 1916, the slight but confident figure of Señor Reed Rosas took possession of a flat not far from the German embassy, where he would meet with Krohn and Eberhard von Stohrer, a first secretary, later to become ambassador, to discuss Allied shipping movements and other ways in which Germany's position could be strengthened. Reed Rosas, or rather Canaris, was never invited to the German embassy and the few operatives in the mission who were aware of his existence only knew him by his code-name 'Kika', his childhood nickname, meaning 'peeper', although, as was later to have fateful consequences for Canaris, the name Reed Rosas was not unknown at the embassy.

With the intuitive brilliance of a born networker, 'Kika' set about gathering agents and informants to track Allied shipping. Soon his web embraced all the principal Spanish ports. In Valencia, he secured the services of the vice-consul, Carlos Fricke. In Cadiz, a friendly business-man offered his services, while German captains of Spanish merchant ships, such as Captain Meyer, of the *Roma*, also supplied information. Soon, 'Kika' had acquired the services of several Spaniards who worked each day in Gibraltar, returning to the Spanish mainland at dusk.

Any useful intelligence gleaned from these sources was given to Krohn, who would then signal Cattaro, where the information could be passed onto the U-boats. In this way Allied shipping began to come under more pressure. As yet, however, the U-boat fleet still did not have the luxury of supplies beyond their bases in the Adriatic. This situation was about to change. Canaris was now going to build for Germany a fleet of ships that would provision the imperial submarines under the very noses of the Allies.

In any country, wealth and power are the preserve of a small minority.[8] In war, it is the task of the professional spymaster to secure access to these personalities. In wartime Spain it was a small group of financiers who pulled many of the strings that could assist Canaris, and these men had close links with German banks. Indeed, some were descended from that culturally rich bourgeois environment of nineteenth century *Haut-Banque* Germany, whose sons were to become such an influence in the financial capitals of the world as the century progressed. Such men were the target of all senior diplomats on both sides, but Prince Ratibor, the German ambassador and scion of the Metternich family, was at some advantage when dealing with the likes of men such as Ullmann or Echevarrieta, to name but two of the most powerful financiers in Spain.

Ullmann was descended from a wealthy assimilated German Jewish family that had migrated to Spain. Introduced to Canaris via Ratibor, he was destined to play an important role in Canaris' life and be the bridge between Canaris and Spanish industry. Horacio Echevarrieta, a Basque, was the wealthiest man in Spain, owning newspapers and banks but, more interestingly from the point of Canaris' immediate needs, the proprietor of a number of shipyards. Ullmann and Echevarrieta were hard men. Whatever their sympathy for the German cause, they were according to a German diplomatic telegram 'not people especially interested in supporting Germany. Primarily they are interested in making money.' And in wartime even more than peace, that meant armaments. The sympathy of such men towards Germany was indicative of the dependence of the Spanish armed forces on German weapons, much to the chagrin of the great English arms companies of Vickers and Armstrong.

Here Canaris, equipped with a wartime budget, could influence events. He needed ships which could resupply submarines. Moreover, he needed

Spanish crews that could disguise the true purpose of the ships' missions. So it came about that the ships were commissioned by Reed Rosas, a Latin American, for use in South America to where they would eventually sail, although it was noted that their sea-going trials often took them to the bay of Cadiz. Here, under the cloak of darkness, they would rendezvous with the U-boats, supplying much needed fuel and provisions.

By March 1916, British intelligence in Madrid could ominously write: 'The situation with German U-boats is especially serious. They do what they want in the Mediterranean.' By this time, Canaris had achieved most of what he had set out to do. German submarines could supply tribesmen in North Africa more or less at will and sink Allied shipping even in convoy.

But successful though his intelligence work was, Canaris was keen to see active service again and return to Berlin. Perhaps he found the constant clandestine activity wearing on his nerves: both British and French agents had begun to home in on Reed Rosas. Perhaps he felt the residual distaste of a conservative regular officer for espionage work. Perhaps he felt that the war was now entering a more desperate stage. His friends Ullmann and Echevarrieta would have had no doubt realistic views on the outcome of the war, the imminence of America's entry into it and the equation of commercial power that implied.

One of their contacts, one of the most influential British allies of the war, had also in the course of the winter of 1916 surfaced in Madrid. He was the man who more than anyone else may have 'spotted' Canaris as a personality to be reckoned with by the British military-industrial elite. He was also the most powerful arms King the world had ever seen: Basil Zaharoff, Director of Vickers, partner and confidant of every arms company in Europe, the most notorious of the 'merchants of death', had ambitions in Spain.

Zaharoff, barely eight months into the war, had said he would put 'a strong spoke into the German wheel in Spain.' His plan was to form an organisation to oppose the AEG-Siemens monopoly of hydro-electric plant in Spain. His visit to Spain was to prepare all the elements so 'that the moment peace is signed we can form the Spanish company and begin working.' This would be the prelude to arming the Spanish navy with Vickers (Whitehead) torpedoes as opposed to the existing German Schwarzkopf torpedo and generally filling the vacuum a defeated Germany would leave. Significantly, he never entertained the slightest doubt that the Allies would win, and said as much to his Spanish friends.[9]

There is no evidence that Zaharoff and Canaris ever met. Yet there is no doubt that they had many friends in common including Juan March, the Mallorquin banker who was later to be Canaris' main conduit to Franco. Zaharoff and Ullmann knew each other and perhaps, if for no other reason than that both Canaris and Zaharoff were proud of their – in both cases far from transparent – Greek connections, they might have remembered each other's names. In any event, it is a fact that at the end of the war, Zaharoff sought Canaris out in Berlin for the most delicate of missions, something which suggests more than a passing acquaintance.[10]

Nor should it be forgotten that, although a firm ally of the British, Zaharoff was not beyond keeping in with all sides. Admiral Hall, chief of the Naval Intelligence Division, never trusted Zaharoff (with reason, for Zaharoff detested Hall and persuaded Clemenceau to ban him from Lloyd George's delegation to Versaillles after the war) and while the arms merchant remained on the British side, it was still the task of the British secret service to keep him within their own orbit.

At times, his activities must have puzzled London, for it was never clear what subtle long-term game he was playing: 'Often it seemed as though he saw the war as something to be run in his own interests first and those of the Allies second.' [11] Zaharoff had persuaded the Allies that it was important for them that he should maintain underground links with enemy firms. This resulted in some extraordinary anomalies, the most famous being the withdrawal of French troops to a distance of twenty-two kilometres behind their frontier to leave the blast furnaces and arms factories at Briey and Thionville in German hands. Throughout the war, no action was ever taken against these works, which were of vital importance to the Germans for key mineral supplies.

Juan March, Zaharoff's and Canaris' friend, played a similar deep game. He first appeared on the radar screen of the British vice consul in Palma at the beginning of the war: 'An extremely wealthy native named March, whose enormous revenue is derived from tobacco-smuggling, is strongly pro-German and is a personal friend of the German consul.' [12] Moreover, as the vice-consul noted in his dispatch: 'These smugglers through Juan March have already been working for Germany even though many of their boats are registered at Gibraltar and fly the British flag.' [13]

These boats had even been employed running German agents across to Italian territory. 'The further step of the supply of submarines would,' the consul ruefully noted, 'arouse no scruples, for agent, master and crew of these boats are Majorcan men, Spanish subjects who owe no allegiance to Great Britain and merely use our flag as a defence against Spanish supervision.' [14]

Canaris worked closely with March and another Mallorquin, Jaume Sabra. As the British noted: 'The configuration of the Balearics, especially of the islands of Cabrera and Espardell, are excellently suited for the surreptitious supply of submarines. The population includes a section of lawless smugglers, uncontrolled by the authorities.' These men were ruled by Juan March and Sabra and while both were cordial with the British authorities, Consul-General Smith realistically noted: 'I have not much faith in Mr Sabra's profession of friendship for either side. He is no doubt strictly neutral in the sense that he would be prepared to serve both sides alike for a consideration.' [15]

These reports elicited a demand from London for more information on March and his oil trading concerns. The reply was terse: 'March is in touch with all the owners of importance and his power for good or evil in connection with liquid fuel running is unquestionable.' [16] March was 'largely responsible for furnishing submarines with supplies of all sorts.'[17]

London could not oppose March directly. They therefore sought to neutralise him by offering an inducement to collaborate. Smith was instructed to point out that March's ships registered in Gibraltar would lose their flagging and be impounded unless March proved more sympathetic. Financial sweeteners were also offered with the result that towards the end of 1915, London was telegraphed that 'March is in general in agreement with our proposals for cooperation and offers unconditional support.'[18]

With March being forced to collaborate more and more with the British, his involvement with Reed Rosas would have to become more circumspect, though he continued to help Canaris with submarine refuelling, perhaps for a higher price. It is more than likely that Canaris may have believed it imperative to report in person to Berlin the pressure under which the British were putting March. The embassy ciphers were not secure and if March was playing both sides, it would require careful explanation to Berlin, who would want to ensure their money was not being wasted.

In any event, whatever the reason, Canaris left Madrid suddenly on 21 February 1917 to return to Berlin overland. He did not get far. On 24 February he was arrested by the Italians in Genoa. Canaris had constructed the not implausible disguise of travelling to Switzerland because his health needed recuperation at a clinic in the Alps. But this was not proof against a tip-off from French intelligence that Reed Rosas was a German agent. The tip-off had come from a French spy within the German embassy in Madrid. This mole had heard the name Reed Rosas on the careless lips of the ambassador a couple of times, but not in any context and with no clue as to who he was. Nevertheless, he had diligently told his handler the name and it had been put on file. Canaris wriggled out of the Genoan interrogation, but at the border station at Domodossola, the frontier guards took him off the train and he was locked up.

To this day the events in Domodossola remain shrouded in mystery. One rather sensational version maintains that Canaris escaped by murdering a priest and making off in his cassock, a dramatic but implausible event even by the cloak and dagger standards of the times. Another version maintains the priest was a travelling companion and that they were both arrested.[19]

More likely is that through the priest Canaris was able to get word to his friends in Spain and they appear, at the highest level, to have intervened with the Italian authorities, possibly even through the Vatican, to get Canaris released. This version is supported by a telegram sent by the German Admiralty on 3 March, noting his arrest but pointing out that 'his release appears probable'. His release by the Italians, in the teeth of objections by French and by now British intelligence, suggests that Canaris could call on some powerful friends in Spain whose links with Italy went through some unusual channels. The Italians predictably compromised. They released the German, but put him on a ship bound for Marseilles and a no doubt well-prepared reception committee from the French authorities. The ship's captain, however, was Spanish and no doubt open to a serious bribe which Canaris would have no difficulty in procuring if the Spaniard took him to a Spanish port rather than a French one. The captain was also most probably convinced by the sincerity of this charming, fluent Spanish-speaking man who explained that a call at Marseilles might well be fatal to him. Canaris was landed at Cartagena, feverish with malaria, and by 15 March was back in Madrid re-applying for an active service posting.

But Berlin was reluctant to see him leave Spain. The German Admiralty wired: 'There is no alternative at the moment to this officer remaining in Spain.' More and larger submarines were on their way to the Mediterranean. At the same time, British naval intelligence, in the shape of the formidable Admiral Hall, had realized that Spain, as the war developed, was increasingly a critical battleground. Spain was not only the base for subversive activities against Allied interests in Mediterranean, it was also the key link for the great offices of state in the Wilhelmstrasse and the overseas world. What Canaris was up to in Spain and what the Spanish government was thinking became priority targets for Hall.[20] Moreover, at the same time Krohn's activities became more transparent thanks to Room 40's interception and decryption of his signals.

For the next six months Canaris remained in Madrid building his organisation, though it may be wondered how useful this was given the fact that by now most of the embassy ciphers had been broken by British naval intelligence. Canaris appears to have travelled, reinforcing his networks and contacts, for most of the following months. It is not known therefore whether he was involved in the gruesome suggestion wired to Berlin by Krohn in June 1917 that 'in order to close the Spanish–Portuguese frontier and to make communications difficult between the Portuguese and the Allies, I suggest contaminating the frontier with cholera bacilli ... two glass phials of pure culture ...'[21]

To be fair, Berlin replied the next day, declining this proposal. However, as the blockade of Germany continued and fodder and fertilisers stopped reaching German farmers, the idea of retaliating by the use of germ warfare against livestock in neutral countries, especially Argentine beef, which was shipped every week from Buenos Aires, was taken up again. This idea met with a more favourable response and Krohn was tasked with finding a suitable method of shipping the tiny sugar cubes which concealed the ampoules of anthrax from the Spanish port of Cartagena to the Argentine. Almost certainly they would have been transported by the ships of Reed Rosas, which would have picked them up from a U-boat, probably the U-35 which reached Cartagena later in June 1917 with a personal letter from the Kaiser to the King of Spain and then returned a few months later to pick up Canaris. (Certainly U-35 was believed to have anthrax sugar lumps in February 1918, some of which were sent to Hall, who lost no time in ensuring the King of Spain was informed, an event which may well have contributed to Prince Ratibor's recall a few weeks later.)[22]

Canaris, meanwhile, was only with some difficulty able to rendezvous with U-35. Once again the French mole inside the German embassy was earning his keep. First, U-35 was held up off the Balearics by Allied ships, then Canaris, on board one of 'his' ships, the *Roma*, was almost intercepted by a French warship as he transferred to the submarine. Reports indicate that the rising sun (it was 6.40 a.m.) helped shield this manoeuvre, which took four minutes, from the French. Irrespective of how close this particular shave was, Canaris landed at the Austrian base at Cattaro on 9 October, where his activities in Spain were rewarded with the order of the Iron Cross First Class. The citation quoted the 'extraordinary skill with which he had carried out his mission.'

Back in Kiel, the submarine arm of the Imperial German Navy beckoned Canaris, as it appealed to many other officers who saw its remarkable possibilities and its scope for courage, imagination and resourcefulness. A long period of training began, enlivened by his meeting Erika Waag, whom he would later, after hostilities ended, engage and marry.

Fraulein Waag was a sensitive, musical and capable girl then aged twenty-four, whose brother was a colleague of Canaris. However, at this stage of the war, such ties were unthinkable. Canaris was posted to Pola and on 28 November finally achieved his ambition to command his own ship when he was put in charge of UC-27. However, a sudden vacancy for a second in command on the submarine U-34 gave Canaris the opportunity to engage the enemy more aggressively.

Canaris proved a success in submarines and U-34 had its fair share of victories against armed British merchantmen in the Mediterranean. The name Canaris even reached the Kaiser's attention: 'Is this man any relation of the Greek War of Independence hero?', he added to the minutes of one report.

But the entry of the US into the war had turned the tide decisively and the Habsburg Empire's disintegration had become a war aim of the Allies. Serbs and Croats were already eyeing up the assets of the Imperial Austrian Navy and Cattaro was deemed, in early October 1918, to be no longer secure. All submarines of the German navy were ordered to return to Kiel, and the Cattaro contingent sailed into Kiel on 8 November. Canaris, by this time, had his own submarine, U-128. As it powered into Kiel, he mounted the conning tower. He would never forget the sight which greeted him: from all the ships of the Grand Fleet there flew the red flag of mutiny. Within hours the Kaiser would have fled to Holland. Two days later the armistice was signed. The world which Canaris had been brought up to respect and imagine would last at least another hundred years was finished.

It is hard to imagine the effect this total breakdown of discipline had on an officer class raised on the dictum of unhesitating obedience. Nothing in Canaris' childhood or background had prepared him for the shock of such complete disintegration. The world Canaris had been born into was at an end. While the lessons he had learnt as part of Nicolai's organisation would never leave him, he might have been forgiven if in this moment of crisis he had turned his thoughts not to the future but to the past, and that happy childhood in a prosperous Germany which now lay about him, to all intents and purposes, entirely in ruins.

CHAPTER THREE

A GILDED YOUTH

Talent ist nur ein Spielzeug für Kinder. Erst Ernst
macht den Man und Fleiss das Genie. [Talent is only
a toy for children. First seriousness makes the man
and diligence the genius.]
THEODOR FONTANE [1]

At twelve o'clock promptly, the carriage drew up at the gates of the Duisburg
Steinbart Gymnasium and a short, wiry youth with a mop of dark blonde
hair, shot through with a hint of Titian red, carrying a parcel of books,
climbed in, to be driven home at a brisk trot through the January snow.
A new century had been born barely two weeks earlier and the sense of
optimism and comfort that pervaded Germany was immense. Techno-
logical advances on every front, a sense of progress, and above all an ever
increasingly diffused wealth, all gave a powerful momentum to those who
saw the coming twentieth century as the dawn of a new age.

The young pupil, who was now whisked away to the classical villa and
park at 110 Wörthstrasse, was only one of countless young men who were
being quietly but confidently groomed to assume responsibilities in a
Germany that would offer far greater possibilities than those available to
an earlier generation. These thoughts, however, would have been remote
from the young man who, deposited at home, flew not to his books but

to his favourite companions, his dogs. Isolated from the world beyond the walls that surrounded his family's gardens and tennis courts, the child's existence was relatively cut off from social interaction with his contemporaries. In the tradition of home and family, social life revolved around the hearth and a self-sufficiency that the febrile world of the late twentieth century would have regarded with astonishment.

This comfortable childhood was considered by one writer on Canaris as a 'silver spoon' existence. It was certainly one in which this youngest of four and second son enjoyed in every way. Later, he would recall these days with unalloyed fondness. If he was teased at school on account of his height or, by German standards, strange name, his villa was his castle, over which the sun always shone. Born on 1 January 1887 in a small mining town near Dortmund, he may have observed the sacrifice and hardship of miners against the backdrop of well-honed German organisation, as one writer has suggested,[2] but it is far more likely that he was principally influenced by his parents and the solidly bourgeois home they had created for him, his elder brother and two sisters.

Ironically, given later events, the cultural inspiration for such Germans came from that bastion of privilege and effortless superiority, England. English hunting prints adorned the walls of the villa. The silver tea service was English and there would have been many references to the self-discipline and values of the English ruling class. Uniformed governesses were also English and introduced the strange habit of placing lettuce in bowls at strategic places around the house to enable the children to satisfy any sudden yearning for food in the healthiest of ways.

However, these were by no means the most important influences. The young boy who excelled at riding and tennis was (with his father frequently absent at work as manager of the local factory) the only man in the house. His elder brother, Carl, had left home early to take up an important position with Thyssen. Wilhelm's stature and his dark skin set him apart from the more macho and athletic of his male contemporaries.

The predominantly feminine environment at home also invested his character with more sensitive influences. He seemingly enjoyed the attention lavished on him by his doting sisters but was nevertheless introspective and far from transparent. His schoolfellows, when later asked about him, found him difficult to remember; so low a profile did he have, so shy was he in many ways.

This shyness, which betrayed a sensitive nature, was disguised by a powerful sense of humour which constantly amused his three sisters and parents. It was the mask of irony, which so many outsiders deploy in dealing with a world that seems challenging and unknown. It may partly have been his response to the most important influence on his life, his parents' rather different personalities. His father appears to have been a gruff, overbearing, socially ambitious but capable businessman; while his mother, Auguste Amelie Popp, was a woman of more refined bearing, the daughter of a Franconian forester and a descendant of a Silesian Catholic family who had always preserved their Austrian as opposed to Prussian identity. Indeed, Catholicism had also been the Canaris family's religion until Wilhelm's grandfather had converted to Protestantism for social reasons on marrying a Protestant, certain professions in Prussia, for example the military, at that time being barred to Catholics.

As is often the case in liberal times, the household limited churchgoing to high days and feast days, but there is no doubt that Canaris was brought up with a strongly Christian ethos, reinforced by his mother's piety. While never later belonging to any religion in a regular confessional way, he nevertheless was brought up to believe that there was a higher authority watching and judging the affairs of men. In his closing months of freedom, he would derive great comfort from the interiors of the great Spanish Cathedrals and be dubbed by British intelligence rather disparagingly as 'a kind of Catholic mystic'.

No less doubtful is the fact that as a privileged son and heir to a protagonist of bourgeois capitalism, the young Canaris would have been brought up with a degree of suspicion towards Marxism and its growing influence on the working classes of the Ruhr, as more and more workers from the East diluted the local labour force and old local loyalties were broken down, to be replaced by ideological ties. While the socialist measures of Bismarck – state pensions, social welfare – were praised by Canaris' father, the 'poison' of Marxism would have been regarded as a threat to the wealth and future of the strata of society to which the Canaris family belonged.

Throughout his later career, Canaris would combine these two traits: a strong sense of responsibility for the welfare of people subordinate and less well off than himself, and an instinctive rejection of Marxism and extremes. It was a point of view shared by many of his background and articulated perhaps in its most magisterial form by the hugely influential 1891 papal encyclical of Leo XIII, *Rerum Novarum*.

Such a family, with an almost uninterrupted ancestry of solid bourgeois achievement, had never aspired to the higher echelons of German society. The Canaris family tree is traceable back to the sixteenth century, but one looks in vain for any sign of aristocratic or military pretensions. But the Germany of the early twentieth century, with its colonial opportunities, naval expansion and powerful industrial development seemed to offer even the arriviste bourgeoisie access to careers that had hitherto been the preserve of an aristocratic caste.

Nevertheless, it appears to have come as a great surprise to his family when the young Canaris, following a cruise around the Aegean with his parents, announced that he would like to join the Imperial German Navy. It is important to remember that not by the furthest stretch of the imagination could anyone have seen the Canaris family as in any way related to the officer or *Junker* class that traditionally made up imperial Germany's officer corps. There had never been a professional soldier in the Canaris family, although that did not mean that the family was hostile to the military. Canaris' father had served in a territorial pioneer regiment in

Metz, but the idea of arms as a profession struck most industrialists like Canaris' father as too poorly paid to be taken seriously.

This attitude also extended to the relatively parvenu service of the navy. But during his cruise the young Canaris had not only seen the impressive new ships of the Imperial Austrian navy in Pola and Trieste, but also something which appears to have had a profound effect on his psyche: namely, the statue erected in Athens to the memory of Admiral Canaris, hero of the Greek war of Independence. Perhaps struck by the unusual sound of his name, perhaps mocked by his fellow German students, the young Canaris seized on this heroic figure and learnt all his daring exploits off by heart, as if to embrace him as an honorary member of his family tree. In fact, despite Canaris' fascination with the Greek hero, there was no evidence of any relationship.[3]

His family was of Italian origin, as was later shown in an elaborate family tree, lavishly produced and bound as a present by Cesare Amé, chief of the Italian Military Intelligence Service S.I.M. The Canarisi were a north Italian family who came to Germany in the seventeenth century and were assimilated entirely into German culture. Nevertheless, certain Latin traits appear to have been recognisable generations later, and Canaris was known for his aversion to the cold – rarely did this officer ever remove his greatcoat – his love of the countries of the Mediterranean and his quick thinking.

Ultimately, however, Canaris' passionate interest in a remote Hellenic figure who was no blood relation of his family cut unsurprisingly little ice with his father, even though he had at first encouraged his son's interest and even procured a small copy of the statue to be erected in their house. A row ensued, in which his son was told in no uncertain terms that if he were to break family tradition and join the armed services, he would be allowed to seek a posting only in a solid cavalry regiment where social etiquette still counted for much and where the young Wilhelm would meet the right sort of person. This dispute is the only documented incident that casts a light on the young Canaris' relationship with his rather distant father. It certainly implies that the relationship was not an easy one and that the ambitions of the father were being heaped on the shoulders of the son, irrespective of the latter's feelings. The element of tacit competition between these two males of the family was, even without the benefit of psychological insight, an important factor in the young Canaris' development. His 'feminine' side was strongly developed by his doting sisters and would later lead to his ability to bond with younger men, such as Heydrich or Szentpetery, at a most intense platonic level.

A suitable commission was sought in a Bavarian heavy cavalry regiment. The young Canaris was an excellent all-round equestrian. It is interesting to reflect on the possible future development of Anglo-German wartime relations had Wilhelm taken this opportunity to appease his father and joined one of the many cavalry regiments which were to be slaughtered by machine guns as unhorsed infantry in the mud and blood of Flanders; though, ironically, in the Second World War, the German cavalry regiments would be very much in tune with the resistance and considered politically highly unreliable.

Mercifully for Canaris, however, fate intervened to save him from a career that almost certainly, at the very least, would have repressed many of his desires and talents. In 1904 Canaris' father died of a stroke. The routine of stables, mess pranks, buckles and boots was spared him. With the successful completion of his 'Abitur', his high school exams which he passed with flying colours, the route to Kiel, the home of the German navy, was now clear.

For the German navy, unencumbered by the feudal baggage of the imperial German cavalry, Canaris was an ideal candidate. First, he came from what would be termed today a good family. He was clearly a bright fellow. He had passed his final school written tests with such brilliant results that he had been, most unusually, spared a viva. In an increasingly technocratic service, this also counted for much. Moreover, the German navy prided itself on its sense of honour and here the quiet piety Canaris had inherited from his mother made a good impression. Despite his mordant wit he exuded that gravitas which German writers such as Fontane have praised. The young man's linguistic skills also impressed the examiners. He was already fluent in three languages. Perhaps most important of all, and here the German navy was no different from any other in imposing this far from nugatory requirement, he had impeccable manners.

On 1 April 1905, Cadet Canaris entered the Imperial Naval Academy, along with other eighteen-year-olds joining a young but already proud elite. Conditions, while not as primitive as those inflicted on much younger Royal Naval cadets at Dartmouth, were nevertheless tough. A strict military infantry course was followed by nine months on a sailing training ship in the North Sea where the skills of seamanship, navigation and gunnery were all taught. A fellow cadet noted that Canaris never had any difficulty in the exams: 'He was slow to speak but quick to listen.' His sense of humour was also frequently deployed. He showed himself to be stoic and surprisingly tough.

Early in 1908, the cadets at Kiel received a visit from a Royal Navy training ship, HMS *Cornwall*, under the command of Captain William Reginald Hall, later to become the head of British Naval Intelligence. There is no evidence to suggest Hall took any interest in Canaris, but as he was gathering intelligence on all aspects of the German navy during his visit, he may well have noted some of the cadets he would have met.

Later that year, Canaris was appointed the German equivalent of a midshipman on the cruiser *Bremen*, which fortunately brought him in contact with the Latin American world where he could perfect his Spanish, immersing himself in the culture and history of the countries he visited. It was also an opportunity to study the Royal Navy at close quarters, as the fleets of all the great powers cooperated in defending their commercial interests in the region. Here Canaris already displayed the 'finger tip instincts and ability to handle people' [4] that were to prove his great gifts in later years. His command of Spanish and young seriousness of manner endeared him to many and the Greek connection was appreciated by well-read Latin Americans who themselves, in younger days, empathised with the Greek struggle for independence. The Chileans in particular took to him, and the links between the two navies were intimate. He was even decorated by the Chileans with the Order of Bolivar. By this time, Canaris spoke excellent Spanish with a Chilean accent and was an expert on all the political trends and personalities of the country.

Within a year, however, it was back to Kiel and the demanding schedule of duty officer on a small torpedo boat in the North Sea. Even in peace, this was a challenging environment requiring high standards of seamanship and technical skill. According to reports, Canaris was virtually alone in not suffering from sea sickness. Those, including Admiral Dönitz, Hitler's successor, who later claimed (in his case during his trial at Nuremberg) that Canaris was 'never a proper naval officer', confused loyalty with training. By the autumn of 1912, the twenty-five year old, now a lieutenant, was considered one of the best naval officers of his generation. By the time Canaris came to his beloved light cruiser *Dresden*, he had already made a firm reputation for being capable and reliable. A naval report describes his possessing a calm temperament well beyond his years, and an ability to deal with people that would be most 'helpful in the political sphere'. But first Canaris had to learn about politics as they were practiced at the time, at their most *haut-politique* level, away from the banana republics of South America.

The Balkan Wars and the need to secure German interests in the eastern Mediterranean provided a suitable occasion. Canaris was posted with the *Dresden* to the Adriatic and then Istanbul where, for the first time, the political problems of the time were thrown into sharp relief. One development in particular was sharply silhouetted: Anglo-German rivalry.

Istanbul, as a diplomat before the First World War pointed out, was not just the capital of a state; it represented many powerful global commercial, political and religious interests which in the run up to 1914 seemed, to an intelligent eye, to be well embarked on collision course. If the British, in the guise of Sir Ernest Cassel, had founded and owned the National Bank of Turkey, and through Vickers owned the Golden Horn and Stenia Docks, German commercial interests were gathering momentum fast. Siemens was deeply involved in the Berlin to Baghdad railway. Krupp was busy bribing politicians, and the formidable Liman von Sanders was about to transform himself into Liman Pasha and turn, with the help of his military mission, what the American ambassador described as an 'undisciplined ragged rabble' into a force 'parading with the goose-step ... clad in field grey'.[5]

For the young and sensitive Canaris this was a spectacular introduction into the game of geo-politics. On shore, as the guest at innumerable receptions given by German interests, the young officer would have heard countless times how, in the words of one expert on German Turkish relations: 'Our common political aims and Germany's interest in keeping open the land route to the Indian Ocean will make it more than ever imperative for us to strengthen Turkey economically.'[6]

More ominously, these ideas went hand in glove with the view that: 'England can be attacked ... on land in one place only ... in Egypt. With the loss of Egypt, England would lose not only mastery over the Suez Canal and the link with India and Asia, but also her possessions in Central and East Africa.'[7]

Such was the influence of the Baghdad railway, supported as it was by all the most powerful commercial interests of Germany, including Deutsche Bank, Dresdner Bank and the giant engineering company Siemens, that news of its progress found its way into State dispatches and dominated conversation.

With his keen brain, Canaris digested all of this with the enthusiasm of a convert. He noted the latest developments and watched for the signs of future moves. He was aware that Germany had supplied four torpedo boats, built in the Schichau yards in Danzig, two years earlier. A few months earlier, Deutsche Bank had acquired twenty-five per cent of the Turkish Petroleum Company, while the Hamburg-Amerika line had so successfully captured a large proportion of the transport business to and from Basra that it had ended Britain's virtual monopoly of the seaborne trade of Mesopotamia, forcing the British to compromise on something like dictated terms.[8]

If, by the close of 1912, Canaris had added some European political insights to his seamanship skills, the next year, the last of peace, would cement these two qualities with renewed exposure to and experience of the Latin American world. By now a senior lieutenant, confident and handsome, Canaris was ready for the challenges of political instability that awaited him.

In Mexico, revolution once again stalked the streets. The country that had seen so much turmoil in the nineteenth century and was destined to be the scene of competing European and American spheres of influence for many years to come, was having one of its periodic struggles between different commercial interests. While the majority of European ships kept their distance, the *Dresden* risked the last twenty miles of the Tampico river to rescue President Huerta from the rebels, despite their threat to set the river ablaze with oil from the nearby refinery. In addition to Huerta, several hundred Americans were rescued by the *Dresden* and taken to an American warship that had been unwilling to risk the rebels' threats. Huerta was deposited in July 1914 in the relative safety of Kingston, Jamaica.

With the outbreak of war a few weeks later, Germany's interest in Mexico became even more intense, though with the then unforeseen consequence that this interest, already resented by America, would eventually bring the US into the war, thanks inevitably to British naval intelligence's interception of the infamous Zimmerman telegram, offering

German support for a Mexican invasion of Texas.

But all that lay ahead. As the *Dresden* prepared to sail back to Germany only the news from the Balkans was disturbing but as Canaris well knew, 'Auf den Balkan ist immer etwas los.'* The disturbing signal that, with the expiry of the ultimatum to Belgrade, the Austrians and the Russians were at war, foretold the full brutal reality of what was imminent. With war declared by all the major powers within days, orders to return to Germany were cancelled and the *Dresden* set off on her final journey. In a ceremony redolent of the end of the era, the ship's crew began consigning important papers to the furnace and jettisoning all unnecessary cargo. The ship's pianos, which had offered such pleasures to the officers in the evenings, went the same way. Memoirs noted that the disposal of the pianos afforded many tears from the more musical of the officers. The world Canaris had grown up in was about to end once and for all, and as the British Foreign Minister Grey noted: 'We will not see its like again in our lifetimes.' [9]

* 'There is always something going on in the Balkans.'

CHAPTER FOUR

FINIS GERMANIAE

Wealth measured in billions has been blown into the
air ... Nothing in fact, economically, politically or
socially, would ever be the same again.
LORD HOME, LETTER TO HIS GRANDSON [1]

The end of the war saw Canaris in his submarine, surrounded by the red
pennants of revolution flying from every capital ship in Kiel harbour.
Imperial Germany was in ruins. The flag of Communist revolt had been
raised and the days of the officer corps, once the arbiter of Germany's
destiny, appeared numbered. Canaris laconically noted in the submarine's
war diary: 'With three hurrahs we lowered our flag.' [2] With it, seemingly,
disappeared decades of discipline. It is hard for those in countries that
have enjoyed centuries of stable continuity to imagine the chaos and bit-
terness that attends social meltdown and revolution. Anarchy, fed by the
countless masses of starved and defeated men and women, was rampant
on every street corner. No authority; no discipline; the revolutionaries of that
November found, as revolutionaries generally find, that it is easier to
destroy an old system than to replace it.

Around Kiel, barracks were turned into brothels or shops; thugs ruled
every main thoroughfare on the lookout for anyone with officer rank or
middle class appearance to intimidate, rob or indeed murder. The Imperial

navy, the pride of Germany and the Kaiser, was no more; worse, it had been the catalyst for revolution. It had been sailors who had first trained their weapons on their officers. Not the sailors who had served under Canaris in relatively small vessels such as submarines or torpedo boats, or even the cruiser *Dresden*, but sailors from the great Dreadnoughts where social tension was more marked. Canaris would never forget how Marxism had infiltrated the crews of these ships to wreak such destruction on the institution that had been his life. Later, in the 1920s, he would defend the navy to the hilt, rejecting any criticism of the relations between officers and sailors. For him, the mutiny had been almost entirely caused by subversive elements on shore which had infected the crews with the virus of revolt.[3] It would make him a life-long anti-Communist despite his relatively liberal views.

In this moment of twilight the officer corps rallied. In Kiel, a naval officer by the name of von Loewenfeld began secretly gathering officers into a network of self-protection which could, when the moment arrived, restore discipline in the navy. This movement, which included distinguished submariners with whom Canaris was on close terms, inevitably attracted him. At the same time, however, Canaris also found himself in touch with the social-democrat Gustav Noske, whose aim was to draw the teeth of the Communist insurgents and establish a more moderate, albeit socialist, authority. Bearded and belligerent, Noske had a natural grasp of the equation of power and was determined to consolidate his position by exploiting his links with the military. This he could do only with the help of officers who knew how to handle the unruly 'people's naval units', nominally under his command. Canaris, aware that order could only be restored by a strong personality, was impressed by Noske and, after a meeting, offered some support.

Meanwhile, in early January, a Communist putsch led by Karl Liebknecht and Rosa Luxemburg – revolutionaries known as Spartakists – had once again exploited mutinous sailors, this time to pave the way for a Soviet-style republic. The sailors from the so-called 'People's Naval Division' had occupied the Wilhelmstrasse and broken into the Chancellery. In many streets Spartakists had set up barricades with machine guns. A few weeks earlier the first Soviet congress, perhaps inspired by its temporary refuge in the imperial stables, had demanded the abolition of Germany's armed forces. This was a radical step and a challenge to the traditional elite of Germany; but it was not all the two agitators wanted. Liebknecht, in a pamphlet, had attacked the arms industry, placing all society's ills at the feet of the merchants of death. He was in favour of entirely disbanding Germany's arms trade which, he maintained, was part of an international arms trade ring dominated by a handful of powerful capitalist figures, whose only driving force was profit rather than patriotism. This rang alarm bells in many quarters, not least among the great German industrialists for whom the spectre of Communism taking over their factories had, a few months earlier, been a factor in ending the war.

The army, however, was not going to comply with its extinction so easily. The terrified socialist chancellor, Friedrich Ebert, had turned to the army as the only credible force to support his administration. In return for this support, the civil administration would impose order and outlaw anarchy. The army now called for this agreement to be honoured. Ebert looked for a man the officer corps trusted and found a minister of national defence in the guise of Noske.

To add to this combustible mix, a figure from Canaris' past in Spain had chosen to arrive in Germany a few weeks earlier. This smartly dressed gentleman, wearing the buttonhole ribbon of the Légion d'honneur, was Basil Zaharoff.[4] Appalled at the apparent success of Communism in Germany, a country where he had maintained substantial armament interests, and no less concerned by the direction of Liebknecht's agitation, he found Noske and Canaris in Berlin. No record of his conversation with Canaris has survived, but an aide-memoire, which Zaharoff addressed to a colleague of Canaris', noted:

'The immediate problem is to counteract the Bolshevik propaganda, which deliberately seeks to make mischief so that all forms of arms trade are controlled or disbanded. Speak to Canaris about Liebknecht; the latter should be in no position to talk further by the end of the year.' [5]

Zaharoff's wishes appear to have been conveyed at a most opportune moment and his relationship with Canaris, begun in Spain a few years earlier, seems to have consolidated. Noske's *Freikorps* (Free Corps) of officers and volunteers, supported by the army, dealt with the insurgents vigorously, storming the stables and arresting Liebknecht and Luxemburg on the night of 15 January. They were taken to the Eden Hotel, where the headquarters of the Guards Cavalry Division had been established under General von Hoffmann, and operations against the rebels were being directed by Captain Waldemar Pabst. Canaris was appointed liaison between the Guards Cavalry and the navy. Pabst and Canaris hit it off, the former later calling the latter 'My best man'. Canaris returned the compliment, describing his time in the Frei Korps as 'those wonderful days'.

For Rosa Luxemburg and Karl Liebknecht, however, time was running out. For Pabst, as for most of the officer class, these two were the human expression of all they detested in Communism. Luxemburg's shrill and harsh voice, which it was said had even caused members of the Soviet Politburo to wince, was, as one officer described it, a 'perpetual insult to civilised Germans.' [6] The two were subversive, foreign (Luxemburg was a Jewish Pole), rootless and fanatic. Pabst was determined to liquidate them as soon as possible. A guard was detailed to escort them to the Moabit prison and shoot them on the way when 'they tried to escape'. There are several versions of what happened next. An official statement declared 'Karl Liebknecht was shot while trying to escape and Rosa Luxemburg was killed by an unknown person while being taken to prison.'

In fact, Liebknecht, already suffering from wounds inflicted by the crowd near the Hotel Eden, was shot by his escort, Horst Pflugk-Hartung after the car stopped for 'a repair'. Luxemburg was shot earlier, near the hotel, but Vogel, the soldier commanding her car, lost his nerve and dumped the body in the Landwehrkanal, where it was not found until May. With these macabre and brutal moves in the cold January night air, Pabst's and Zaharoff's aims had been realised.

Canaris, meanwhile, was ordered to Bavaria to compile a report on civil defence movements that were being organized there. At least three writers on Canaris (Abshagen, Buchheit, Brissaud) put this trip to Bavaria before the murders of Luxemburg and Liebknecht. Canaris himself always denied any complicity in the crime but, at that stage in his life, it is hard to imagine he would have felt regret at the death of the two. His relationship with Noske would have depended on a ruthless approach to them. Noske, later questioned on the murders by his anxious comrades, replied: 'You are like old women. War is War! You were not even there.'

Moreover, Canaris – thanks to his time in Spain – had become a willing if junior partner in the international arms ring that Liebknecht had denounced. His brother Carl, now with the armaments firm of Thyssen, would later become director of Krauss-Maffei, the manufacturer of German tanks to this day. Canaris could scarcely have operated so effectively in Spain without it, and this ring, as Zaharoff's career so vividly illustrated, operated on the basis of more complex loyalties.

It is beyond any doubt that Canaris knew the two were murdered, not least because the officer who ordered his journey to Bavaria was his old friend and comrade, Pflugk-Hartung, the main protagonist of the events of the night of 15 January. It is hard not to see Canaris' trip to Bavaria as an attempt to distance him from the murders, though as will be seen they would cast a long shadow over his future career. Canaris' exact involvement may never be fully explained, but he was an accomplice and his right wing anti-Communist credentials were vividly forged by his connection, however shadowy, with this event.

For the next few months, however, his life was one of careful and constructive alliances. As liaison officer with the Guards-Cavalry, as a significant voice at the Admiralty, above all as the confidant of Noske, he enjoyed insights that gradually made him a key observer of that most important fault-line in post-war Germany, the interface between politics and the military. At the same time, he managed to find time to track down his love of three years earlier, Erika Waag, in Pforzheim, and within two days the couple were engaged. With all the passion that romance against the backdrop of political unrest can engender, this must have been an absorbing time, but Canaris' sense of his own mission, then as later, never allowed him to be ruled by matters of the heart.

His mission in Bavaria completed, he returned to Berlin to find his friend Pabst under investigation by a military tribunal looking into the deaths of Liebknecht and Luxemburg. Vogel, who had driven Luxemburg, had been arrested; while shortly afterwards, his accomplice Pflugk-Hartung was also placed under arrest. A full trial now appeared inevitable.

Canaris visited the prisoners and briefed them on their defence, rehearsing with them every detail so that no clue could be traced to his friend Pabst. Canaris also explored the possibility of helping the officers escape abroad with the help of money and false papers. Already at this stage, Canaris was a versatile exponent of the art of subterfuge and deception.

In the event the officers were acquitted, except for Vogel, who was sentenced to two years for 'failure of discipline and abuse of power.' But he did not remain in prison for long. On the afternoon of 17 May, a young lieutenant, announcing himself as Oberleutnant Lindemann, arrived at the guard room of the Moabit Prison with instructions, signed by the highest judicial authority, to transfer the convict to another prison. In a few minutes both men had disappeared. Both the documentation and the Oberleutnant Lindemann were fakes. In a few hours, Vogel was safely over the frontier in Holland. 'Lindemann' meanwhile, if Pabst is to be believed, reverted to his real identity: Canaris.

The removal of a prisoner, by one German officer impersonating another, equipped with a forged release order signed by the chief military prosecutor, was even by the standards of the time a highly unconventional event. Unsurprisingly, the authorities demanded an explanation and a new inquiry was established to work out how Vogel could have escaped. Arrests were made of suspects within his immediate circle and one of those was Canaris. But after eight days in custody, he was brought before a military tribunal consisting of several officers, most of whom had, in some way, been themselves involved in instigating the entire affair. Canaris was released, his reputation among the military higher than at any time hitherto. Here was the man whom right-wing politicians and soldiers could trust for missions involving subtlety and subterfuge. Now thirty-three years of age and shortly to be married, he was the man whose name would be discreetly mentioned when officers gathered to discuss how they could restore Germany to her former glory by 'breaking the rules'. [7]

Unsurprisingly, it was perhaps only a question of time before another political intrigue enveloped him. This time the intrigue came firmly from the ranks of the right and would set him against his old patron, Noske. The punitive terms of the Treaty of Versailles were rejected by the officer corps and the desire of the government to sign inevitably led to friction. Into this explosive atmosphere the Allies threw a grenade, in the form of a list of 800 'war criminals' whom they demanded to be handed over. As the list included members of the German royal family, Admiral Tirpitz, Ludendorff and Hindenburg and practically every important leader in German public life during the war, the note provoked outrage.

Supported by Ludendorff (in the shadows), Wolfgang Kapp, a pale bureaucrat from East Prussia, surrounded by a motley group of officers, staged a putsch aimed at restoring Germany to her former feudal glory and repudiating the Versailles treaty.

Faced with the choice of supporting his fellow officers or Noske, Canaris chose the former, but a general strike called by Noske paralysed the rebels and much of the Reichswehr remained aloof. Expecting a heroes' welcome, but greeted with hostility, the Kappists quickly crumbled. Kapp himself crept out of the Chancellery he had arrived at three days earlier in top hat and tails, wearing a trenchcoat and trilby. Most of the leaders went into exile in a wave of similar low-key and furtive departures.

Within two days the dream was over and Canaris found himself once again under arrest. He had, however, played both sides in the drama well, even if he had miscalculated the finale. This time, a spirit of consensus – remarkable for the times – prevailed. The government saw little point in being vindictive, as it would need the support of the officer class. On their side, the officers realised that they could achieve far more by working through the republic rather than against it. Thus, there were no courts-martial or firing-squads. Noske was replaced as minister by Otto Gessler, and the rounded-up conspirators were released, though each one was now subject to judicial investigation for their role in the coup. Canaris, however, as a relatively junior officer, escaped any serious censure. Moreover, Gessler needed help with the navy which once again had shown itself to be bitterly divided at the time of the putsch, with ratings and non-commissioned officers disarming the officers and taking over command with alarming ease.

Posted to Kiel on 23 July, Canaris was given the task of assisting in some restoration of normality to what had become a demoralised, and in many ways paralysed, naval station. With the sinking or handing over of many ships to the Allies, naval personnel were now mostly based on land. Unsurprisingly, discipline had collapsed, important installations were abandoned or under the slightest of guard; naval stores, including munitions, plundered and lost. Every ship, meanwhile, had to be approved by the terms of the Versailles treaty, while the loss of the Bay of Danzig to Poland, together with that country's imminent creation of a navy, reinforced the sense of hopelessness that prevailed. If the Ost See station was to play the important role of linking the thousands of Germans stranded in East Prussia by the terms of the Versailles treaty with the rest of Germany, huge progress would have to be made

Canaris and his fellow officers were undaunted by the task. Gradually discipline was restored and the natural talent of the Germans for organisation was harnessed to restore order and regulation. Each week, Canaris would lecture the ratings, detailing the progress made and how everyone in the service had a role to play in rebuilding the navy. This was unconventional by the standards of the times, and progressive. Also, with his undoubted talent for persuasion, Canaris was able to put his experience to good use to secure ample provisioning in adverse circumstances. By March the following year, the Ost See Squadron was a functioning entity made up of four capital ships and nearly a dozen torpedo boats.

With these, however, the limits of the Versailles treaty were reached. Moreover, under the terms dictated by the Allies, naval personnel were reduced to 15,000 of whom no more than 1,500 were to be officers. Canaris was not one to be put off by such formalities. He was already drawing in the best officers of the disbanded, post-putsch naval brigade to be incorporated into the new navy. Now he set about forming a secret reserve, which would be invisible to those sent to enforce the Versailles treaty, in this instance the Allied Naval Control Commission at Kiel.

To achieve this, Canaris needed money. His encounters with Zaharoff and others had left him in no doubt how to acquire it. The sale of weapons was the easiest way, and there were plenty of old contacts who would help procure and sell them on. A Danish intermediary was found with links to customers, notably in the recently created Baltic States, who were desperate to equip new national navies. Indeed, demand soon outstripped supply, as the Danes proved highly energetic. As they took a forty per cent commission, their enthusiasm was perhaps justified.

Within months, assisted by his old comrade Leutnant Richard Protze, who would later troubleshoot on arms deals with Canaris in the thirties, a complete arsenal and training area was constructed under the very noses of the Control Commission. The many radical, right-wing groups of dis-enchanted officers were now tapped by these two. Canaris became more and more involved in groups that had no desire to see the republic survive. One of these was led by a seemingly unimportant Austrian called Adolf Hitler. There is no evidence to suggest that the two ever knew each other personally at this stage, although they both must have heard something of each other in the twilight world of right wing conspiracy.

However, if he did not meet Hitler at this point, he was now going to encounter someone with whom his fate would be inextricably bound. In June 1923, he was posted to the cadet training ship *Berlin*. It so happened that his appointment coincided with the arrival of a singularly dashing, if histrionic, cadet by the name of Reinhard Heydrich.

Canaris found many aspects of the training ship tiresome, not least the overbearing quality of some of his fellow officers, who lacked the finesse Canaris had enjoyed among his wartime naval comrades. Moreover, the isolation from the intrigues and machinations which had so marked his life in the last three years was a hard penance. Conspir-acy had become an addictive drug for him, as important as family and career. His relatively junior position on a training ship seemed a sad use of his talents. Depression and melancholy set in; only interrupted by the young and sensitive cadet, Heydrich, whose highly strung nature appealed to Canaris.

Heydrich was, perhaps to the eternal credit of the German navy, the most unpopular cadet on board. The son of an opera singer and a painter, his passionate, artistic temperament, moulded by naval discipline into arrogance and brutality, Heydrich was mocked for his high-pitched voice. His fellow cadets called him 'the goat'. He was mercilessly teased and bullied. Canaris, who himself had known some teasing at school and had always felt, with his name, diminutive stature and sensitive nature, something of an outsider, experienced a strange rapport with Heydrich. The two met often on shore and the young cadet, who was a proficient violinist, played duets with Canaris' wife while the senior officer donned his chef's cap and prepared supper.

Whether Canaris found out at this stage that the even then staunchly anti-semitic young man was in fact partly Jewish is not recorded, though it is clear that Canaris knew this in later years but never breathed a word of it to his colleagues or friends (see chapter twelve). Problems over ancestry appear to have acted as a bond.

The rapport that began in Kiel lasted to the end of his life, though the two were to become deadly rivals. As a later secretary of Canaris, who knew both men, recalled : 'With Heydrich and Canaris there was always a kind of unstated understanding as if to say to the rest of the world, we have shared experiences in the Navy together which places us apart from everyone else.'[8]

Heydrich did not last long in the navy. Cashiered for breaking off an engagement, then as in other navies an act bringing disrepute onto the honour of the service, he left for more political pastures. But it seems possible that through his relationship with Canaris he had indeed learnt perhaps a little about the world of intelligence, enough to whet his appetite and find in that world an outlet for his strange ideas and inferiority-complexed personality.

Canaris, meanwhile, went into decline. Malaria and depression both took their toll. He had made up his mind to resign from the navy unless he was offered more stimulating duties. However, events once again took control and he was summoned to the Admiralty to discuss whether he would consider a 'delicate' mission overseas.

Having survived the initial shocks of the immediate post war period, with both extreme right and extreme left for the moment exhausted, there was time for Germany's authorities to contemplate how the country could wriggle out of the straitjacket of the Versailles conditions. Most pressing of all was how the military and naval arms could be reconstructed far from the prying eyes of Britain and France.

Under the guiding genius of Colonel-General Hans von Seeckt, the chairman of the preparatory committee of the Peace Army, the 'poison' of the disarmament articles of the Treaty of Versailles began to be neutralised. Moreover, thanks to the creation of Poland by the Allies, there was in the form of the Soviet Union a country eager to cooperate with these military aims. Poland was for Moscow as much as for Germany a negative factor in their security arrangements. Bismarck's old Prussian policy to safeguard relations with Russia was back and, notwithstanding ideological differences between Moscow and Germany, the two military hierarchies found mutual benefit in the business of avoiding the demands and prying eyes of the West.

But while Moscow could offer the location for secret armies and embryonic air-forces to train and re-equip, her lack of warm water ports offered no such facilities for the German navy. Moreover, the navy was, after the traumatic experiences of the Kiel mutiny, among the officer class at least, highly anti-Communist. One country, however, that was geographically suitable for such activity and desperately in need of building-up its own naval arm was Japan.

In the spring of 1924, Canaris, dressed as a civilian, set off for Osaka to help supervise what was in many ways the most deadly of the breaches of the Treaty of Versailles: the secret U-boat construction programme in Japan. The U-boats had been denounced by the Allies as the most aggressive arm of the aggressive state. If it had been left to the Allies' Control Commissions, there would have been no submarine construction capacity left in Germany. However, Japan was keen to acquire submarines and the Germans desperate to retain their expertise. Together the two countries worked with growing efficiency, not least as the Japanese were convinced that only the Germans had the know-how to construct submarines suitable for the Pacific Ocean.

A blind cover firm was established in the Netherlands to deal with the Japanese and Canaris was sent to Osaka to ensure the Germans understood the needs of the Japanese and that there were no difficulties caused by the cultural differences involved. The mission lasted barely twelve days and the report Canaris made upgraded the relationship, allowing the two countries to lay the foundations of what would become an ever more intimate cooperation. Given the strong ties which linked Japanese and British navies in those years this was a formidable achievement.

Indeed, the Royal Navy may well have got wind of what was afoot and brought pressure to bear on the still weak German republic. In any event, a new chief of the navy, Vice Admiral Adolf Zenker, was appointed, with a very different brief: to end all secret rearmament activity and replace it with nothing less than cooperation with the Royal Navy. Zenker believed that, as the Royal Navy had imposed most of the restrictions on the German fleet, it would make sense to win over its goodwill and work for the more restrictive articles to be lifted. Moreover, Zenker was convinced that any clandestine rearmament would be picked up by the all-seeing eyes of British intelligence.

On 3 October 1924 Zenker announced that cooperation with the Japanese navy would no longer be a priority. Moreover, Zenker was keen to limit the activities of the industrial and commercial interests that were behind the sinews of the secret armament programme. 'Naval policy,' he wrote, 'cannot be led by commercial interests.' Canaris was given a desk job which, although he discharged it capably, was not his natural environment, a fact not lost on his superiors. Captain Arno Spindler, who saw a lot of him at this time wrote: 'His troubled soul is appeased only by the most difficult and unusual of tasks.'

The Zenker policy, however well-intentioned, could not deflect those interests and personalities who were determined to throw off the shackles of Versailles. One such man was Captain Walter Lohmann. This roguish descendant of a Bremen merchant, whose father had been a director of the powerful North German Lloyd shipping line, was a dedicated intriguer with a passion for secrecy and backstairs deals. Lohmann and

Canaris linked conspiratorial hands across a sea of Zenker caution.

Secret funds were channelled to a score of front companies ostensibly engaged in shipping or sailing boat construction. In 1923 Navis GmbH was set up as an undertaking ostensibly carrying out work for north German sailing clubs. Other companies, all well capitalised, followed suit. Trayag GmbH, the same year, was followed within eighteen months by half a dozen others. These included Berliner Oeltransport GmbH, Caspar Werke, and the film company Phoebus: an important addition for Lohmann which he hoped would help combat American penetration of German industry by propaganda.

In this maelstrom of secret activity, it was perhaps inevitable that as soon as Canaris mentioned submarines to Lohmann, yet another shell company was established to further the secret submarine programme. But with Japanese cooperation stymied by Zenker, it was necessary to look for another friendly navy closer to home. It was time to reactivate Canaris' links to the Spanish navy, now and since the end of the war being supplied by that old friend Basil Zaharoff. Happily, this coincided with the German admiralty's keenness to set up a network of agents in Spain. Canaris was the obvious man for this job and within two days of arriving in Madrid in June 1925 he had rekindled his old links and begun to set up a web of agents covering all principal ports.

In Barcelona, Carlos Baum, a businessman, was employed under the codename Martha. In Valencia, it was Carlos Fricke (code name Fernando). In Cartagena, Alfred Menzel (Edoardo), in Cadiz, Riccardo Classen (Ricardo). These agents were supported by networks resurrected by Canaris from his wartime experiences.

In addition to this sterling work, his official task, Canaris now set about ensuring a home for his submarine projects. With the help of his old friends Ullmann and Echevarrrieta, he rapidly disabused Berlin of the value of working with the 'third rate' Banco de Cataluña as a partner and noted that the only financial house worth having as a partner was Echevarrieta. By happy coincidence, Echevarrieta, 'the richest man in Spain', was running short of funds. He was by no means the first, nor indeed the last, industrialist at the centre of a country's power structures to suddenly require capital replenishment. If German money was available to help Echevarrieta escape bankruptcy and enable him, with Ullmann, to realise the dream of establishing an independent arms industry for Spain, what reason could there be for not helping Germany with her illegal submarine programme?

Fortunately for Canaris, these powerful interests were in tune with the younger officers in the Spanish navy who had not been suborned like their superiors by Zaharoff. Like most officers of junior rank they resented the 'sweets' lavished on their superiors. They knew the reputation of German submarines from the war and were eager to have them for their own navy. By another stroke of luck, a few weeks later a Spanish naval delegation was in Berlin. They soon came to the conclusion that the only man they could do business with in Germany was Canaris. Only he understood their language and their foibles. Thus, in a matter of a few months, Canaris had placed himself at the centre of the interlocking circles of German and Spanish naval rearmament. From now on nothing concerning relations with the Spanish Navy in Berlin took place without Canaris' approval.

Events now moved relatively swiftly. Echevarrieta was invited to sail his yacht, the magnificent *Cosmo Jacinta*, to Kiel. Lohmann opened him a generous line of credit from Deutsche Bank and the Spanish King was 'inspired' to ask Echevarrieta to build torpedo boats for the Spanish navy. Echevarrieta, however, needed capital to do so. Zaharoff and other British interests had got wind of what was going on and had offered the distressed industrialist financial support if he would support British, or at least Vickers' interests in Spain. This move, however, only strengthened Canaris and Lohmann's hands in Berlin to secure yet more credits from Deutsche Bank, one of whose directors, the aptly named (from Echevarrieta's point of view) Dr Luck, travelled to Madrid to draw up the financing agreements with the industrialist, ably assisted by Ullmann.

At a stroke, the stranglehold on Spanish military affairs exercised by the Bank of England and the Zaharoff-backed pro-British Constructora Naval, which had dominated Spanish arms procurement, was broken. Zaharoff, it appears, was distracted by events in the eastern Mediterranean. He may also have chosen to remain neutral partly out of respect for the King of Spain, whose goodwill he would need in order to continue his affair with the King's cousin, the Duchess of Marchena. Another factor, of course, was that Zaharoff himself, along with all other armament interests, could only eventually prosper from a resumption in Germany's armed capabilities. In particular, his interests in France could only be encouraged by a revival in German arms or at least the semblance of rearmament.

As was pointed out by Philip Noel Baker: 'A ceaseless propaganda ... indoctrinated the French people with the view that Germany was being prepared for a war of revenge ... .in this way a constant anxiety was maintained in France which ... facilitated the passage through the French Chamber of huge annual appropriations for the purchase of war material.'[9]

For Spain, these developments heralded the beginnings of a new and significant financial orientation. With the neutralisation of Constructora Naval, Spanish society from the King downwards felt liberated from what might be described as the pressure of British capital. Canaris reported that the resentment at all levels of the Spanish navy towards the British-backed company was intense, as it was felt 'the company put its own interests ahead of those of Spain.'

The gratitude of the Spanish was, as always, immense. Lohmann was invited to Spain to demonstrate new German technology on board a German merchant ship; the high point of the demonstration being no less than a visit from the King himself, flying his standard from the German ship as he inspected a new propulsion system. As Lohmann was at pains to point out to his superiors in Berlin, this was the first time the King of Spain had flown his colours in a foreign merchantman.

More importantly, it was noted by Lohmann how Canaris, with his fluent Spanish, had the ear of everyone of importance in Spain. 'Our cooperation with the Spanish navy owes much to the fact that he has the confidence of Echavarrieta, naval officers and members of the court and not least the King himself.' [10]

This confidence was fully exploited by Canaris to lay the foundations of what would be a lasting cooperation with the important organs of the Spanish state. In 1928 he initiated a formal agreement with General Bazan, head of the secret police. Other connections were consolidated with the intelligence service and the counter-intelligence service of the Spanish navy. At the same time he made contact with the military intelligence chiefs in Spain and procured their approval for a training scheme for German air force pilots, who would join the Spanish air force and with them enjoy combat experience as Spain put down the Morrocan revolt. In this way, Canaris came to work with Colonel Alfredo Kindelan, a senior air force officer, and the colonial minister General Gomez Count Jordana. Meanwhile, he added to these contacts a plan for joint police cooperation between Germany and Spain. He later negotiated this in detail with the minister of the interior, Martinez Anido. Without exception all these men would, in ten years time, be key advisers to one young officer whom Canaris at this stage had not yet met but who would dominate his country for decades to come: Francisco Franco.

Meanwhile, commercial projects came hand in glove with military cooperation. A Spanish airline was established as a joint venture with Luft-Hansa. Banking and insurance joint ventures followed. Moreover, Canaris did not limit his activities to Spain but exploited that country's links with Latin America to push for similar ventures in Argentina – another attack on, at that time, a diminishing but still important bastion of British capital influence. [11]

Unsurprisingly, in this ever more successful career, Canaris made enemies who, allied to his old foes on the left of German politics, began to counter attack. In this they were helped by the spectacular bankruptcy of one of Lohmann's most adventurous business forays, the film maker Phoebus. Lohmann's health had begun to deteriorate as he failed to keep track of the finances of the many-headed monster he had created. As one shell company after another required the discipline of detailed and regular audit, Lohmann adopted the tactics of a hunted man: he kept on the move. From train to motor-car to aeroplane; dictating the odd memo to bewildered subordinates, he found the only way to deal with the labyrinth he had created was to avoid dealing with it.

Unfortunately, when Phoebus collapsed, the left wing press all too easily found evidence that it had been a pack of cards constructed on the firm but secret foundation of Admiralty funds. *Die Weltbühne*, the newspaper that had had Canaris in its sights over the Liebknecht affair, now returned to the charge. Canaris, though largely innocent in the case of Phoebus, was brought back from Spain, questioned and given a posting in Wilhelmshaven, miles away from the spotlight in Berlin. The defence minister, Gessler, was forced to resign and was replaced by General Groener, whose thorough investigation exonerated Canaris while at the same time making the awful discovery that no less than twenty-six billion marks had been lost in one way or another through Lohmann's 'investments'.

To move from key negotiator on cutting edge naval technology with the King of Spain and other senior figures to a relatively insignificant backwater, surrounded by out of date ships of no serious strategic value, cannot have been easy. Canaris had the satisfaction of knowing that the work he had initiated in Spain would continue, and that the contacts he had begun between the German naval intelligence and the important organs of Spain would not be lost. There were, however, attempts – as some partly burnt secret documents from the German foreign ministry reveal – to bring Canaris back to Spain. On the recommendation of the retired naval officer Captain Messerschmidt, a German secret agent in Spain, the German ambassador Welczek wrote to the Reichswehr minister, noting Canaris' good relationship with the King and the 'great confidence he enjoys with other important personalities in Spain'. However, both Admiral Raeder, the new head of the navy, and the minister were determined 'on account of the sensitive themes' surrounding Canaris to keep him well away from Spain.[12]

Raeder also knew that as far as the prying eyes of a hostile German press were concerned there was no safer place than a life on the ocean wave. There now began two years of 'conventional' naval service for Canaris as first officer on board the training cruiser *Schlesien*, a ship built long before the war and indeed already obsolete by 1914.

Judging by the correspondence of the next two years, these conventional duties were not without their moments of pleasure. Though obsolete as a fighting ship, the *Schlesien* could at least show the flag and this it proceeded to do, in the best tradition of the old German navy, in a number of cruises around the Mediterranean. On one of these, a gala ball was given in Corfu by wealthy Greeks, who were so charmed by the officer with the Greek name that they gave him a picture of the Greek hero Admiral Canaris, which had pride of place in the Canaris household. The *Schlesien* also visited England, though tantalisingly there are no accounts of meetings between Canaris and his Royal Naval hosts.

By all accounts Canaris was a capable executive officer and his crew and officers found him to be a demanding but fair superior. Unsurprisingly, therefore, on 1 December 1932, Canaris was appointed captain of the *Schlesien*. The world of intelligence, secret deals and clandestine rearmament which had given Canaris so many opportunities for his unique talents must have appeared very remote. But then two months later, together with the rest of the *Schlesien*'s crew, he heard that Germany had a new Chancellor. His name: Adolf Hitler.

CHAPTER FIVE

SPY CHIEF

A naval officer and therefore an intelligent man.
CAPTAIN THOMAS TROUBRIDGE R.N., NAVAL
ATTACHÉ BERLIN 1936-39 [1]

The German navy was at first sceptical of the little man with the lock of black hair, Chaplin moustache and thuggish supporters dressed in those 'extraordinary brown uniforms', as one naval officer called them. The tactics of terror, anti-Jewish attacks and pagan ideology were not obviously appealing to officers brought up, like Canaris, in the imperial navy and monarchist at heart. But at the same time, the anti-Communist rhetoric rang a bell for those who had experienced the trauma of the Kiel mutiny. Moreover, in a stroke of cunning public relations, Hitler visited Wilhelmshaven and addressed an audience that many officers, dressed in mufti, attended. The rhetoric, the dramatic Austrian intonation in the voice, the rolling Rs and histrionic modulations, all played in a strangely convincing way for the north German audience.

The following day, a naval officer, Captain Schroeder, broke ranks and invited Hitler aboard his cruiser, the *Köln*. Here Hitler amazed his host by asking questions of such technical detail that it was clear he understood more about the German navy than any previous politician they had encountered. Signing the visitors' book, he confirmed the good impression with the words: 'In the hope that I can help with the reconstruction of a fleet worthy of the Reich.' [2]

For Canaris, these impressions were positive. Like millions of other Germans he saw in Hitler a saviour and an enemy of the Bolshevism that was his sworn enemy. The extreme anti-Semitism, no doubt given his later acts to save several Jews, would not have appealed to Canaris, – himself a far from Aryan-looking German – but it should be remembered that his worst antagonist in the Reichstag had been deputy Moses and the Communist left was still seen by the officer class in Germany, rightly or wrongly, as the preserve of Bolshevik Jews. Whatever his distance towards Hitler later in his life there can be little doubt that at this stage Canaris was a believer and, as shall be seen, not above playing the Nazis by appealing to their prejudices, anti-Semitism included.

However, such convictions did not avoid a spectacular gaffe when Goering visited the *Schlesien* on 23 May 1933. Goering was so frequently and violently seasick that one of Canaris' officers told him, in a serious voice, as he surfaced pale and ill in the ward room, that he had just heard that the air ace was to be appointed the chief supplier of fish feed for the North Sea and that he would have permission from now on to wear a fishnet over his immaculate white uniform. Unsurprisingly, Goering did not share the joke. He demanded disciplinary action: something Canaris felt obliged to pay some lip service to, although no charges were ever brought and once back in Berlin the Reichsmarschall appears to have forgotten the offence caused.

Irrespective of this episode of humorous if somewhat laboured inter-service rivalry, Canaris was finding relations with his superiors difficult. His immediate boss, Rear Admiral Bastian, appears to have been exceptionally truculent. On one occasion he sent Canaris a signal demanding that the commander of the *Schlesien* pay 'more attention' to the 'personality and desires' of the admiral. A series of disputes arose on petty regulations, which further widened the gap between the two men.

Bastian complained to Admiral Raeder, navy chief since 1928. Raeder, who had never hit it off with Canaris, was happy to hasten Canaris' career into obscurity. Raeder had never appreciated Canaris' gifts and remembered all too well the difficulty he had had in prising him out of Spain in the teeth of diplomatic opposition. An old fashioned officer, familiar as a type in every navy, Raeder was a man who saw everything in black and white. Everything about Canaris displeased him. He was controversial, involved in strange twilight activities and above all kept questionable company. Canaris' past dealings with the dubious financiers of Spain did not endear him to this former head of naval archives and son of a minor government official.

On 29 September 1934 Canaris was posted to take command of the German navy's equivalent of outer Siberia, the coastal defences of Swinemünde. Here, in the exile of the most provincial of provincial postings, Canaris could take solace only from the fact that the long stretch of deserted beach would afford many a happy hour cantering on horseback to escape the tedium of the ultimate sunset posting.

Miles away in Berlin, however, wheels were moving; indeed had been moving for some time, which would thwart Raeder's plans and bring Canaris back into the centre of events. The first major development, which was to have a profound effect on Canaris, was the appointment on 2 June 1932 of Captain Conrad Patzig to the post of Abwehr chief. This appointment was nothing short of sensational. There had never been a naval officer at the head of Germany's military intelligence, the famous section IIIB of the old imperial general staff.

Patzig's predecessor, Colonel Bredow, was, as Patzig later pointed out, 'an ambitious man'. But as the naval officer had also shrewdly noted: 'Such ambitious men are usually especially easy to deal with' and Bredow had come more and more to rely on Patzig, head of the important naval section (V). Poland was the principal target for counter-espionage activity and there was neither appetite nor funds for the Abwehr to undertake much more than a watching brief on the difficult Poles, rattling their sabres fresh from the successes of the Russo-Polish war. Here the ports of Königsberg, Stettin and Danzig were the critical centres of operations and naval intelligence support was the key factor. To the horror of the army, Bredow, on being promoted to a senior position in the Reichwehr ministry, now recommended Patzig to be his successor.

Patzig proved, as his recorded comments suggest, a highly capable intelligence chief. He moved swiftly to reassure the military and earn the respect of their officers serving under him. Patzig was fully aware that German rearmament must gather momentum and that with it, inevitably, came scope for expanding intelligence activities through cooperation with foreign agencies. Thus he initiated a successful joint venture with the Lithuanian service against the USSR. He also built up relations with other agencies, though not with the Italians, despite orders from on high to become more intimate with the Italian service. Patzig, like many Germans and Austrians, never trusted the Italians and was convinced all their codes and ciphers had been broken and that they had long ago been effectively penetrated by British and French intelligence.

Nevertheless, all these activities were gingered up with the advent of National-Socialism. This was the second major event, or wheel, which began to turn for Canaris. As was well-known even at the time, Hitler was obsessed with what he considered to be the key to Britain's power, its secret service. His admiration for Britain and its world empire knew few bounds, and if his favourite film was *Bengal Lancer*, he may well have been familiar with the exploits of clubland heroes as chronicled by Buchan and others in the inter-war period. He certainly admired Kipling, though it seems unlikely that he had ever read that textbook of essential reading for all British agents, *Kim*.

But the mystique of a great power sustained by an all-seeing intelligence service appealed to Hitler and indeed many of his cronies. As Walter Schellenberg, SD officer and the man who would later arrest Canaris, wrote admiringly: 'If we really want to understand the structural essence of British Intelligence we must liberate ourselves from conventional ideas.' (*Gestapo Handbook to Britain*, 1940) German ideas of strict organisation and detail were not always appropriate for a successful spy service. The new bosses of Germany wanted someone who was not conventional to run their service. Someone, moreover, who knew, if only indirectly, a little about the ways British intelligence worked. At the same time, they needed someone who was well connected with the influential interface between the military industrial complex, high finance and politics.

Here the wheel was turning in Canaris' favour, for through his contacts with Juan March he had become known to Zaharoff and Hitler's first paymaster, Baron Thyssen, both of them part of the forces which would 'save' Europe from the Bolsheviks. Given the now urgent desire to step up German rearmament, this world was also keen to deal with someone they knew and could trust. Not for nothing would Zaharoff, in 1934, bracket Canaris and Thyssen together as the only people his old friend George Mandel, Clemenceau's former head of cabinet, could work with in Germany.

In addition to these developments, a fourth, though perhaps in light of later events rather unexpected, wheel also seemed to be turning in Canaris' direction. This took the form of his former naval colleague, Heydrich, now head of the influential domestic security organisation the SD (*Sicherheitsdienst*), which reported to the head of the SS, Heinrich Himmler.

Through relentless card-indexing, extortion and blackmail, Heydrich had built a feared and powerful domestic spy service with access to all aspects of civilian life. He also admired the British secret service, even signing himself in the style of the SIS chief as 'C' though the compliment of imitation may not have been appreciated in the corridors of Broadway Buildings. Heydrich wanted a service that would embrace every aspect of German life in a way he imagined the British security service, through the English class system, dominated England. Inevitably, as he ceaselessly worked to expand the jurisdiction of the SD, he began to tread on Patzig's toes. Already, in April 1934, Goering had been forced to relinquish control of the police to the SD. One by one the provincial police forces became subject to central control. The Reichswehr minister General von Blomberg, described by Patzig as a 'rubber lion', failed to register any meaningful protest as the SD more and more encroached on Abwehr territory.

Patzig, later commander of the famous pocket battleship *Graf Spee* (and to be a great hit at the Coronation Regatta off the Isle of Wight a few years later), was a clear-thinking figure. He quickly saw that Heydrich and the SD would be the defining threat in the long term to Germany, and in the short term to the Abwehr. This perception was reinforced by the Roehm putsch: the 'night of the long knives' in which the tyranny and bloodletting of the SA was replaced by the tyranny and bloodletting of the SS, all with the silent acquiescence of the army. These macabre events, which saw generals murdered in their homes and countless others shot out of hand (including two of von Papen's adjutants, shot across their office desks) only confirmed what Patzig had always suspected: that the new regime was run by gangsters. The fact that among the corpses was his predecessor von Bredow shocked all the staff of the Abwehr. One of them, Major Hans Oster, determined from that day on to work against the regime.

Patzig, meanwhile, was determined to fight a rearguard action while at the same time seeking the calmer waters of an operational appointment. His dealings with Heydrich had become ever more fractious. Heydrich demanded a list of all the armament installations in Germany, which Patzig refused on the grounds that such lists did not exist and would be a risk to national security. This fencing with the SD led to a heated exchange between Blomberg and Patzig, during which the former tried to defend the SS as 'an organisation of the Führer', evincing the reply from Patzig: 'Then I regret that the Führer is not aware of the pigsty he has under him.' Patzig was now isolated and his career at the Abwehr could not last much longer. Whoever would replace Patzig, Blomberg noted, would have to build a more 'constructive relationship' with the SD.

Although there is no evidence to suggest Heydrich may have lobbied behind the scenes for Patzig's dismissal and replacement by Canaris, it is not inconceivable that Heydrich, through Himmler, may have applied pressure to get rid of one naval officer and have him replaced by another they trusted.[3] There is certainly something guarded, if not mischievously evasive, in Patzig's post-war evidence that Canaris got the job simply 'because I could not think of anyone more suitable.'

Canaris may have been the most suitable candidate to replace Patzig but he was not considered by anyone in the navy, with the possible exception of Patzig, as a relevant candidate. But irrespective of any lobbying on his behalf by the SS, Canaris certainly possessed, for those who chose to examine his record, relatively impeccable credentials. He had frequently outwitted British and French intelligence, he was well connected with the magic circle of financiers and industrialists associated with armaments and he even, at the very least, had had a convivial social relationship with that wolf in sheep's clothing, Heydrich. Thanks to the continuing rumours of his involvement in the Liebknecht affair, Canaris possessed good anti-Bolshevik credentials and was therefore ideologically sound. In addition to this, perhaps critically, he was a naval officer.

In the event, it was this last factor which guaranteed him the job. For as Patzig broke the news to Admiral Raeder that they should consider Canaris as his successor, the Admiral spluttered: 'Impossible'. Raeder acidly pointed out that he had not sent Canaris to Swinemünde so that he should be considered eligible to play a future role in the German High Command. Quite the reverse; Raeder expected Canaris to retire within the next four years and bring to a discreet close his controversial, but in Raeder's view, relatively undistinguished naval career.

At this point, Patzig may have played the Heydrich card and suggested that Canaris was the only person who could find a modus vivendi with the SD. He certainly put down his strongest suit. He pointed out that if Raeder was implacably opposed to Canaris' appointment, it would really be quite simple to find a solution. There would be no alternative but to appoint to the post of Abwehr chief someone from the army. Once again, Patzig's insight into character weaknesses proved decisive. He knew that Raeder, as a conservative naval officer, would choose the lesser of the two evils rather than surrender control of military intelligence and signals to the narrow-minded men in field grey.

Whether Canaris was the classic compromise candidate acceptable to both sides and therefore supported by both the SS and the military is difficult to prove, but it seems likely. In any event, within a few weeks of his taking over the Abwehr, relations between the SD and Abwehr had been organized along less fractious lines and a period of calm entered into the relationship, something which is highly suggestive that Canaris was indeed Heydrich's candidate. Certainly, if Inge Haag, Canaris' sole surviving secretary, is to be believed, the two men had a very convivial relationship at this stage.[4] 'Between Canaris and Heydrich there was a relationship which can best be described as intimate. Certain things were taken for granted in that naval tradition whereby they were comrades who had served together at sea and therefore enjoyed a bond denied to other officers around Canaris.'[5]

Heydrich's widow described Canaris' relationship to Heydrich as 'paternal' and even Himmler had a superstitious respect for Canaris. No doubt the tales of espionage that had enabled the two navy men to bond when Heydrich was a cadet had, in their retelling to the former chicken farmer Himmler, lost none of their excitement or plausibility. If Canaris had introduced Heydrich into the world of intelligence concepts and ideas, over the dinners he had prepared more than ten years ago, it would hardly be surprising for Heydrich not to remember his mentor.

Canaris certainly seems to have felt confident that he could work with Heydrich. Patzig had some words of advice to Canaris about how to manage the relationship with the SD, but Canaris shrugged these off, noting that he knew how to deal with 'these young men'. At the same time, as Canaris noted in his diary, Heydrich was 'a brutal fanatic with whom it will be difficult to have an open and friendly cooperation'. For his part, Heydrich never trusted Canaris, always correcting colleagues who underestimated Canaris by referring to him as that 'wily old fox'.

As Canaris well knew, all telephone lines out of the Abwehr offices were monitored by the SD.[6] This would not stop the two men later living near the Schlachtensee as close neighbours with adjoining gardens and reviving the chamber music evenings that had been part of their earlier naval days.

Thus it was on 2 January 1935 that the grey granite five-storey building of the Tirpitzufer welcomed the small, rather understated, sallow-skinned man with grey, almost white hair for the first time as its chief. Two small lifts and a divided staircase lit from above beckoned him past the small concierge's room occupied by a non-commissioned officer. One of the lifts took him to the top floor, where a tall-ceilinged room with twin doors was empty, save for a large desk and a couple of chairs. It was eight o'clock and the offices were largely deserted. Patzig, he noted, had with typical naval thoroughness taken all his furniture.

Canaris' appointment was a state secret and as has been pointed out, in a police state with draconian laws for treachery and the recent memory of summary execution of 'traitors' in the Röhm Putsch vivid in everyone's minds, such secrets were not difficult to keep. The British Admiralty, which had tracked Canaris in Spain during the war, lost sight of him between 1935 and 1939. Its attachés and intelligence officers did not note the change of appointment from Swinemünde. Indeed, their senior naval attaché, Captain Troubridge, addicted to golf and sailing, despite meeting every senior naval officer Germany could offer, diligently recording every name in his diary, (and connected through his wife to the influential Rathenau family), never once, it seems, encountered Wilhelm Canaris.

In fact Troubridge, who would later lunch with Churchill and Bracken to give 'first hand information' about the senior personalities of Nazi Germany, appears to have been 'mentally quite inadequate', to coin his phrase, for intelligence work. Until his recall in 1939, he continued to believe the head of the Abwehr was General Tippelskirch, who was in fact the Quartermaster General of the German army.[7] Not without reason could one historian of that time note that the NID was 'very poorly served in Germany in those years.'[8]

Rather more alert was the Chilean naval attaché, with whom Canaris established cordial relations, partly as a result of the immense help Canaris had been given by Chileans to escape his internment camp after the *Dresden* was sunk.

When Alfredo Hoffmann, a Chilean of German descent, paid a visit to Canaris the conversation turned not unnaturally to those days:

'I shall never forget what the Chileans did to help me. I shall do everything to help you here. How can I help you?', Canaris asked.

Hoffmann had a sensitive request: 'May I see the Baltic fleet exercises?'

What followed was typical Canaris. Raising his voice, he bluntly said: 'Impossible. These exercises are off limits to foreign attachés.' Canaris then lowered his voice and said *sotto voce*: 'As a Chilean and a fellow naval officer, you place me in an awkward position; I have a duty to examine all the possibilities. Someone will be in touch.'

A few weeks later, just as Hoffmann had given up any hope of attending the exercise, an officer of the Abwehr appeared complete with a false German journalist's pass and for the duration of the exercise an entirely new identity for the bemused Hoffmann.[9]

In this way Canaris illustrated his mental elasticity, and built for the future as well as repaying the debts of the past. From that day onwards, any intelligence of relevance gleaned by Hoffmann would be vouchsafed to the Abwehr.

Most diplomats, however, who did run into Canaris knew him as a staff officer working in Berlin, occasionally but very rarely to be seen on the cocktail party circuit. A young English journalist ran into the name but thought him concerned with minor protocol duties.[10] Even when a spectacular spy scandal broke, involving the seduction of two war office secretaries by a Polish officer, Canaris remained in the shadows. As the Polish ambassador Lipski recalled, he never suspected for a moment that Canaris was a spy chief: 'I was visited by an elderly white-haired Admiral. I was struck by his soft benevolent manner ... I never dreamed this was the chief of German intelligence.' [11]

This encounter had been provoked by the Sosnowski case. Jurek von Sosnowski, a tall, handsome 'devil, brave and cool with a charming smile and cold eyes that make you shiver' [12] was a formidable operator. Setting up in Berlin as an impoverished former cavalry officer down on his luck, Sosnowski was literally lethal when it came to members of the fairer sex. One after another he seduced female members of the lesser nobility until he had a certain Frau von Natzmer in his sights. She worked for the staff of General Guderian, then perfecting his tactics of armoured blitzkrieg that would prove so devastating against Poland and France a few years later.

Together with Benita von Falkenhayn, a member of the Berlin society of those times, and a frequent visitor to the races and theatres, Sosnowski worked on Frau von Natzmer. At a bathing party, seduction was soon followed by blackmail, with the result that what had been just a few titbits of information became a steady trickle of documents from I.N.6, Guderian's planning section. The tighter the turning of the blackmail screw the more desperate and informative the hapless victim became. As usual he gave her some money, but not enough to cover the debts run up by the victim, with Sosnowki's encouragement, to complete the web of financial dependency.

It was made clear to Natzmer that if she wished to be released from her 'contract' with Polish intelligence she would have to enlist other girls in the war ministry who might be hard up to replace her. Unsurprisingly,

Natzmer complied, and within a year Sosnowski had more than a hundred documents detailing the secret development of German weapons on Russian territory and the latest developments in German armoured vehicle technology. He even managed to procure the keys to Guderian's safe.

Unfortunately, about that time, the Abwehr had 'turned' the junior Polish military attaché in Berlin, Lieutenant Griff Tchaikowsky. This weak and rather amateur Pole was the exact opposite of Sosnowski; careless where Sosnowski was diligent, rocked by scruples and emotions where Sosnowski was ruthless. Passing on at the behest of his masters false documents purporting to come from Guderian's section, Tchaikowsky was surprised to find one day, hanging up to dry in the darkroom of the Polish embassy, some genuine material from Section I.N.6. Rarely has the old adage of the left hand not knowing the activities of the right in intelligence work had such dramatic consequences. Tchaikowsky showed the genuine documents to the astonished Abwehr, who then proceeded to investigate together with the all-seeing SD of Heydrich. It was not long before Sosnowki's spoor was detected. At a champagne supper given by Sosnowski, the Gestapo suddenly appeared, lining up the hysterical female guests and their nervous male consorts. Sosnowski, with the sang-froid of a Polish cavalry officer of Austrian training, regarded his interrogators impassively.

'You are a spy', shouted the Gestapo.

'No, no nothing of the sort', he replied coolly.

'Then you are a confidence agent.'

'You are quite mistaken', said the smiling Sosnowski.

'I'll tell you what he is,' said Richard Protze, the Abwehr's man on the case: 'You are a Polish intelligence officer.' [13]

When this accusation was repeated in the People's Court some months later, Sosnowski clicked his heels and sprang to attention. Sosnowski was exchanged for some German agents picked up in Warsaw. Both Frau von Natzmer and Frau von Falkenhayn were beheaded in February 1935. The documents so carefully procured by them suffered the fate of much high grade intelligence; it was considered too good to be true and an obvious plant. It was ignored by the Polish intelligence staff. [14]

The incident, with its accompanying sensitive negotiation between Canaris and Warsaw on the exchange of prisoners, was the first joint Abwehr/Sicherheitsdienst operation to run smoothly and set the seal on a period of greater harmony between the two organisations. But the cooperation came at a price that Patzig had been unwilling to pay: the Abwehr was becoming a key building block in the totalitarian architecture of Germany. The lines of engagement between the once aloof military intelligence machine of the Abwehr and the more brutal activities of the SD security apparatus were being blurred.

At first there was some disquiet among Abwehr officers. The relationship with Heydrich so bitterly fought and resisted by Patzig appeared to be easily surrendered by the white-haired Captain. These critical views were not helped by Canaris' own appearance, which his subordinates pointed out could not have cut a more different figure from the energetic, dynamic and smartly turned out Patzig. In contrast, Canaris appeared tired, disorganized and distinctly unmilitary in appearance. One officer noted: 'Compared to Patzig, he seemed decidedly shop soiled and old.' [15] Another noted: 'We were so surprised, he gave the impression of a civilian rather than a senior German officer.'

In his first speech, Canaris made it clear that he expected the atmosphere of resentment towards the SD and Heydrich to change. His opening speech was decidedly pro-Nazi and contained the phrase, which sent a shiver down some spines, 'comradely cooperation with the Gestapo', [16] a point overlooked by some biographers of the Admiral who have preferred to dwell on the oft-quoted Nicolai reference to espionage being the 'domain of gentlemen'. Certainly Canaris made a passing reference to this, for all intelligence officers, comforting remark, but he appears at this point to have been keen to play as straight a bat as possible, knowing of course that his words would within hours be reported to Heydrich by his sympathisers in the Abwehr, of whom Rudolf Bamler, head of section III, counter-espionage, and therefore in closest contact with the SD, was only one.

Moreover, Canaris knew that cooperation between the Wehrmacht and the SD was the theme of the moment. The day after Canaris gave his introductory speech, he was summoned with the rest of the senior military to a speech in the Berlin Opera House in which Hitler denounced the 'rumours of military disloyalty', pledging his faith in the loyalty of his generals and rejecting criticism of them by the party. The speech was delivered to quell rumours of tension between the party and the senior officers of the military and knock on the head once and for all the rivalries that seemed to poison the key relationship of the Reich. In this it was a success, as the appeal to the generals' vanity once again silenced many of the critics in field grey. For a brief time it even looked as if all might yet be sweetness and light with their black-uniformed contemporaries.

Canaris was seated in the stalls behind Keitel and Jodl and under no illusions that he would have to play his own part in this rapprochement if he, and indeed the Abwehr, were to enjoy some freedom of manoeuvre and play the role which the coming years would offer.

In private, Canaris worked on his officers to quickly convince them that the only choice for the Abwehr was to 'run with the party' if it was to develop and grow and expand into an instrument capable of some inde-pendent thought and action. That, however, as he pointed out, did not mean that the Abwehr would adopt the methods of the Nazi party. As one officer who was very impressed by the admiral that day noted: 'All activities would be conducted in a gentlemanly style, the style in fact of our chief.' [17]

In intimate conversation, Canaris made it clear that orders from outside agencies that involved brutal methods would be disregarded by a variety of methods, some involving deceit, others delay, but never any public acts of direct obstruction. Gradually many Abwehr officers realised that far from being some party apparatchik, their chief was a more subtle spirit. The relationship with his subordinates was paternal (as with Heydrich in the old days) and Canaris introduced the naval tradition of calling staff by the familiar *Du* rather than the more formal *Sie* of the German Army.

In discussing events with his officers he rarely missed an opportunity to show his contempt for scurrilous behaviour in espionage. Blackmail he abhorred. Indeed, he took advantage of the Sosnowski case to dwell on the shortcomings of such methods, making it very clear that he would not tolerate for a moment similar tactics in the Abwehr: 'If one of my officers has recourse to these methods,' he sternly warned his section heads as the case wound down to its melancholy conclusion, 'I shall proceed against him with the utmost severity.' [18]

Good intelligence, in Canaris' philosophy, came from neither extortion nor blackmail. The human element was the key. It was far better to establish a relationship of trust with an agent than to deploy the black arts so beloved of spy fiction, though as will be seen, the Abwehr, far from always playing by Queensbury rules, was certainly not above blackmail, especially with regard to its Irish agents during the Second World War. Nevertheless, on the whole, honey rather than vinegar was Canaris' watchword.

For similar reasons, although he had an entire section devoted to sabotage, (Section II), he was also sceptical of its value, not least on account of the danger to innocent civilians. Such groups were difficult to control and often provoked reprisals against the civilian population. Gradually, one by one, the Abwehr officers learnt that they had a strong and wily protector of their interests in the slightly dishevelled admiral and that, as one of the Abwehr officers pointed out a few weeks later, 'There is rather more to him than meets the eye on first impression'.[19]

Canaris, needless to say, made his mark with the Führer. Between December 1934, just prior to his taking over the Abwehr, and March 1935, Canaris had no less than seventeen private meetings with Hitler. Like every chief of clandestine intelligence he enjoyed the right of access to the head of state at any time. But in Canaris' case this privilege appears to have been unusually generously interpreted. No record exists of their first meeting but we can be sure that the qualities Canaris had manifested throughout his career stood him in good stead.

These were, first and foremost, a cosmopolitan outlook on life. Canaris was perhaps the only politically reliable (i.e. anti-Communist) figure close to Hitler who knew something of the outside world. Much has been written about Hitler's admiration for Ribbentrop,[20] the whisky salesman who had traded with the Scots and was therefore, somewhat rashly, invested by Hitler with a broad knowledge of the British empire. If Ribbentrop could appear a man of the world to Hitler, it would not have been difficult for Canaris, with his knowledge of the clandestine armaments and banking worlds, to appear the very incarnation of geo-political wisdom.

Secondly, Canaris was a good listener, a sine qua non of any meaningful relationship with Hitler. Canaris knew well how to listen and charm Hitler, playing to his foibles and character weaknesses. Canaris had a soft spot for the Austrians: a legacy, perhaps, of his love of Europe south of the Alps. While Hitler would come to represent all that he loathed about klein bourgeois Austria, Canaris knew enough about the central European temperament to know how to 'play him'. That meant pandering to Hitler's prejudices, including anti-Semitism.

Following research by Willi Grosse, [21] there is a probability that in one of these conversations, Canaris even mentioned the crass and repellent idea of identifying Jews in Germany by their enforced wearing of the Star of David. It was, of course, long before the death camps had been constructed, but while several biographers have sought to defend Canaris, claiming that he was acting in accordance with geographical rather than racial considerations, this conversation, if it indeed took place, must count as one of the blackest marks against Canaris' record. At this stage, with the first flush of success in reorganising the Abwehr, it is sadly all too plausible that Canaris might have wanted to ingratiate himself with the Führer by suggesting a 'solution' to the Jewish problem inside Germany. As mentioned earlier, Canaris was, in part, as a result of his views on Communism, far from philo-Semitic, yet as has been seen from his time in Spain during the First World War and his subsequent action in saving many Jews by drafting them into the Abwehr, he cannot be branded a typical anti-Semite either. He had worked successfully with Jewish bankers such as Ullmann, and would time and again rescue Jews from the certainty of being sent to the concentration camps by drafting them as agents abroad. Indeed, the conversation in which the question of the wearing of the Star of David arose may well have been provoked by the fact that the Abwehr was, uniquely in the Third Reich, exempt from the Aryanisation laws that barred Jews from government service.

For Canaris, the means justified the end, and if the Abwehr was to play a decisive role in Germany's future it had to be inoculated against the charges of treason, sentimentality and pro-Zionist tendencies, especially as its chief was hardly the embodiment of aryan vigour. That meant not only supping with the devil but imbibing much of the poison on the same menu.

Canaris was ambitious. He knew that his was only one of seven intelligence gathering agencies in Hitler's Germany (*see the diagram on page 109*) and his aim was to make the Abwehr the predominant and best informed of them. The Abwehr had to share the intelligence stage with the Sicherheitsdienst, the Naval Intelligence section, Goering's Forschungs Amt, Rosenberg's Foreign Political Office, the German Minorities Intelligence Centre and the Foreign Ministry. It was by no means clear that the Abwehr could establish the necessary predominance to overshadow these rivals, all of which had Hitler's ear in one way or another. Relations with the Foreign Ministry were especially strained, partly on account of Ribbentrop's jealousy but also on account of that inevitable tension between diplomats and intelligence officers which always casts a shadow over collaboration between these organisations. It is in the nature of diplomacy to strive to avoid incidents which result from espionage activity, while it is in the nature of intelligence work to risk provoking such events, if only because espionage frequently involves people for whom the codes of diplomacy are sadly very far from being second nature.

In order to establish credibility and dominance, Canaris aimed to mend fences on all fronts. He established cordial links with the Foreign Ministry through a former naval officer and colleague, von Weiszäcker, then a state secretary but soon to play an important role at the Vatican as German minister to the Holy See, and to collaborate with Canaris in heading off Hitler's instructions later in the war to kidnap Pope Pius XII.

Later during the war, many of the peace-feelers that would engage London and Berlin would be transmitted through the Vatican. At a stroke, Canaris and Weiszäcker restored cordial relations: the freemasonry of the imperial German navy apparently breaking the ice which had frozen relations between the Tirpitzufer (German admiralty) and the Aussen Amt (foreign ministry).

With the SD, any reserve felt by the Abwehr officers after Canaris' inaugural speech may have been dissipated by a Bierkeller evening specially arranged for officers of the Abwehr and the SD on the evening of 13 January, less than two weeks after Canaris took over as Abwehr chief. The mood was convivial and field-grey and black appeared to mingle on the best of terms. Himmler, predictably well-briefed by Heydrich, hit it off with Canaris: the naval officer with the understated manner, but keen gaze, was the spy chief of all his fantasies come true.

As it happened it was also the day of the Saar plebiscite. The rich coal mining area lying north of Lorraine was detached from Germany under articles 45–50 of the Treaty of Versailles, and the rights of exploitation granted to France for a period of fifteen years. At the close of this period the population were to decide their future status, on this day voting more than ninety per cent in favour of reunion with Germany. Unsurprisingly, the

The viper's nest of competing intelligence in the Third Reich

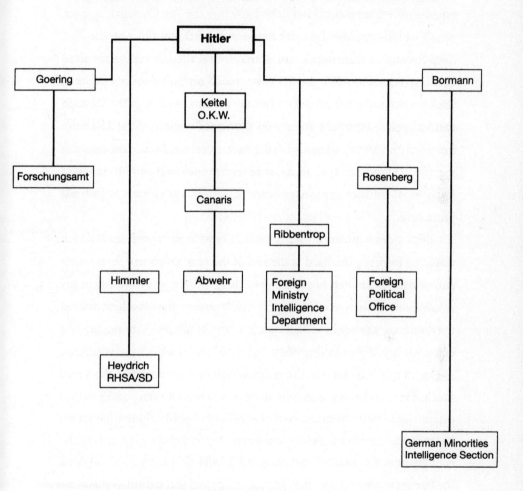

mood in the *Berlin Bierkeller* was *gemütlich* (convivial). Both sides could take pleasure in the fact that the ball of German ascendancy had been set rolling.

Less than a week later, on 17 January, Canaris and Heydrich met to establish the framework, later to be known as the Ten Commandments, which would regulate the work between the SD and the Abwehr. The need for such a framework had, it may be recalled, been the result of Patzig's refusal to allow the SD to encroach on the Abwehr's political work, in particular the Abwehr's right to act *pari-passu* with the Gestapo political police. The agreement now discussed envisaged the Abwehr's monopoly on secret espionage left intact, in return for an undertaking that the SD had priority to act as more than *primus inter pares* with regard to political counter-espionage activity, which was subject to judicial procedure.

Both sides expressed their satisfaction with the agreement, which would be formally finalised at the end of the year. Of course, as no strict definition was applied to counter-espionage, there was needless to say ample room for manoeuvre on both sides. Moreover, the Abwehr remained the dominant agency in military matters and as anyone with the briefest of knowledge of the intelligence world could see, it would not be difficult to extend this interest into the political field in a country like the Third Reich. Even in democracies, the frontier between military and political espionage is rather fluid. Canaris could collect political intelligence on the grounds that it was relevant to military decision making. In this way he could continue to prick Ribbentrop and, as will shortly be seen, outshine the foreign minister's own intelligence credentials and so further ingratiate himself with Hitler.

Moreover, if he offered cooperation with the SD, this was a two-way street. If Heydrich felt he had a window on the military thanks to Canaris, the Abwehr was building up its own surveillance of the party, so that by December 1938, the diplomat von Hassell could note in his diary that the 'one positive approach ... is the surveillance of the entire party through the intelligence section (Canaris) of the army.' [22]

At the same time, Canaris set about building up his intelligence machine. The Abwehr was divided into five sections (*see the diagram on pages 112–3*). Section I, under Colonel Pieckenbrock, was responsible for secret espionage abroad. Section II (Sabotage), under the direction of Major Helmuth Grosscurth, was responsible for preparation of sabotage/commando activity behind enemy lines. Into this section was inserted a formidable special forces unit known, after the area in which they were trained, as the 'Brandenburgers'. These were the true predecessors of todays special forces. Multi-lingual, highly mobile and trained to operate behind enemy lines, these units recruited by word of mouth proved more than a match for the NKVD at Murmansk and even the SAS at the Iron Gates on the Danube, and later at Leros. At the same time, these units may have later formed the secret potential nucleus for an armed revolt against Hitler.

Section III (Counter-Espionage), under Major Rudolf Bamler, was the principal department liaising with the SD and was a domestic security section dealing with infiltration, treason and counter-espionage.

In addition to these three sections, there was the so-called 'Foreign Section' under Admiral Leopold Birkner, a colleague of Canaris from his Wilhelmshaven days, which had the job of evaluating foreign military intelligence and liaising with the military and naval attachés *en poste* abroad and foreign attachés posted to Berlin.

Finally, Section Z, under Major General Hans Oster, was responsible for administration and organisation: perhaps in many ways the most important, if least transparent, part of any intelligence organisation. This section dealt with budgeting issues, although in certain circumstances conflicts were resolved by Canaris himself.

As with other intelligence agencies, a civilian front company acted as a screen for the organisation's financial transactions that could not be

The Abwehr

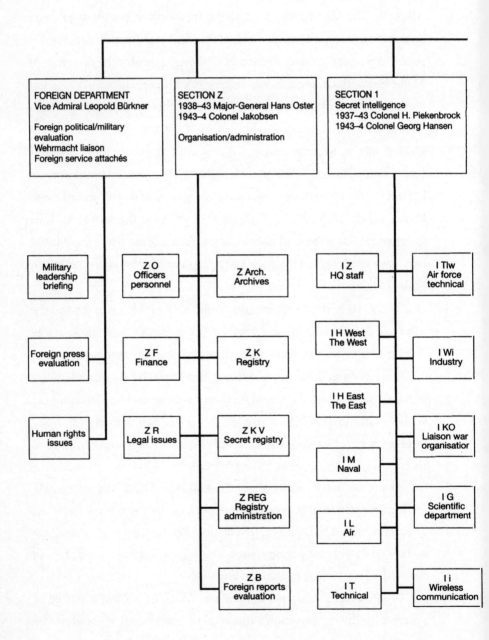

FOREIGN DEPARTMENT
Vice Admiral Leopold Bürkner

Foreign political/military
evaluation
Wehrmacht liaison
Foreign service attachés

SECTION Z
1938–43 Major-General Hans Oster
1943–4 Colonel Jakobsen

Organisation/administration

SECTION 1
Secret intelligence
1937–43 Colonel H. Piekenbrock
1943–4 Colonel Georg Hansen

Military
leadership
briefing

Z O
Officers
personnel

Z Arch.
Archives

I Z
HQ staff

I Tlw
Air force
technical

Foreign press
evaluation

Z F
Finance

Z K
Registry

I H West
The West

I Wi
Industry

Human rights
issues

Z R
Legal issues

Z K V
Secret registry

I H East
The East

I KO
Liaison war
organisation

I M
Naval

Z REG
Registry
administration

I G
Scientific
department

I L
Air

Z B
Foreign reports
evaluation

I T
Technical

I i
Wireless
communication

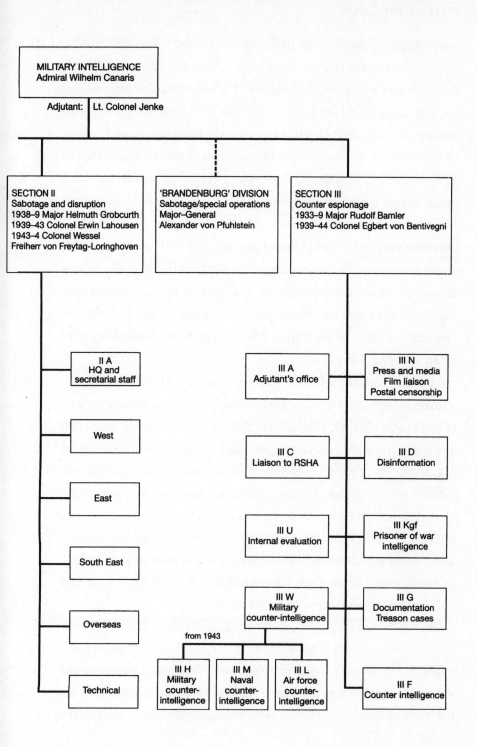

MILITARY INTELLIGENCE
Admiral Wilhelm Canaris

Adjutant: Lt. Colonel Jenke

SECTION II
Sabotage and disruption
1938–9 Major Helmuth Grobcurth
1939–43 Colonel Erwin Lahousen
1943–4 Colonel Wessel
Freiherr von Freytag-Loringhoven

'BRANDENBURG' DIVISION
Sabotage/special operations
Major–General
Alexander von Pfuhlstein

SECTION III
Counter espionage
1933–9 Major Rudolf Bamler
1939–44 Colonel Egbert von Bentivegni

II A
HQ and
secretarial staff

West

East

South East

Overseas

Technical

III A
Adjutant's office

III N
Press and media
Film liaison
Postal censorship

III C
Liaison to RSHA

III D
Disinformation

III U
Internal evaluation

III Kgf
Prisoner of war
intelligence

III W
Military
counter-intelligence

III G
Documentation
Treason cases

from 1943

III H
Military
counter-
intelligence

III M
Naval
counter-
intelligence

III L
Air force
counter-
intelligence

III F
Counter intelligence

handled by the diplomatic bag. In this case the company was called, suitably enough, Transmare and was run by a Levantine Jew known only by his cover name of Baron Ino. Ino possessed Turkish nationality and was, like Canaris, someone whose commercial links were intimately linked with armament interests.[23] Also like Canaris he had forged his early career in Spain, where he first came to the attention of British intelligence in 1916. As early as 1925 Stewart Menzies had called up his file. Ino had a dozen aliases but his real name was Misrachi. The British intelligence Black Book knew him as Baron von Rolland. Canaris would regularly entertain him in Berlin in Hungarian bars. It is a tribute to the power Canaris managed to garner for the Abwehr that Ino was able to pass through Germany unmolested until the summer of 1939. By that time the Abwehr had long had its own passport and visa section and, with the special permission of the Führer, immunity from the Nuremberg rules on aryanisation policy.

Oster, the head of Section Z, was from the moment of Bredow's assassination a determined figure in the resistance movement. A cavalry officer of impeccable turn-out, who believed that life was an obstacle course that had to be surmounted with intelligence and wit, he was at first suspicious of Canaris. The relationship between them was tense. Where Canaris was cautious and ambivalent, Oster was direct and honest to the point of folly. Nevertheless, both men were deeply if not formally religious and for both, ethical considerations were paramount. Moreover, Oster felt he could always speak his mind in an Abwehr under Canaris: a circumstance which, as Abshagen points out, 'only those who knew and experienced the Nazi police state can understand what that meant.'

Between 1935 and 1937, Canaris expanded this core framework considerably. From an organisation of less than 150, the Abwehr grew rapidly to nearly a thousand in less than three years. The intake was mixed and as has been documented elsewhere, [24] fell into three categories. First were the traditional imperial officers, men who had grown up in the Kaiser's service and adhered to nineteenth century values. Then came the post-1918 intake made up of officers of the Reichswehr, the small force permitted by Versailles and groomed by von Seeckt, highly qualified men with a technical training without equal anywhere in the world at that time. They were, nevertheless, bureaucratic in outlook. Both these cadres were apolitical. The third group, made up of younger officers who had completed their training after 1933, were more indoctrinated by the party: Hitler, after all, had given them a career with possibilities.

All three groups had in common an above average intelligence in comparison with many of their military contemporaries, but they were not as cohesive as a whole as might be imagined. If Bamler was pro-nazi, Oster was his opposite. If 'Piecki' (Pieckenbrock) was the dry technocratic Rhinelander, 'Benti' (Bentivegni), who would replace Bamler in 1939, was as Prussian an officer of the old school as one could find, complete with spurs and monocle.

In 1938, following the incorporation of Austria into the Reich, this disparate group would be joined by yet another type, in the form of Colonel Lahousen, the 'purest example of the typical Imperial and Royal officer corps of the old Austria'. Detached, sardonic, charming and when appropriate refreshingly frivolous, Lahousen was at the same time at ease with the most Balkan of intrigues. With his Austrian *k.und k.* (imperial and royal) training – Lahousen had even served in the old imperial and royal Austrian secret service known as the Evidenzbüro – came an utter contempt for the Prussian officer corps type (though Lahousen was careful to refrain from ventilating this prejudice too loudly until after the war, when he denounced several of his former colleagues as 'born Prussians, typical Berlin philistines.' [25]

If this was an eccentric group of officers to form the core of a powerful secret organisation, they only reflected the foibles of their chief. Canaris was, his regular siestas on his iron camp bed apart, a workaholic and prone, like most men obsessed with their work, to be capricious in their judgements of personalities. He loathed men with too small ears and large physical frames. 'That is a kidnapper', he would say, deploying the English word after meeting someone whose appearance somehow threatened him. At other times he would tolerate intellectual lightweights if they had the requisite manners and were 'handsome or dashing'.

A similar lack of convention governed the furnishings of Canaris' office. Here austerity ruled, as elsewhere in his modest life-style. If his wife had had to sell her violin for him to build their modest house on the Schlachtensee, Canaris' office was also dominated by few trappings of comfort. A military camp bed, a sofa and a threadbare carpet, which he obstinately refused to repair, greeted foreign ministers of state and visiting chiefs of staff. On his desk was a model of his beloved cruiser *Dresden*, on the wall a map of the world. Otherwise the only memorable details appear to have been a portrait of his 'ancestor', the Greek admiral Kanaris, a hazy photograph of his illustrious predecessor Colonel Nicolai and the three small bronze apes: seeing no evil, hearing no evil and speaking no evil, which some took to be the motto of the Abwehr but in fact had a wider symbolism, with echoes of Kipling and the Anglo-Saxon world of the Great Game. Nearby a small safe completed the picture of an otherwise unmemorable office.

Given the pace with which events moved from January 1935, it is tempting to conclude that Canaris simply had no time to consider richer furnishings. In any event, he loathed desk work and no trappings of office could soften the tedium which the thought of office life provoked.

Meanwhile, the momentum of German rearmament continued. In February, the Abwehr was asked to monitor France, Britain, Czechoslovakia, Poland and Spain for possible reaction to an eventual German announcement of conscription and rearmament. In the first week of March, the French announced they were extending national service from eighteen months to two years. This was the opportunity for which Hitler had been waiting. The announcement on 16 March that the German army would expand to thirty-six divisions was, as has been written, the 'epitaph of German disarmament.' [26]

The French and British were caught off guard and handsomely *brûlé* but the reaction, in the form of the Stresa Front, offered little impediment to Germany's plans, though the resulting international hullabaloo afforded Canaris an opportunity, on 29 March, to dictate a directive rather in the style of Nicolai, noting: 'Times of foreign political tension are a test for intelligence organisations and their abilities. I expect from all ranks their best efforts in the service of the Fatherland.'

There now began a period of rapid transition. The Reichswehr became the Wehrmacht, the Truppenamt the Generalstab and the Reichswehrministerium the Kriegsministerium. The Abwehr did not change its name but its activities and budget expanded. In particular it began to infiltrate potentially hostile foreign agencies by expanding cooperation with friendly intelligence organisations. Canaris now began to establish closer relations with the head of the Hungarian military intelligence and Colonel Roatta, the chief of the Italian service. These officers were all Anglophiles and had insights into French and British intelligence activity that were at that stage denied to Berlin. Here, Canaris, thanks to his naval background, was able to effect formidable connections. He had served with Hungary's regent, Admiral Horthy, in the First World War, while his establishing of close links with Roatta, long neglected by Patzig, came with the blessing of Hitler and Mussolini.

At the same time, the Abwehr, again cooperating with the SD, drew a tight net over French and British agents monitoring German armament firms. The trawl brought several agents to book, including Captain Demphoff, nominally in the pay of the Czechs but whose intelligence was being passed to Paris and London. Demphoff was hanged for treason after he had, in Canaris' words, 'sacrificed life, honour and the fortunes of his family by betraying the Fatherland.' The net fell also on Marxists, Communists and thousands of other politically unreliable people who were sacked from jobs in sensitive industries and often rounded up with ruthless efficiency by the Abwehr and SD. In contrast to those who might have imagined the Abwehr to consist solely of dilettantes and patriotic eccentrics, it is as well to recall that at this stage it was proving both a formidable adversary to those intent on prizing military secrets out of Berlin, and an instrument of internal repression. Hotels were now staffed almost exclusively by informers and agents of the SD and Abwehr. Every industrial complex in Germany had its Abwehr representative at board level.

A year later, by the time Hitler came to reoccupy the Rhineland, the Abwehr's reputation was in the ascendant. The events of spring 1936 were to consolidate its position even further. In a meeting with Hitler, early in February 1936, Canaris showed the Führer an invasion plan of Germany jointly prepared by the French and Czechoslovak general staffs. Its immediate effect (though it was later proved a forgery) was to spur Hitler into bringing forward to March his plan to remilitarise the Rhineland. However, before giving his final consent to operation 'Winter Manoeuvre', he demanded an accurate intelligence assessment of London's possible reaction. Here the Abwehr, to the chagrin of the foreign ministry, proved woefully accurate in its assessment of the British government's reaction. While the service attachés in the embassy in London, having been called in to the Admiralty and shown plans to mobilise the fleet, cabled Berlin tersely: 'Situation Serious. War 50/50', Canaris assured Hitler that London would not react. His sources, which by this time must have included someone very close to the highest political intelligence circles in London, had made it clear that London would not oppose Hitler's move.

Vindicated by Britain's and France's failure to offer any robust response to this flagrant breach of international agreements, with its unilateral abrogation of the Locarno treaties, Canaris would later draft a memorandum urging service attachés *en poste* to 'keep their nerve' in times of international tension. Geyr von Schweppenburg, the military attaché in London who had, with his air force and naval colleagues, signed the ill-starred telegram, was unamused. He had always rejected anything more than superficial cooperation with the Abwehr and Admiral Birkner's foreign affairs section. He remained obdurate, noting tersely; 'I shall remain a gentleman in London'. Unfortunately for Canaris, who must have savoured this moment of victory over his rivals both internal and external, von Schweppenburg would not be *en poste* in London for much longer. Britain was moving more and more towards appeasement and a degree of cooperation was beginning to take place at many levels in the wake of the Anglo-German Naval Agreement a few months earlier, in which London had already given, for those who could see, the brightest of green lights to German rearmament.

Nevertheless, an event was about to take place that hot July which would once again enable Canaris to exploit his strengths: in Spain, a conservative politician by the name of Calvo Sotelo was murdered by Republican policemen. Within days the Spanish Civil War had broken out and Canaris would have a new field for his talents.

CHAPTER SIX

SPAIN

I left him to retain as I shall ever retain the impression
of those words exchanged in the noble sombre room
of a Spanish palace, majestic as all those proportions
are in that land of majesty ... I had been in the air of
what has always been the salvation of Europe — I mean
the Spanish Crusade.

HILAIRE BELLOC [1]

The Bishop's Palace in Salamanca in October 1936 resounded to the crack of brisk commands and the zing of spurs on limestone. Here in this great cube of Spanish masonry, all the paraphernalia of armed rebellion had been constructed and stored; ordnance, guard posts, sentries, and horses were, with the more modern instruments of telephone and telegraph, harnessed to the headquarters of the new 'saviour' of Spain, General Francisco Franco.

The assassination of Calvo Sotelo, leader of the monarchist opposition, had lit the long prepared fuse with the result that within days the army had called for an insurrection against the Republican government. While the army fought successfully in Navarre, Aragon and Galicia, the military insurgents suffered grave setbacks in Madrid and Barcelona. In Tetuan, however, the army of Morocco remained firmly under the control of General Franco and Franco was now in Salamanca, expecting a certain Latin American, Juan Guillermo, for lunch. According to his papers, Juan Guillermo was an Argentine. Fortunately, the plane that had flown from Stuttgart at high altitude had not needed to refuel in France. Señor Guillermo's seat was among petrol cans in a cabin stripped down to give maximum range. Señor Guillermo was of course Wilhelm Canaris.

Two months earlier, Franco had asked two Germans in Tetuan, Johannes Bernhardt, a businessman and Adolf Langenheim, the Nazi party chief in Morocco, for help in organising an airlift between Tetuan and Seville on the Spanish mainland. Franco's army lacked ships and transport to cross the Strait of Gibraltar. The Spanish air force had declared for the government, and in the navy the crews, mostly Communist, had massacred their officers. Pinned down in Morocco, Franco needed desperately to move his troops to the mainland. Colonel Saenz de Buruga asked Franco: 'What shall we do if we cannot get the Army of Africa across?' Franco typically replied: 'We shall do everything that is possible and necessary but not surrender.' [2]

Everything possible included asking Mussolini but *Il Duce*, on receiving a telegram from Franco asking for help, scribbled in bold blue pencil on the telegram, 'NO!'

France, then supplying arms to the Spanish government, was even less inclined. London took the moral high ground of neutrality and awaited developments. At first, Berlin appeared no less indifferent. When Bernhardt and Langenheim arrived on a Lufthansa flight in the German capital, armed with a letter from Franco to Hitler, their reception was distinctly cool. In the foreign ministry in those pre-Ribbentrop days, caution and discretion were still the currency of German diplomacy. Herr Dieckhoff, the director of the political department of the foreign ministry, noted: 'It is absolutely imperative that the German authorities and the party maintain the utmost reserve in the present state of affairs. Deliveries of arms to the rebels would very soon become known

... our merchant shipping and navy would be heavily compromised.'

Dieckhoff considered the secret delivery of aircraft as 'impracticable and not at all realistic.'[3] He went further: 'We might consider allowing Franco's representatives to make agreements here now for when they have attained power. However, even if that eventually happens, the German authorities must for the present remain at a distance from the whole affair.' The German foreign minister von Neurath added in his neat hand in the margin of this memorandum: 'Precisely'.

Not to be put off, the two Germans went to party headquarters where Gauleiter Böhle of the foreign party organisation introduced them to Rudolf Hess, who sent three party officials with them to Bayreuth, where Hitler was attending a performance of Wagner's 'Ring' cycle. Langenheim and Bernhardt had to wait until the epic performance of 'Valkyrie', conducted by Wilhelm Furtwängler, was over before being ushered into the Führer's presence to deliver the letter from Franco. Hitler received them cordially and then, despite the late hour, immediately summoned Goering, Blomberg and Canaris, who had all been attending the opera, to a meeting to discuss the issues involved in helping Franco.

Both Blomberg and Goering were sceptical of intervention, though Goering later, somewhat artificially, recalled he saw it as an excellent opportunity for his air force to train.[4] Goering, always conscious of relations with the West, wanted to avoid the risk of serious differences with France and Britain. Only Canaris formed an immediate argument in favour of support. He was the Spanish expert and knew the developments of the recent weeks better than most. It was clear to him from the intelligence he had received that Stalin was determined to subvert Spain by bringing the Communists to power. Should Stalin succeed, Canaris argued, south-western Europe would be lost to the Kremlin. France, already in the throes of a popular front government, would rapidly follow suit and Communists would then threaten Germany.

Quietly but resolutely, Canaris continued to build up the case for intervention. While Goering thought the military rebellion too uncertain to support, the intelligence chief, having established the wider strategic rationale, developed his theme by dwelling on the unusual personality of Franco. He had got to know Franco very well in Madrid during the course of 1935, when there had been meetings with him and members of the defence ministry to discuss German arms sales to Spain. Like Hitler, he was a man of personal austerity, Canaris said. Like the Führer, Franco did not smoke, did not drink alcohol and avoided involvement with women. Canaris recalled how Franco had told his officers in Morocco: 'I want neither women nor drinking bouts'. Moroever, Franco was a gifted military leader, a man of rock-like calm and at the age of thirty-three the youngest European general since Napoleon. As Canaris drew this attractive portrait of Spain's 'saviour' he did not, of course, dwell on Franco's fiercely independent nature, his contempt for 'foreign systems' nor indeed his firm belief that Spain was superior to any other European state.

Gradually, the fluency and conviction of Canaris' arguments began to tell. Having planted a certain sympathy for Franco at a personal level with Hitler, he proceeded to move with ease to the financial advantages of assisting Franco. There was, Canaris noted quietly, a chance to earn a not 'negligible' amount of foreign exchange by supplying arms. Here the old henchman of Zaharoff, Juan March and Ullmann was in his element. The logistics of smuggling in the Iberian peninsula were very familiar to him. Canaris' network covered every city in Europe, including London. He had intelligence that Franco was being backed financially by some important interests in London. These interests would be prepared to pay for German aid and weapons. Spain was a country rich in resources and would also contribute handsomely in the event of a victory.

Like a conjuror whisking rabbits out of a hat, Canaris had yet another card to play. There was a risk that if Germany did not support Franco, Mussolini would eventually support the nationalists and extend Italy's sphere of influence in the Mediterranean without Germany's support.

It is hard to underestimate the effect of such fluid and worldly reasoning on provincial political and military minds, especially as it was doubtless delivered with that gravitas which is the preserve of all great experienced intelligence chiefs. Those who argue that intelligence and spymasters cannot materially affect military events or decisions [5] are unfamiliar with the interplay of rigid military minds on the one hand and subtle masters of elasticity on the other. Canaris' softly spoken *tour d'horizon* is as pure an example of the decisive influence of well-informed and argued intelligence as one can find. By the time the meeting broke up at 4 a.m., Goering and Blomberg had been persuaded to meet the Spanish delegation with Canaris later that day. Canaris had persuaded Hitler that the success of the rebels would depend entirely on the aid Franco received. Hitler's decision to support Franco was therefore to have tangible implications for Spain's future.

From Canaris' point of view, Germany's support for Franco would place him at the centre of German–Hispanic relations; a development which was to have far reaching strategic consequences when it came to 1940. Hitler had to rely now on Canaris' knowledge of the country and his relationship with Franco to deal with any problems that might arise. It would enable Canaris to cement his relationship with Hitler, while at the same time winning the confidence of Franco. It would also bring him into contact again with British intelligence, whose network of agents was understandably extensive throughout the western Mediterranean.

Goering, Blomberg and Canaris moved quickly to agree aid to the nationalists. The army was predictably cautious. The Chief of Staff, Beck, rejected outright the idea of any direct intervention. Colonel-General von Fritsch no doubt expressed the scepticism of many of the Prussian-trained generals when, screwing his monocle tightly into his eye to peruse a map of Spain to evaluate transport facilities, he stared in disbelief: 'Remarkable ... what a strange country, it does not seem to possess any railways.'[6]

While the staff officers struggled with their maps and European rail timetables, the Abwehr swept into action. Canaris' old network of agents in Spain was reactivated to produce raw intelligence reports on Republican munitions, arms dumps and military strength. Then, front companies were established to channel the aid programme. Bernhardt was made director of a new company called Hisma (Hispano-Marroqui Transport Company). Goering then helped establish Rowak (Raw Materials and Wares Purchasing Company). Further companies were set up and grouped into a new holding concern called Sofindus (Sociedad Financiera Industrial Ltd). Nor were these companies limited to German capital. There was plenty of capital backing to be found in London for Franco. The more internationally minded of the British merchant banks were prepared to channel funds through Canaris' old friend Augusto Miranda, who would become Franco's arms agent in London and was, of course, well plugged into Canaris' old acquaintance Zaharoff and the Vickers Empire. Vickers had long coveted Spain and had a long-standing interest in that country moving to the right. Whatever the protestations of the British government concerning non-intervention, Vickers could only view the emergence of Franco as a highly positive development. As early as March 14 1934, Sir Charles Craven of Vickers-Armstrong had written thus to his fellow merchant Mr Spear of the Electric Boat Company in the United States:

'I can tell you at once that there is every possibility of the Spanish government approving the construction of certain warships ... Of course things look very stormy in Spain at present, and I sincerely hope nothing will be done to check the swing to the Right which has recently taken place, because the present Government look as if they are going to be most sympathetic to the Sociedad and give us a modest naval programme which I can assure you is very sorely needed to keep the place going.' [7]

Indeed the first aircraft Franco ever received, enabling him to cross the Strait of Gibraltar to the army of Africa in Tetuan, was chartered in

London.[8] It could be argued that without that particular craft, his ambitions would have been stopped in their tracks.

If the British Labour party could sympathise with the Republicans and Clement Attlee warn of strikes if London showed any sympathy for the insurgents, there were many interests in London prepared to profit from a weak Spain, as well as one that needed armaments.[9] Equally unsurprisingly, it was London where most of Franco's financial debts to Germany were met.[10] The Spanish aristocracy had important friends in the City and the likes of Juan March were not unknown in the square mile.

Twenty Junkers 52 and six Heinkel 51 fighters were earmarked for transport to Spain, together with supplies, spare parts and ammunition. Then a sympathetic army officer, Colonel Walther Warlimont, code name 'Waltersdorf', was appointed to represent the German armed forces in Spain. A personal letter from Canaris to Franco expressing support accompanied Bernhardt and Langenheim back to Spain. It promised imminent material aid. In particular, it hinted at the supply of the aircraft vital for Franco's efforts to step up his airlift.[11]

At the same time, aware that Mussolini would not hesitate to climb fervently aboard once he was informed of German involvement, Canaris initiated discussions with his Italian counterpart Roatta. Roatta, codename Mancini, soon to be commanding Italian units in Spain, and Warlimont were dispatched to Tetuan to discuss aid requirements with Franco. By the end of the summer more than 15,000 men of Franco's Moroccan forces had been transported by German and Italian aircraft to the mainland. These men of the African army were disciplined, brutal and hard. They were, however, more efficient than anything else the nationalists had at their disposal and began to affect significantly the balance of forces on the peninsula.

By the time Canaris arrived at Salamanca, a mood of optimism was palpable and talk was of the offensive against Madrid to be launched the following month. Already, the outskirts of Madrid had been captured,

Toledo had fallen and Oviedo invested. At lunch the conversation between Franco, General Luis Orgaz, the director of military training, and Franco's brother, Nicholas, was of a swift conclusion to the war. Only the recent ominous eruption of Soviet tanks in Esquivia under the command of a Russian general, Pavlov, which had badly mauled Franco's cavalry, cast a shadow over the proceedings. The German kept his counsel during the lunch, listening carefully to the conversation but keeping his remarks to superficial comments until he was alone with Franco. Then, with the same intuitive skill with which he had convinced Hitler of the need to intervene in Spain, he convinced Franco of the necessity of his dependence on German support in a dazzling report compiled by the Abwehr of the French and Soviet intentions towards the Spanish conflict.

Speaking again in that calm understated way, which is so effective with military men, Canaris proceeded to give Franco an intelligence update. It was not reassuring. The General may have thought the war was proceeding well but the Soviet Union, the Comintern, France and Britain were active and an estimated 50,000 volunteers were on their way to constitute the formidable International Brigades.

Moreover, attached to this serious fighting force there were tanks, aircraft, machine guns and ammunition flowing in from France and the Soviet Union. At first Franco stared at the German in impassive scepticism, but Canaris had prepared his brief. He could name the eight Russian supply ships that had passed through the Dardanelles in the last month, laden with supplies. He could even furnish lists of their cargo. The *Kurak* had just delivered to Barcelona forty trucks, twelve armoured cars, six artillery pieces, four aircraft, 700 tons of ammunition and 1,500 tons of food. Another ship, the *Komsomol*, had delivered a further eight tanks, 2,000 tons of ammunition and 100 tons of medical supplies. The international Left had, with its brilliant cross-border structures for coordination, created a new factor. Moreover, it was one that would dramatically alter the situation on the ground. As one Englishman who fought in Franco's forces against the International Brigade remembered, they were men 'almost impervious to death or fatigue.' [12]

Canaris, of course, knew Franco's character well enough to realise that such foreign interference in the affairs of Spain would strike a particularly sour note. Franco's response was brisk: 'International mercenaries are trying to impose on Spain a foreign ideology and the rule of Moscow.' He accepted that a new force would be required to resist it, but such a new army could only be equipped by Germany and perhaps Italy. Canaris realised that Franco would be unwilling to accept outside support in so heavy a measure. So he stressed that Hitler's support would not impinge on Spain's independence. However, having made this point Canaris went on to stress that Berlin's only demand was a less methodical and hesitant approach to the war. Berlin wanted decisive action to take Madrid. This would soon lead to recognition of the national government by Berlin, Rome and Lisbon and it would justify Hitler developing a much bolder aid programme.

Franco's reply was predictable: 'I cannot exterminate the other side or destroy towns, agriculture, industrial installations or means of production ... If I made haste, I should be a bad Spaniard. If I made haste, I should not be a patriot. I would be behaving like a foreigner.'

The general continued in the same proud vein: 'Give me aircraft, give me artillery, give me tanks and ammunition ... and I will be very grateful. But above all do not require me to hurry. Do not force me to win at any cost as that would mean a large number of Spaniards killed ... and a less firm basis for my government ... I will occupy Spain town by town, village by village and one railway line after another. Nothing will oblige me to change the pace of my programme; there may be less glory in it, but there will be a greater peace at the end of it.' [13]

This bravura performance, combining as it did utter confidence with an almost mystical sense of national identity, impressed Canaris, who like many intelligence officers operating in a world of subtly shifting sands and cynical allegiances could not fail to admire the utter clarity and noble sentiments with which Franco enunciated his ideas. The unshakeable faith, so bound up with Franco's devout Roman Catholicism, which so impressed Hilaire Belloc and other English politicians and writers, gave Canaris an image of a fervent autocrat, imbued with a sense of responsibility towards God and Spain, against which the pagan paladins of the Third Reich seemed an inferior breed. Henceforth, the many disputes which would inevitably arise between Berlin and Franco would be brokered by Canaris, and where possible in the Spaniard's favour. It suited Canaris' own Christian ethics that Franco was proceeding according to a programme of slow reclamation rather than through a scorched earth approach. Later he would be profoundly distressed by Franco's violent reprisals against the Communists, warning Franco that summary justice and mass executions were not consonant with Christian ethics. But even when Franco's purges got into their full sanguinary stride, Canaris refused to bracket the Spaniard with Himmler or Heydrich, though a long shadow began to fall over their friendship.[14]

One of the reasons he may have had for this was that while Franco proceeded against his political enemies mercilessly, believing them to be incapable of pardon, he shared none of the racial theories of Nazi Germany. In one later recorded conversation between Canaris and the Caudillo, the German warned the Spanish leader of the dangers of totalitarianism: 'If I have understood you correctly, Spain will be a Kingdom without a King and you will be a King without a crown,' Canaris said. 'Are there not in this totalitarian form of yours risks of a sort that I have already detected in Germany?', he continued, subtly alluding to Germany's racial laws. Franco handed Canaris a copy of the weekly *Noticiero de España* and asked him to read a tolerant article about the Jews, rejecting anti-Semitism. As Franco's biographer Brian Crozier observes, the fact that Franco chose to surround himself with the panoply of fascism 'did not mean that he accepted the Nazis should dictate his behaviour and still less that he should subscribe to their anti-Jewish theories.' [15]

The fact that Madrid would not fall for many months did not, however, inhibit Berlin from announcing a few weeks later diplomatic recognition of the nationalist government.

Canaris soon hammered out an agreement for the supply of German bomber and fighter formations. He explained to Franco that such a German air corps, to be known as the Condor Legion, would be commanded by General Hugo Sperrle and that a military chargé d'affaires, in the form of Hitler's former commanding officer in the First World War, Lieutenant General Wilhelm Faupel, would be accredited to the nationalist government as soon as Madrid fell. The German proposal included the following terms:—

1. That the German formations in Spain be placed under a German commander, who will be the sole adviser to General Franco in matters concerning the German air corps and responsible to General Franco only for its overall activities. Outwardly the appearance of a Spanish command would be preserved.

2. That all German units already in Spain be attached to this German air corps.

3. That the German air bases be adequately protected, if necessary by infantry reinforcements.

4. That the conduct of both land and air operations be more regular, active and co-ordinated, having in view a more rapid occupation of the ports which Moscow might utilise to increase its reinforcements.

Such terms inevitably would allow full rein for Canaris' negotiating skills, not least as many of the senior German officers involved had little finesse in dealing with the Spaniards. More than once, the fury of Prussian officers over the poor condition in which the Spaniards looked after their weapons would lead to heated exchanges between Franco and his senior advisers. Canaris, as always, understanding both sides of the argument, defused the debates when they showed signs of escalation.

When this proved impossible, he never criticised Franco but merely worked hard to remove the German officer involved. Thus he was able to liberate Franco from the Prussian pedantry of General Faupel and replace him with a career diplomat and old friend, Eberhard von Stohrer. When the officer commanding the Condor Legion, Sperrle, began to get on Franco's nerves, one report from Canaris was enough to have him replaced.[16]

Hand in glove with this diplomatic activity, Canaris continued to develop more practical ways of assisting Franco in his cause. In a devilishly cunning scheme, if Richard Protze of Abwehr IIIF is to be believed, Canaris also sought to exploit, on Goering's suggestion, the time-honoured practice among arms dealers of supplying inferior material to one's opponents. Canaris directed a German-Dutch arms dealer, Josef Veltjens, to buy up all the superannuated weapons of the First World War which Canaris had helped to sell abroad after the Treaty of Versailles. Rifles, carbines, ammunition and grenades were bought up in Czechoslovakia and the Balkans. These weapons were then tampered with by German armourers, who filed down the striking pins, doctored the ammunition, reduced the grenade charges or inserted instantaneous fuses. The consignments were then distributed to the arms dealing 'ring' in Poland, Finland, Czechoslovakia and Holland, from where they were sold to the Republican government for gold. This dubious but common practice was an act of sabotage that would have appealed to Canaris, as the casualties would be limited to Republican soldiery.

Within a few months Canaris had concentrated in his hands little formal power but immense informal influence, which was, as always, far more effective. Hardly any decision involving Germany and Spain did not pass through his hands. Nor was such influence limited to those two countries. Canaris, who by this stage was actively involved in the plans to coordinate aid with Italy, even managed to persuade Mussolini to write to the German ambassador in Rome asking that the German intelligence chief be given negotiating as opposed to observer status in conversations involving Italian aid to Spain. This development swiftly resulted in far closer cooperation between Italy and Germany than had hitherto taken place.

Collaboration between the two countries was now to be forged on the anvil of aid to Spain. Hitherto Canaris had been – for all his personal rapport with Roatta and affection for Italy – wary of too close an involvement on the political, as opposed to intelligence, plane with the Italians. Indeed, the Abwehr had supplied weapons through London to the Abyssinian insurgents in 1935.[7] (Canaris always feared that unilateral action by Italy was an unfortunate example for Germany, which the Nazis would inevitably be eager to one day imitate.) But Spain, more than Abyssinia, was the litmus test for those who saw Bolshevism as the enemy and the scale of Soviet intervention in Spain was a dramatic warning of Moscow's ambitions and capabilities.

Diplomatic relations between Berlin and Rome now warmed up at a cracking pace. No longer would Roatta ask his Austrian counterpart, Lahousen, to peer over the Alps to see what he could discover about German military strength. By November the 'Pact of Steel', with its secret provisions giving support to Italy in the Mediterranean and Germany in Eastern Europe, was signed and Italy's and Germany's fates were seemingly irreversibly linked. As Italy became more and more embroiled in the conflict, she became less and less capable of independent diplomatic action. France and Britain began to isolate her, throwing Rome into Berlin's welcoming arms.

At a stroke, the intervention in Spain, as well as eventually stalling the tide of Communism in that country, also sealed the Italo-German alliance. By the time Canaris sat down with the Italian foreign minister Ciano on 6 December 1936, a 'methodical and effective programme for the future' was virtually worked out. While Germany sent the Condor

Legion, Mussolini began to send well-equipped fascist militia to cooperate with the Spanish army. By the beginning of 1937, this force equated to an infantry division of 50,000 men, though after initial victories it was spectacularly routed by the International Brigades on the Guadalajara front. Given that one of the International Brigades in this action was composed of German Communists and Jews, this gave the western liberal media much to crow over the Italian intervention.

Even the nationalist soldiery made fun of the Italians. In this difficult situation, Canaris forbade any criticisms of the Italians among his officers and travelled frequently to Spain to iron out disagreements, actively encouraging the senior officers of the Condor Legion and the Italians to fraternise even when they were barely on speaking terms with each other.

On the whole, the German infiltration was far more subtle, and while German ordnance and anti-aircraft weapons were extensively tried out in Spain, German personnel were sworn to strict secrecy. It was related at the time that a few officers who had talked to their families about the mission had been arrested and sentenced to death for treason. Later, with the war going more favourably, Franco was able to make the tentative suggestion to Canaris that the Condor Legion be withdrawn. There was never to be any secret military alliance between Hitler and Franco, though in April 1939 Canaris would be entrusted with the mission of persuading Franco to join the Anti-Comintern pact. Nevertheless, even after military aid of 5 billion Reichmarks, described as an 'unconditional gift' to Spain, Franco would never be a German stooge and his policy would be one of subtle insubordination: a policy in which he was ably assisted by Canaris.

As Franco himself pointed out in the decree establishing his authority on 19 April 1937: 'As initiator of the historic epoch in which Spain will fulfil its destiny ... the Caudillo will exercise absolute authority ... The Caudillo is responsible to God and to History.'[18]

Thus, while adhering to the Anti-Comintern Pact, Franco also courted France, promising Paris neutrality in the event of a war between France and Germany in return for the end of French aid to the Republicans. As von Weizsäcker commented to the Spanish ambassador when the latter was called into the German foreign minstry to explain this *démarche*: 'When he alluded to the continuity of Spanish policy, I observed to him that we had nevertheless been somewhat astonished at the haste with which Spain had promised France to remain neutral in the critical days of September 1938.' [19] Canaris would have briefed Franco fully on the European situation and it was Canaris' firm view that Spain should keep out of any impending European war. In any event German supplies would be cut back as Berlin deployed all available material to central Europe.

As the crisis in Europe developed, the conflict in Spain lost the character of a civil war and became more and more the battleground of powerful foreign interests. It was perhaps only to be expected that the intelligence chiefs of both the Soviet Union and Germany should become personally involved. While Canaris, disguised as the Argentine Guillermo, travelled between his various agents in the peninsula, the Soviet spy chief Jan Karlowich Bersin was operating in the guise of the military attaché Colonel Gorjew in the Soviet Embassy in Madrid. [20]

Already the Abwehr had set up a station in Algeciras to monitor Soviet agents and activities under Korvettenkapitän Wilhelm Leissner (cover name Colonel Gustav Lenz). This station rapidly began uncovering Communist agents, especially those linked to Soviet companies exporting arms to Spain from London and Holland. In the Hague, they found a powerful Soviet network of arms traders under the control of General Walther Krivitski. The Spanish Civil War was offering a unique and unprecedented opportunity to infiltrate agents across Europe, and the Soviet Union embraced the chance with vigour. Working closely with the Gestapo, the Abwehr stations began rolling up enemy networks with the utmost ruthlessness. On the other hand, Eberhard Funk, one of Canaris' best agents, who supplied useful information on Republican forces, was caught and shot.

Unfortunately for Canaris' long-term plans, one agent of the Comintern he failed to unmask was the correspondent of the *Times* attached to General Franco's forces, Kim Philby. Philby was to play a significant role in derailing all of Canaris' attempts to help bring about an Anglo-German understanding during the Second World War. Krivitski, Canaris' opponent in Holland, almost identified Philby when he told the Foreign Office after he defected to the US that Moscow had an 'Englishman who was sent to Spain as a journalist.'

In Spain, Philby – already a recruited Soviet agent complete with ciphers – made the acquaintance of the Abwehr and saw how influential the organisation was. It was clear to his keen mind that Franco was winning the war on account of German support and advice and Anglo-Saxon capital. In his attempt to supply his Communist masters with information he made all possible efforts to ingratiate himself with the German officers attached to Franco's headquarters.

One of the German officers in Spain, Ulrich von der Osten, (codename Don Julio) [21] was visited often by Philby, who even tried to insinuate himself into the German's company by effecting an introduction to his English lover Bunny Doble. Philby would later claim that von der Osten was far more important than he was and that the German regularly invited him to 'Abwehr headquarters', a fantastic exaggeration as the Convento de las Esclavas in Burgos where Philby went was a logistics depot. Von der Osten was relatively junior and only tangentially linked to the Abwehr, but his acquaintance gave Philby the chance to pose as an expert on German intelligence, elevating the unsuspecting von der Osten into a senior Abwehr officer. This would be something that would prove to be of extreme importance in Philby's soon-to-be flourishing career in British intelligence.

It was thanks to these encounters in Spain that Philby could be considered a suitable officer to evaluate intelligence from Canaris during the war: the man the Soviets considered the 'most dangerous man in Europe'. Had the admiral known how decisive Philby would be in sabotaging his later plans, he would have doubtless proceeded with more ruthlessness against the *Times* correspondent. There is some circumstantial evidence that the Abwehr had its suspicions, but naturally could not easily proceed against the correspondent of what was then the most prestigious newspaper in the world. Nevertheless, on his first trip to Spain as a journalist, Philby had been arrested in Cordoba and only just managed to swallow his cipher, which was made of specially treated rice paper.[22]

The Abwehr would have seen the file concerning the arrest and may even have provoked it. Together with the Gestapo, they advised the Spanish police on foreigners in Spain. But at that time, the thought of war between England and Germany seemed remote while the struggle with the Soviet Union was just beginning to crystallise. Abwehr and British intelligence agents cooperated with each other, exchanging information on the Soviet networks in the country. The idea of a future alliance between England and Moscow would have struck most people in both Germany and England at that time as absurd.

But as the Spanish war ground on to its conclusion barely weeks before the outbreak of the Second World War in 1939, it proved the backdrop to a series of seismic shifts of the European diplomatic plates. As Hitler focussed more on his ambitions in central Europe, Spain came to play the role of a useful source of continuing tension. As Hitler would later declare during the military conference of 5 November 1937: 'A total victory for Franco is not desirable in the German interest and we have a greater interest in the war continuing.' [23]

Canaris was under no illusions that German policy aimed to defeat the Republicans while leaving Franco dependent on Germany. While the war in Spain continued, it afforded some distraction from Hitler's moves on the Sudetenland. At the same time, Hitler calculated that by involving Mussolini more and more in the affairs of the peninsula, Italy would no longer be in any position to resist Germany's designs on Austria.

As the storm in Europe began to gather momentum, Canaris

found increasing solace in his tours of Spain. He found Spain a welcome distraction from the events of growing crisis in central Europe. For Canaris there was a 'constant exhilaration' associated with Spain. He loved Spain, not because of its sights or landscape, but because he sensed an empathy with its soul and character. His staff noted how his spirits rose when he was in the Iberian peninsula. The ruinous Spanish roads, the undeveloped, in some areas almost feudal, conditions seemed so remote from his homeland of modern Germany and yet thanks to his superb command of the Spanish language, his unteutonic appearance and his intelligence, he could pass as a Spaniard whose home these worn sierras, windowless churches and mud-built villages were.

If Spain was to underline the fault-lines in European ideological conflict, it would impress upon Canaris how strongly drawn he was by a culture which was not German. In the long months of visiting little wayside inns, savouring southern dishes and contemplating the near-impenetrable gloom of great cathedrals, Canaris may well have reflected on the irony that though he was increasingly a Spaniard-*manqué*, it was the very fact of his being a German which allowed him his power and influence in the peninsula. But the loyal servant of the German state and the German patriot were about to collide as the focus of diplomatic and military activity moved away from the dusty plains of Spain and towards the snow-clad peaks of the eastern Alps.

CHAPTER SEVEN

FALLEN BASTIONS

War means a catastrophe far greater and beyond comprehension for Germany and all mankind in the event of the victory of this Nazi system.

CANARIS, QUOTED BY LAHOUSEN, *SECRET DEBRIEFING TO BRITISH INTELLIGENCE* 1946 [1]

As Germany and the Soviet Union became more and more embroiled in an intelligence duel in Spain, Soviet and German agents were increasingly pitting their wits against each other in other parts of Europe. The relationship between the German army and the Soviet military inevitably continued to deteriorate.

In barely ten years, it had gone from fulsome cooperation to mutual suspicion, reinforced by Hitler's denunciation of the secret training treaty of 1926 and his unwinding of all the former Chief of the General Staff, von Seeckt's, careful networks of cooperation.[2] The two biggest armies in the world had been forcibly separated and arranged in opposite camps. But it remained one of Hitler's obsessions that his army had never abandoned the policy of secret understanding with the Russian army that had prevailed in the Weimar republic under the inspiration of von Seeckt. Hitler was haunted that the two armies would preserve a sympathy that would one day turn them against their respective regimes.

As Ian Colvin speculated: 'Suppose then that the German and Russian generals ever met each other secretly and complained: "We soldiers understand each other – it is these two political systems, Bolshevism and National Socialism, which make our people enemies".'[3]

The military training agreement of 1926 had been signed on the German side by General von Seeckt.[4] The Russian signatory was Marshal Tuchachewski, a distinguished officer, trained in the Czar's army and the embodiment of the Russian military tradition. Tuchachewski had represented his country at the funeral of George V in February 1936. The Abwehr received intelligence that while in London he had secretly met emissaries of the White Russian, General Miller. On his way back to Moscow, the Abwehr also noted that he had met with some White Russian émigrés in Berlin. Significantly, though the Marshal was expected to return to London for the coronation of George VI, he was posted to an obscure Volga command.

Canaris duly noted these events. He was building up contacts with anti-Soviet intelligence chiefs throughout Europe that year and had just rekindled some old contacts from his days with the Austro-Hungarian navy in Pola during the First World War. His former colleagues from the 'imperial and royal' naval station, Adria, were now heading up the Hungarian service and Canaris had been charmed in particular by a young Hungarian officer called Szentpetery. Szentpetery and his Magyar colleagues were well aware of developments in their neighbour to the east.[5] Budapest, then as now, carefully monitored events in Moscow and Canaris came to rely on their reports. He even became so fond of Szentpetery that a photograph of the young man adorned his desk. [6] At the same time parallel contacts were being developed with the Baltic States and Japan, this last encouraged by Ribbentrop, who was dreaming of securing Japanese adherence to the Anti-Comintern Pact against the Soviet Union.

But with the distractions of the events in Spain, Canaris forgot about Tuchachewski until in the first half of June 1937 Canaris heard the news reports from Tass announcing that Tuchachewski and seven other generals had been found guilty of treason and shot. This was the signal for a huge, bloody purge of the Soviet High Command. More than 35,000 officers would be executed, including ninety per cent of the generals.

Canaris may have recalled Heydrich asking a year earlier for the loan of Abwehr handwriting experts who could forge the signature of Tuchachewski. At the same time, Heydrich had wanted facsimiles of the expired German–Soviet military training agreement. But Canaris did not see the connection and it was left to other Abwehr officers to point out that Heydrich was gloating that he had orchestrated the entire affair. For with the forged signatures, Heydrich had created imaginary letters between Tuchachewski and German officers. These compromising documents had then been planted on the Czech secret service in the full knowledge that they would find their way first to the Czech president, Benes, and then to Stalin in Moscow.

Heydrich was working closely with some elements of the Soviet secret service through the double agent General Skoblin, an exiled Russian general living in Paris, who worked both for the Soviets and the SD. Heydrich had produced the documents on Hitler's instruction. As he later explained to Canaris, it was the Führer's idea that the leadership of the Soviet army should be decimated. Moreover, both Hitler and Heydrich convinced themselves that their forgeries contained a germ of truth. The Soviet high command may have been in truck with the German generals. When Canaris confronted Heydrich with his responsibility for the bloodbath, Heydrich's cynical indifference appalled him. 'Why in Heaven's name did you get involved in such a scheme?' he demanded.

Canaris was not to know that Heydrich's contribution to the purge may only have only been minor because Stalin was, in any event, determined to destroy his generals, but the fact that Heydrich had falsified documents which had been instrumental in any way in a massacre of Russian officers in peace time showed that his old protégé was no longer a German officer bound by any accepted tradition of honour. Colleagues who saw Canaris after this meeting with Heydrich described him in a state of 'deep spiritual shock'.[7] This affair, more than any other, convinced him of the moral abyss into which the leadership of his country was falling.

As Richard Protze, Canaris' Abwehr colleague, noted, 'this was the time when Canaris began to turn from Hitler.'[8] It was also the time when Canaris' final illusions about Heydrich were lost. His one time protégé in intelligence affairs and, indeed, later protector had become a monster over which Canaris had no control. Henceforth the 'master', while remaining ever cordial and helpful on a personal level, would use every trick in his formidable armoury to cut the ground from beneath his former 'pupil' and his more sinister machinations.

In the Tuchachewski affair, the SD moreover had operated in a sphere normally the preserve of the Abwehr. Everywhere the signs of encroachment were seen in the Abwehr. At first, Heydrich no doubt thought that having helped to give Canaris his job, he had little to worry about from the Abwehr. They would no doubt fall into line. In the excitement of his success in the Tuchachewski affair, Heydrich even began investigating German officers. On 22 March he arrested Ernst Niekisch, who had helped negotiate the 1926 agreement with the Russians. A further nineteen Germans were arrested, including one of Canaris' own officers.

But here Heydrich overstepped the mark, and he soon began to realise that the Abwehr was not going to submit without a struggle. At the trial the admiral sat in the court to hear the evidence. When the hearing was over and the Gestapo had been unable to prove his officer's guilt, Canaris walked forward in court, demonstratively shook the accused's witness by the hand and loudly asked him to let his office have a note of his expenses.[9] This act of almost ostentatious bravado went down well among the officers of the Abwehr, who realised their chief would look after his own and that they should not submit to the demands of the SD. The tension between SD and Abwehr gathered apace. Only those who have worked in an established organisation of any size can understand the myriad of bureaucratic techniques that can be deployed to delay the requests of hostile outsiders. The Abwehr continued to promise the SD full cooperation, but such appearances increasingly began to bear little relation to reality. These developments did not go unnoticed by Heydrich, who began warning his officers to not be taken in by the 'mild little man'. Canaris, Heydrich hissed, was a 'crafty old fox'.[10]

At the same time, Heydrich moved against the General Staff on another front. Perjured evidence was trumped up to destroy the commander in chief, von Fritsch, and a scandal arranged to remove the war minister, Blomberg. Blomberg had married a woman of dubious background, and even though leading members of the regime, including Hitler and Goering, had attended his wedding, this did not protect him from the scandal 'ventilated' to the press that his wife had briefly been a prostitute. The union, first seen as a glorious example of the breaking down of the rigidities of the old Prussian officer caste – the new Frau von Blomberg was wonderfully *petit-bourgeois* – quickly became a scandalous cause célèbre.

In the case of Fritsch, a delinquent named Schmidt was bullied by Heydrich into denouncing Fritsch as his lover. In fact, Schmidt had had a homosexual relationship with a certain Captain Frisch. Canaris got Protze to take a photograph of this officer before the SS spirited him away. But though the case collapsed, Frisch and Schmidt were both murdered by the SD and General Fritsch was never reinstated. The scandals had served their purpose of weakening the General Staff, thus allowing tighter political control. The staff was further deprived of some of its most important functions as a new high command, the OKW, was created under the direct control of Hitler on 4 February 1938, a duality of reporting lines which was to have fatal consequences later in the war.

Richard Protze was convinced that these events began to mark a crisis of loyalty between Canaris and Hitler.[11] In the summer of 1938, Hitler spoke at a parade in Gross Born warning 'I, too, would not recoil from destroying ten thousand officers if they opposed themselves to my will.' The obvious reference to the Russian purges was not lost on those present as Hitler continued: 'What is that in a nation of eighty million? I do not want men of intelligence. I want men of brutality.'

The intrigues against the generals and the Moscow purges showed Canaris all too vividly the weakness of the traditional German officer class in the modern world of the Nazi police state. No longer could the officer class see itself as the kingmaker in German politics. It was gradually, but relentlessly, being outmanoeuvred. Dining at Horchers with his predecessor Patzig, back from the Coronation Review off Spithead where he had commanded the *Graf Spee* pocket battleship, Canaris dicussed not only England but also outlined the crimes of Himmler and Heydrich in angry detail.

Patzig was about to be made chief of naval personnel and offered some advice:

'You cannot continue to direct the Abwehr. Submit your resignation from the service. I will see you get transferred to an important command.' The route of resignation was to be taken shortly afterwards by the Chief of the General Staff, General Ludwig Beck. It was a route always open to Canaris. But Canaris was not Beck. He was not an officer in the Prussian mould, though he adhered to the ethics and values of the German officer class. He was a worldly operator, totally at home in intrigue and yet, like others addicted to espionage and its broad curriculum of sharp practice, he was desperate for the counter-balance of a noble cause.

Canaris by now believed that tempting though Patzig's offer might be, he had a new destiny awaiting him. From now on he would not only be the man who preserved the integrity of the Abwehr against the predatory demands of the SD, he would fashion the Abwehr into an instrument that would do all it could to prevent the war which the methods of Heydrich, Himmler and Hitler would make inevitable and which would be a disaster for Germany and all Europe. 'I cannot resign', he told Patzig simply, 'because after me would come Heydrich.' [12]

From now on, as if struck by an intense Damascene conversion, Canaris saw his duty in opposing Hitler from within his lair rather than from without. Fate had placed him in a position to monitor the regime – he began keeping a diary – and even prevent some of its excesses. At the same time, he would preserve an organisation that would demonstrate that there was an honourable Germany capable of independent action in the gangster state. The organisation would be imbued with the ethics of European civilisation; a small but effective Trojan Horse within a criminal regime, a beacon of decency and honour in the ever darkening night of moral disintegration.

Canaris now began to divide his instructions to his fellow officers into 'open orders' and 'secret directions'.[13] The open orders already marked a line in the sand between the Abwehr and Heydrich's SD. They included the following:

1. Limitation of all Abwehr activity to military tasks with absolute non- interference in political activities.

2. Sharpest rejection of all methods employed by the SD and the Gestapo.

The 'secret directions' were listed at the end of the war by Colonel Lahousen as aiming to prevent war under any circumstances:

1. The formation of a secret organisation within Abwehr II with the purpose of consolidating anti-Nazi forces and preparing them for all illegal acts that might be possible in the future against the system.

2. The systematic removal of fanatical Nazis or SD spies from the Abwehr.

3. Protection of those personalities threatened by the Gestapo, SD, NSDAP and Foreign Office.

4. Passive conduct of Abwehr II (Sabotage) activities with external show of apparent very great activity.

Later, when war became inevitable, these instructions were reinforced with more detailed methods of outwitting the SD and a strict policy of 'failure to carry out any orders relating to kidnapping, assassination or poisoning.' [14]

As can be seen from the first of the 'secret directions', Canaris was, in the utmost stealth, collecting around him such men as might be able to prevent Hitler from carrying out his plans. At the same time, he also made his views known discreetly to important sources in the West, including London. The *News Chronicle* correspondent in Berlin, Ian Colvin, began to have 'his first glimpses of his separate diplomacy.' [15] Also, about this time is the letter attributed to Juan March to a friend in Madrid:

> Hitler's regime bodes ill for the future. Basil Zaharoff who knows his Germany and who has tried to get along with the National Socialist riff-raff agrees with me. More important, Canaris thinks the same and does not love or trust his new masters. He is our best ally in Europe at the moment ... Zaharoff is horrified at the idea that Germany may once again perpetrate another world war.
>
> Canaris is not what he seems. He has learned a lesson and will now merely hold on to his powers in the intelligence world to find out Hitler's plans and to thwart him until some new rulers can be brought to power. [16]

Canaris felt, as one colleague later wrote, that 'he must remain at his post because that mattered more than his opinion of Hitler or the Third Reich. He felt it was his duty to maintain this powerful organisation, the Abwehr, with its thousands of agents, its network throughout the world and its enormous budgetary resources which he controlled. He wanted it to be identified with a high concept of human rights, of international law and morality.' [17]

Canaris was convinced after the small conference held secretly on 5 November 1937 that Hitler was determined to go to war, hence his beginning to draw Abwehr officers around him who could, in accordance with the 'secret directions', work to 'prevent war'. Canaris did not attend the conference himself. Only the three service chiefs, Hitler's war minister and foreign minister and the adjutant, Colonel Hossbach, whose memorandum of the meeting was used in evidence at the Nuremberg Trials, had attended.[18]

Germany, Hitler had told his somewhat startled audience, 'had nothing to gain from a prolonged period of peace.' Germany needed 'Lebensraum' and her superiority in weapons would last only until 1943. Austria and Bohemia were to be incorporated into the Reich with 'the speed of lightning'. As Goering made plain a few days later to the American emissary William Bullitt, who was in Berlin in November 1937, what Germany feared most was a union between Vienna, Budapest and Prague with a restoration of the Habsburg Monarchy.[19] Such a development would be an immediate *casus belli*.

But if Canaris and other Germans were beginning to see all too clearly where Hitler was leading, the lesson was lost on London. The British Lord President, Lord Halifax, was in Berlin at this time, ostensibly at the invitation of Prince Löwenstein, to visit a hunting exhibition. Chamberlain had encouraged Halifax to accept this invitation so that Halifax could meet Hitler and Goering. The visit would, he wrote to his sisters, embody the 'far-reaching plans I have for the appeasement of Europe.'[20]

Chamberlain had been much affected by the economic collapse of 1931 and he was afraid that the steeply rising costs that were bound to accompany a massive rearmament programme would reverse the economic recovery, which five years of prudent finance had fought so hard to achieve.

Moreover, Chamberlain had no confidence in France as a reliable ally. The French were the people most affected by German remilitarisation of the Rhineland but they had shown no sign of wanting to intervene.

The German leadership adopted a softer tone, assuring the diffident but fair-minded peer that Germany would seek a peaceful revision of her frontiers. Halifax returned to London convinced that 'the Germans have no policy of immediate adventure.' [21] Halifax told the Cabinet that Germany was too busy building up its own country to cause any alarums or excursions. 'Nevertheless,' he added, ' I expect a beaver-like persistence in pressing their claims in central Europe, but not,' he concluded loftily, 'in a form to give others cause or probably occasion to interfere.' [22]

It is worth pointing out that none of Halifax's colleagues, who included Eden, demurred from this assessment that implied a negotiated settlement with Hitler was possible and indeed desirable. Nor was the Foreign Office, despite subsequent myths woven around the names of Vansittart and Wigram, against the Conservative government's policy of trying to find a negotiated settlement that could deflect Hitler from war. In a document prepared by Sir Orme Sargent in 1937 for circulation to the Cabinet, the senior Foreign Office official noted:

> The fundamental idea, is of course, that the ex-allied Powers should come to terms with Germany, in order to remove grievances by friendly arrangement, and the process of give and take, before Germany again takes the law into her own hands. This is the only constructive policy open to Europe.
>
> The alternative policy of drift and encirclement are avowedly policies of negation and despair. There will in this Memorandum be no suggestion that the policy should be abandoned. [23]

But if no one in the British establishment could see the implications of Hitler's 'forward policy towards Austria', in Berlin, General Beck, the Chief of the General Staff, was profoundly disturbed at the thought of occupying Austria. He knew, as all intelligent German strategists knew, that occupying Austria was, is, and always will be the prelude to German penetration of central and south-eastern Europe. It meant a Balkan line, a south-eastward thrust in German policy, assimilation of alien races, the subordination of the successor states of the Habsburg monarchy and eventually a clash with powerful foreign interests.

It was noted by Canaris' colleagues that following meetings with Beck, Canaris spent more time with Colonel Oster. With the creation of the OKW, Canaris began reporting to its chief, General Wilhelm Keitel, a very dull officer from Württemburg who had made a 'good' marriage to Blomberg's daughter. Keitel and Canaris never really hit it off. Later, at the Nuremberg Trials and in interrogation sessions with the Allies, Keitel, like Jodl, would recall 'I always had problems with Canaris.'[24]

However, at this stage, Canaris, while determined to undermine the regime, was in no position to prevent the imminent invasion of Austria. According to Jodl's diary on 12 February 1938 he even orchestrated a clever deception plan to spread false but credible rumours which gave the impression of military preparations against Austria through fictitious troop movements. Canaris had no choice if he was to remain head of the Abwehr but to pursue a twin-track policy of simultaneously supporting and checking Hitler where possible. While carrying out to a high degree of professionalism the deeds required of the Abwehr to establish German hegemony in central Europe, the admiral remained committed to explore every avenue that could prevent a European war. This also included circumventing where possible Hitler's moves to strengthen party control of the military and encouraging the liberal democracies to stand up to Hitler.

At this stage in early February, Hitler was concerned at the effect on world opinion if German troops were mobilised to the Austrian frontier. The sham military action did not deceive the Austrian chancellor, Schuschnigg, who suddenly announced a plebiscite on 9 March. The plebiscite was expected to bring a strong majority for the monarchists, Jodl noted in his diary. Hitler, incensed at the prospect, ordered a march into Austria, Operation Otto, named after the Austrian heir to the throne, the same day as the plebiscite. Greeted with flowers by an hysterical Austrian populace, it was a bloodless victory, arousing no harsh words from London. With almost indecent haste, the British embassy in the Metternichgasse was converted into a consulate-general.[25]

Canaris was among the first arrivals in Vienna. He formed a special team to seize any files concerning him from the Austrian archives. Known as ZL, the unit was to lay its hands on anything they could find mentioning Canaris before the SD arrived. Canaris was clearly worried that the Austrian files might contain references to his links with London through the armaments circle and other details on his background.*

Canaris knew one of the heads of the Austrian service well: Colonel Lahousen. Lahousen and Canaris had exchanged information on both services' common intelligence target, Prague. Lahousen was as typical an Austrian officer as one could find – diffident, amusing, languid in speech, utterly charming and immensely subtle, he was, despite his great height, a kindred spirit for Canaris. As the admiral set about absorbing elements of the Austrian intelligence service into the Abwehr, he reportedly fixed Lahousen firmly with a keen eye and said: 'Bring me real Austrians. I do not want any Austrian Nazis in my service.'[26]

A month after the *Anschluss*, on 21 April 1938, Hitler summoned Keitel, ordering him to draw up plans for the invasion of Czechoslovakia, the so-called Operation Green. As the second officer of the OKW, according to seniority, Canaris was fully informed and like Beck, the Chief of the General Staff, disturbed. The risk of war was obvious and it was Canaris' fear that an attack on the Czechoslovak Republic would bring about a European war that Germany could not possibly win. Again however, Canaris had to pursue a dual policy of preparing supplies to Sudetenland activists undermining the Prague administration, while taking some steps to head off the crisis. However, this was not 'hedging bets', as some have speculated.[27] Rather, it was a conscious decision to preserve the influence

---

*Of some concern to Canaris would have been information linking him to other intelligence chiefs, notably in Hungary and the Baltic States, who were members of secret societies outlawed in the Third Reich. Since the eighteenth century the Austrian service had traditionally close links to such organisations and like any other service kept personality files on the intelligence officers of neighbouring countries.

of the Abwehr so that when it was needed for resistance, it would not be compromised and therefore deprived of its considerable freedom for manoeuvre.

One of those opponents of the regime with whom Canaris was in touch was Ewald von Kleist-Schmenzin, leader of the old monarchist conservatives and the embodiment of the Junker Prussian landowning tradition. Kleist had strong connections with England. He even mentioned the name of Canaris to English journalists he knew and suspected were in touch with British intelligence.[28] Canaris was determined to discover England's position, which was to outsiders far from clear. Ribbentrop was reporting that England would not resist German action against Czechoslovakia, but General Beck refused to believe the reports. One day in July 1938, Kleist met with Colvin and asked him if he thought England would fight.

Then he dropped his voice and said 'The admiral wants someone to go to London and find out. We have an offer to make to the British and a warning to give them.' [29]

Hitler, meanwhile, sent his adjutant, Captain Wiedemann, to sound out Lord Halifax: a most unconventional mission hatched with the help of Wiedemann's lover, Stefanie Hohenlohe, a Viennese Jewess who was also Hitler's go-between with Lord Rothermere. Rothermere, as recent documents published in Germany reveal, appears to have been much taken with her and bankrolled her until his death.[30] Princess Hohenlohe's (the title came to her through marriage) relationship with Rothermere was a grotesque counterpoint to the serious efforts of Anglo-German go-betweens, but vividly illustrates the desperate clutching at straws by Berlin to keep lines of communication open to pro-Nazi circles in London.

The piquant idea of the Olympian Halifax holding a serious conversation with the athletic, stupendously unintellectual, former heavyweight boxer Wiedemann must belong to one of the most picaresque chapters in Anglo-

German diplomatic relations. It inevitably left neither side the wiser. While Hitler was satisfied with Wiedemann's somewhat glowing account of his meeting with Halifax who, *pace* Wiedemann, would like nothing more than to see Hitler ride with the King down the Mall (!),[31] Beck noted in his diary: 'I think it is a dangerous error to believe that Britain cannot wage a long war. The war effort of Britain has always been long-term because her strength lies in the immeasurable resources of the Empire.' [32]

He continued: 'If she fights, it will not be so much to succour Czechoslovakia as to defeat the new Germany that has become a disturber of peace and a threat to the principles of statesmanship, recognised by the British: Law, Christianity, Tolerance.' [33]

Wiedemann, like Hohenlohe and her doting admirer Rothermere, was not taken seriously in the Abwehr. Indeed, Wiedemann's pedantic correspondence with Canaris over hostile press reports concerning Hohenlohe and Rothermere [34] illustrates a completely naive and superficial reading of events. If England needed further convincing of what was in store, the admiral would try to undeceive the British in his own way. Together with Beck and Kleist, they formed a plan in a brief conversation in Beck's office.

'Through yielding to Hitler,' Beck observed, 'the British government will lose its two main allies here, the General Staff and German people.' The general then continued in a conspiratorial tone: 'If you can bring me from London positive proof that the British will make war if we invade Czechoslovakia then I will make an end of this regime.'

Kleist asked him what he would regard as proof. Beck replied: 'An open pledge to assist Czechoslovakia in the event of war.' [35] It was decided then and there to send Kleist, with Canaris' help, to approach London and bring this news directly to the attention of certain persons in British political life who might influence the formulation of policy.

The choice of Kleist was wise. He was pre-eminently a gentleman, an unwavering opponent of Hitler, had charm of manner, honesty of bearing and 'deep sincerity'.[36] Getting Kleist to London was a challenge for Canaris. Kleist was watched by the Gestapo and officially at least would need their permission to leave the country. In London, there was, however, the risk that British intelligence might treat him as a German spy. Kleist used Colvin to tip off British intelligence and Canaris, who had the spy-chief's usual cavalier attitude towards the passport system, procured a fresh identity and some sterling for Kleist. By the time Kleist arrived at the great semi-circular arcade of Tempelhof airport, he was no longer just a patient German traveller waiting for his passport to be stamped, but a civilian whose escort was a German general (his nephew) and whose car was a Mercedes belonging to the OKW. The car drove onto the runway without making any detour towards customs or passport control and the civilian was escorted by the general to the plane. There was no question of interference. The civilian sat back in his seat and the escort, a kinsman, General von Kleist, got back into his car and drove off to the war ministry.

At Croydon, British security officials noted his arrival and watched him board the bus to London and take a taxi to the Park Lane Hotel, where Lord Lloyd was waiting to take him off to dinner in a private room at Claridges. Lloyd spoke no German, Kleist no English. The two men communicated in French. Kleist impressed upon Lloyd that the mobilisation plans for the invasion of Czechoslovakia were complete. Then he related the reluctance of the generals, the fear of war among the people, the unpreparedness of the armed forces. If England took a firm and positive stand against Hitler, the generals had plans to arrest him and make an end of the Nazi regime. These plans were well advanced. Beck had told him that 30 September was the last possible day of peace. Thereafter events would gather their own momentum.

Later, Kleist went over the same ground with Sir Robert Vansittart, former Permanent Under Secretary and then the chief diplomatic adviser to the cabinet. Kleist, according to 'Van', was the living embodiment of the Junker tradition and was not prepared to compromise on Poland.

Vansittart later claimed: 'Of all the Germans I saw, Kleist had the stuff in him for a revolution against Hitler. But he wanted the Polish corridor, wanted to do a deal.' [37] This rather off the cuff remark suggests a certain unease, if not a guilty conscience, about the meeting. On the one hand, it confirms that Kleist, who would later be hanged for his efforts, left no doubt in Vansittart's mind that the generals were serious. Kleist had listed some of the officers involved in the conspiracy. But it also contradicted Kleist's own version of the conversation and even the British official documents published since the war which made no reference to Poland. [38] 'Van' was either being studiously disingenuous as well as, predictably, cautious, or keen only to probe Kleist's sources of backing and not to offer anything in return.

Steeped in the tradition of the 1906 Eyre Crowe Memorandum on Germany, with its implication that Germany, irrespective of her leadership or intentions, on account of her size and capabilities would always be a threat to British interests, [39] 'Van' was temperamentally opposed to a deal with Germany. Accused by one German diplomat of being a well-known Germanophobe, [40] he would later prophetically warn another German *en poste* in London at that time, Theo Kordt, that 'if necessary Britain would follow the example of Samsom, tear down the pillars of the British Empire and bury Hitler along with themselves beneath the rubble.' [41] This 'temperamental opposition' to a deal with what A. J. P. Taylor called that 'recurring figure in European history, the good German', was a dynamic that was to repeat itself grimly in subsequent rounds of conversations between the German opposition and the English diplomatic establishment. As Colvin icily noted, 'Lord Vansittart's remarks did not seem to me to relate to the main problem.'

One thing seems certain, however: in his explanation of the forces hostile to war, Kleist would have mentioned Canaris' name. If he had breathed it to Colvin he would certainly have mentioned it in London, as Vansittart demanded more details of the aims and organisation of the secret opposition to Hitler. Kleist, therefore, in giving details of the conspiracy against Hitler, was assuming that these delicate conversations would remain confidential and that his interlocutor was a man of *bon volonté*, ill-disposed to Hitler and the Nazis rather than Germany. Kleist naturally assumed Vansittart was on the same side. In this the old gentleman may have committed a fatal error.

The conversation was repeated the following day at Chartwell, where Churchill received Kleist with solemn precautions. This appears to be the formal beginning of the 'conversation' Canaris, according to Sir Stewart Menzies, the head of British intelligence, 'initiated' with Churchill. Kleist left Churchill, like 'Van', in no doubt that the generals were preparing a coup. (The specious view that Kleist was somehow unaware of what Halder, Beck's successor, was planning in relation to these plans holds no water.) [42]

Kleist's request for an official letter that Beck could use to win the support of the generals offended every protocol of established diplomacy. No government could issue an informal démarche of such importance to someone not in the acknowledged government of Germany, but Halifax asked Churchill to send a letter. It was delivered by secret courier to Kleist after his return to Berlin and he laid it on Canaris' desk a few days later.* If London had still not woken up to the imminent Czech crisis, Churchill's letter showed that there was considerable foresight in some circles of what was coming:

My dear Sir,

> I have welcomed you here as one who is ready to run risks to preserve
> the peace of Europe and to achieve a lasting friendship between the
> British, French and German peoples for their mutual advantage.
>
> I am sure that the crossing of the Czechoslovak frontier by
> German armies or aircraft in force will bring about a renewal of world
> war. I am as certain as I was at the end of July 1914 that England will

*The letter was delivered to Kleist via Fabian von Schlabrendorff, a lawyer in the Abwehr service.

The man who outmanoeuvred both Churchill and
Admiral Fisher in 1915, *Korvettenkapitän* Wilhelm
Canaris. *ullstein bild*

ABOVE The *Dresden*, shortly before her scuttling in neutral Chilean waters, flying a parley flag. *Topfoto*

RIGHT Admiral Canaris at the height of his career as head of the Abwehr. *akg-images*

Canaris and Heydrich: a sense of camaraderie based
on shared naval experiences masked a bitter rivalry.
akg-images

ABOVE Basil Zaharoff: merchant of death and Knight of the
Bath, linked through Thyssen to Canaris, with whom he shared
a similar far from straightforward Hellenic background.
ullstein bild

OPPOSITE TOP For the Kremlin he was 'the most dangerous
intelligence man in the world.' Canaris with Himmler and
Goebbels. *SV-Bilderdienst*

OPPOSITE BELOW The traditional king-maker of German
politics: the Prussian officer corps. Von Fritsch, Ludendorff and
Blomberg. Hitler would outmanoeuvre them all. *Topfoto*

Brilliant, precocious and dangerous. Barely out of his teens, Julian Amery worked up the forces which led to the Belgrade *coup d'état*, derailing Anglo–German peace-feelers and delaying Hitler's invasion of the Soviet Union by six fateful weeks. *Portrait by Jane Bown, Camera Press, London*

The most underestimated politician of his generation. Leo Amery's broadcast to Belgrade on 26 March 1941 was the signal for the *coup d'état* against Prince Paul. *National Portrait Gallery, London*

Reinhard Heydrich, Canaris' protégé, later rival, and the
most feared of Hitler's paladins. *Corbis*

ABOVE Heydrich as *Reichsprotektor* of Bohemia, determined
to 'deal firmly with the Czech
vermin.' *Topfoto*

RIGHT Heinrich Himmler, head
of the SS in 1944. He would try
to exploit Canaris' contacts with
Western intelligence so as to
replace Hitler. *Corbis*

Colonel Lahousen as a witness at the Nuremberg
trials. His evidence revealed to the West Canaris'
policies and actions. *ullstein bild*

Hitler and Franco at Hendaye. Despite the smiles Hitler would bitterly recall his failed attempt to persuade Franco to help Germany take Gibraltar as like 'pulling teeth'.
Getty Images

ABOVE Pius XII, day by day tortured by his failure to openly help the Jews, mediated between London and Berlin, convinced that peace was the only way to stop the slaughter. *ullstein bild*

LEFT Count Michael Soltikow, Abwehr man, confidant of Canaris, bon viveur and anti-Nazi. After the war Churchill told him that Britain owed much to Canaris. *ullstein bild*

Aristocrat, Catholic and socialist, Stauffenberg came closer than anyone else to killing Hitler, but the last minute change of venue thwarted his and the German opposition's plans. *akg-images*

Walther Schellenberg, SS man and rising star in the viper's nest of Hitler's competing intelligence agencies. Canaris enjoyed weekly rides with him but warned his staff to treat him with great caution. *Topfoto*

'C', Sir Stewart Menzies, rumoured to be the illegitimate son of Edward VII. Churchill described him as a 'terrific anti-Bolshevik'. *Portrait by Vandyk, National Portrait Gallery, London*

ABOVE The 'Holy Fox',
Halifax, and the coming man,
Eden. At this stage both men
were keen to come to terms
with Berlin despite German
intentions in central Europe.
Hulton Archive

RIGHT Churchill and Halifax.
Both men cooperated over
Canaris' first unofficial
advances in 1938, receiving
his emissary Ewald von Kleist-
Schmenzin. *Topfoto*

Chamberlain at Northolt. By deliberately publishing
Hitler's declaration of wishing to settle disputes between
Britain and Germany peacefully he hoped to bind Hitler
before the opinion of the world. *Popperfoto*

ABOVE Chamberlain with his PPS Lord Dunglass, later Sir Alec Douglas-Home. Home noted: 'His miscalculation, which he shared with others, was that he could not conceive that any man could positively get his way by war.' *IWM (HU 5538)*

LEFT Canaris after his dismissa as chief of the Abwehr, with his two faithful friends, whom he often noted – unlike the two-legged variety – would never betray him. *Photos12* march with France, and certainly the United States is now strongly anti-Nazi. It is difficult for the democracies in advance and in cold blood to make precise declarations but the spectacle of an armed attack by Germany upon a small neighbour and the bloody fighting that will follow will rouse the whole British Empire and compel the gravest decisions.

Do not I pray you be misled upon this point. Such a war, once started, would be fought out like the last to the bitter end, and one must consider not what might happen in the first few months but where we should all be at the end of the third or fourth year.

Churchill predicted Germany would be utterly and terribly defeated. Kleist 'might ponder these words' with such patriotic Germans as he had come to represent.[43]

For Beck, the letter, which went on to quote with official approval Halifax's view that if 'war broke out, it would be impossible to know where it would end', was hardly a ringing official call to arms but it was sufficient in many ways to get things moving. Sceptics in London would for decades say the naive player in this was not Halifax but the German opposition, who were, with Churchill, 'star-gazing'.[44] However, the evidence shows that the Generals were ready to act even if Beck by that stage had decided to resign. Moreover, Beck knew all the details of the plan to invade Czechoslovakia, Operation Green, including the projected date in late September, before he resigned.

Beck had resigned in early August after Hitler announced in a speech to his generals at Jüterbog that he intended to solve the Czech question that autumn by force. Beck's logical mind saw that, as sure as night followed day, Germany's disturbing of the balance of power in Europe would unleash a world war which 'with mathematical logic' would utterly destroy Germany. His successor, General Franz Halder, a Bavarian, was more cautious. Dohnanyi, the Abwehr lawyer, noted that Halder lacked any revolutionary spirit and seemed obsessed with the details of his uniform. But even Halder – who to Dohnanyi's dismay produced at their first meeting a handkerchief which he carefully placed on his right thigh in order to protect the cut of his trousers before crossing his left leg over his right – was prepared to fall in with the plot and develop the existing plans, convinced, as he was, that Hitler was leading Germany to ruin.

Beck's resignation, far from causing 'opposition plans to collapse' [45] actually stiffened the resistance. The vital new factor was the discovery in this phase of the planning of several generals commanding troops who, in deference to the leadership of Beck, were prepared to enter the conspiracy. By 14 September General von Witzleben, commander of the Berlin area, had made arrangements with Halder and others to arrest Hitler as he returned from Berchtesgaden to the capital. Count Helldorf, the Berlin police chief, would arrest the other party leaders while General Hoeppner, in command of the Third Panzer Division, would march on Berlin at the signal from Witzleben. Count Brockdorff-Ahlefeld, in command of the Potsdam garrison, would support Witzleben while Count Fritz von der Schulenburg, son of the German Crown Prince's former chief of staff, would secure the government sector of Berlin. These plans were clandestine and drawn up with ruthless precision.

Canaris left the detailed planning to Oster who, in addition to the military timetable, constructed an extensive legal case against Hitler with the help of the lawyers von Dohnanyi and Dr Sack of the judge advocate-general's department. A panel of psychiatrists was even prepared, under the chairmanship of the eminent professor Dr Karl Bonhoeffer, who would certify the Führer as insane so that he could be immured in a lunatic asylum. Canaris himself was personally opposed to the idea of a military putsch against the Reichskanzlei by the Potsdam garrison. He favoured the kidnapping of the Führer by a small group of determined young officers as being easier and less complicated. Hitler would be held incommunicado until after the revolt had succeeded. All the conspirators agreed that a civilian-led government, or initially a military regime, would then be installed to consult the country on the form of government it desired for the future. 'By the beginning of September,' Halder could write, 'we had taken steps to immunise Germany from this madman.' As Churchill noted in *The Gathering Storm*, these were formidable steps. 'There could be no doubt of the existence of this plot and of serious measures to make it effective.' [46]

But the vital factor for the conspirators' success, on which the entire conspiracy was predicated, was that France and Britain would state that they would intervene in the event of a German attack on Czechoslovakia. But as the days wore on, the chances of such intervention began to recede. As Wheeler-Bennett has written, the conspirators and generals were 'playing with fire in every sense of the term ... No balancing feat, no trick of prestidigitation, demanded a greater control of nerve, timing and equilibrium.' [47] For London and Paris the challenge was to 'screw their courage to the sticking place and maintain a firm and united front.'

But London had other intentions. Within days of Kleist's return to Berlin on 23 August, Nevile Henderson, the British ambassador in Berlin, who had vehemently opposed Kleist being received in official quarters, was summoned to London for discussions with Chamberlain. Chamberlain, who had initially commented on Kleist's visit dismissively, noting that 'like Jacobites, a good deal' of what Kleist had said 'must be discounted', had changed his mind. Perhaps intelligence reports had confirmed Kleist's 'offer'. As one distinguished historian has written 'the official documents and files are silent. Perhaps some relevant papers are still kept secret or have been destroyed.' [48]

Whether this is the case or not, the documents show that on 28 August Chamberlain gave Henderson two important instructions: first, to prepare a 'serious warning' to the Führer concerning action towards Czechoslovakia but then to 'very secretly' prepare for a personal contact between Hitler and Chamberlain. The fact that the first of these instructions would be entirely negated by the second did not seem to impinge on the two men's logic. Henderson, moreover, succeeded within forty-eight hours in having the first instruction withdrawn 'on his own earnest insistence'. [49] Chamberlain's meeting with Hitler was thus being planned less than a week after Kleist's return and not, as has been generally assumed, on the spur of the moment two weeks later after Hilter's anti-Czech diatribe at the Nuremberg rally on 12 September.[50] Plans were already well advanced for the meeting by the evening of 5 September.

Theodor Kordt, a member of the German embassy, reinforced Kleist's message that evening in a private meeting with Sir Horace Wilson, the chief industrial adviser to the government, and Lord Halifax. Halifax, after the Munich Conference some weeks later, apologetically told Kordt: 'We were not able to be as frank with you as you were with us. At the time you gave us your message we were already considering sending Chamberlain to Germany.' [51]

Kleist had, in a British official's own words, 'come out of Germany with a rope around his neck to stake his last chance of life to warn Britain.' But Chamberlain, Henderson and even Vansittart had no desire to deal with the generals or help install a non-Nazi regime in Germany. It is very hard not to sense that there was at work here something beyond the reluctance of any government to treat with conspirators. Chamberlain no doubt hoped to win Hitler's gratitude and make him more amenable to a deal. He was convinced that 'reason and example would influence a dictator.' [52] If Chamberlain could show he was a man of integrity, surely Hitler would realise he could reach an agreement with him. How better to demonstrate this integrity than by refusing to help the generals stage a *coup d'état*? Moreover, as Lord Home, who as Lord Dunglass knew him better than most, points out, Chamberlain believed that in Hitler he had 'an unwavering ally against Communist Russia', something that was not necessarily the case with the German generals brought up in the tradition of von Seeckt. If fear of offending the Soviet Union would destroy later attempts to reach a settlement with Germany, at this stage fear of depriving Britain of an ally against Moscow would have the same effect.

Vansittart, was, as we have seen, reluctant to do a 'deal' with the generals; and Nevile Henderson, ever keen like every ambassador to cut the ground from beneath negotiations behind his back, was, in a fit of almost prima-donna like pique, determined to frustrate the conspirators. Though to be fair, like all diplomats, Henderson believed diplomacy was far too important to be left to outsiders, especially soldiers, even his admired Prussians.*

To regain the initiative and frustrate the conspirators, Henderson and Chamberlain knew they had to work swiftly. Canaris and Oster had ensured the British military attaché in Berlin was informed of the date of Hitler's projected invasion of Czechoslovakia as 'towards the end of September, most likely 28th'. The warning was delivered on 21 August, the same day von Kleist was in London telling the British of the generals' decision to act by the end of September. Both warnings hinted at Hitler's speech at the Nuremberg Rally on 12 September being the prelude to mobilisation, and therefore the coup would, according to the plans already discussed, take place shortly afterwards, on Hitler's return to Berlin on 14 September. Taken together, these two pieces of information left Henderson and Chamberlain in little doubt that the generals were planning to move swiftly after the 12th. As A. J. P. Taylor mischievously would note, for some 'intuitive reason' Chamberlain was convinced he had to take steps by 12 September.[53] The information had been confirmed by further secret emissaries from the German diplomatic corps, notably Kordt and Böhm-Tettelbach, to Halifax and Vansittart, respectively.[54]

Hitler, about to be betrayed by nearly every one of his generals, was facing a well-thought-out *coup d'état* which, given the anti-war sentiment of the German people at that time,[55] would receive mass support. At this

---

* Henderson had had a German governess and preferred speaking German to English when addressing Germans.

point in his career, his future looked at best as if it would be lived out in an institution for the criminally insane.

However, he was about to be saved – not by the SS or the Gestapo or Ribbentrop, who had no inkling of the conspiracy – but by the only people who did, the British. Chamberlain had persuaded himself that 'where neither concessions nor persuasion nor power' had changed Hitler's mind, 'his own reasonable approach could do so.'[56] Chamberlain gave his support, fully aware that the German leader was almost certainly about to be deposed if it were not forthcoming. World peace, perhaps he reasoned, would be preserved a little longer if Hitler could be brought to see reason.

Though some have argued that the generals were 'star-gazing',[57] there is extensive and consistent evidence from both sides that the plans for the coup were well-advanced. [58] As well as the determined military plans, the coordinated actions of Halder and Witzleben, sympathisers in other parts of the government apparatus were on the alert. In the foreign ministry, side arms were being distributed to supporters.[59]

An awful calm hung over the roofs of the Bendlerstrasse on the afternoon of 14 September, the date selected to announce Operation Green, the invasion of Czechoslovakia, which would be the signal for the Generals to act. But the afternoon passed without incident and by dinner Canaris knew why. He was sitting with Lahousen, Piekenbrock and Groscurth when a message came to him from the war ministry. Chamberlain had announced he intended to fly to Berchtesgaden to discuss a solution to the Czechoslovak situation. Lahousen recalled how the Admiral quite lost his appetite and laid down his knife and fork.

At that time, as Chamberlain's secretary Lord Dunglass [60] noted 'statesmen did not fly to meet each other.' Chamberlain had never flown before. His journey was 'novel, daring and spectacular'. He flew with no agenda, no interpreter and no detailed brief. This strongly suggests the event of his flight being the purpose as much as the talks that followed it. The search for peace may have demanded such unconventional behaviour, but it had also, indeed, been essential for him to fly out if the generals' plan was to be forestalled and Hitler prevented from returning to Berlin and certain arrest. Henderson had, as instructed, prepared the visit in great secrecy, not least with regard to the Foreign Office officials who would normally have been involved in the planning for such a trip and who were conspicuously left out.

These factors suggest that the kernel of Kleist's message, 'his warning and offer', as Kleist confided to Colvin, was not an entirely negligible factor in Chamberlain's calculations. Even Wheeler-Bennett, no friend of what he called the 'mythology' of the German opposition, notes: 'There is evidence indeed that plans which had existed for a putsch had been abandoned at the time of Mr Chamberlain's first flight to Germany.'[61] However, he insisted that only the 'flimsiest of evidence' offered support for the idea that Chamberlain forestalled the generals: a point of view fashionable at the time he was writing, shortly after the war, but belied by the consistent testimony of witnesses on both sides: Gisevius, Halder, Kordt, Colvin, Bartlett and others.

Certainly Vernon Bartlett, one of the newspaper men who accompanied Chamberlain to Munich, was approached by a former acquaintance on the general staff who told him that Chamberlain's decision to meet Hitler had spared the Führer and his gang from immediate arrest.[62]

David Astor would later write that the failure to act on the Kleist disclosures was 'the saddest missed opportunity of the whole hellish experience leading up to World War Two.'[63]

'What! He ... visit that man?'[64] Canaris exclaimed. He rose from the table utterly distracted and ate no more dinner. Half the world may have been rejoicing, but the other half, including Hitler's intelligence chief, the Reich's leading banker Haljmar Schacht[65] and many other prominent Germans were horrified. Operation Green was postponed, and with it the opposition generals and their units in Potsdam and elsewhere had no choice but to stand down. Canaris was experiencing a sensation few spy chiefs enjoy. He had opened his hand to the British and they had politely listened, but the result had been neither support nor cooperation but a betrayal in substance, if not in detail, of his entire stratagem. Given Henderson's almost pathological, though honourable, determination to avoid war with Germany and to see the positive side of Hitler, it is not improbable that in arranging Chamberlain's visit so rapidly and secretly he obliquely impressed on the Führer his knowledge of Hitler's vulnerability to the generals and the need to act swiftly.

Both Chamberlain's message to Hitler, noting 'I shall be ready to travel as of tomorrow morning' and Hitler's immediate acceptance, imply a mutual understanding that the stakes on a personal plain were high. Canaris could have been forgiven if his deep knowledge and admiration of the British Empire took something of a knock that afternoon. Anglo-German intelligence cooperation had always been a desired objective, but the chief of the Abwehr had not envisaged quite such a response to the Kleist visit. He had underestimated Chamberlain's determination to do a deal with Hitler. But there were other disturbing thoughts. Did forces in Britain in some subtle way want a war with Germany? Did they fear a restoration of the monarchy and the generals who would prove no less menacing to the balance of power? Were fate and destiny, as Canaris often later remarked to his officers, not to be cheated by the sincere attempts of men of good will to save Germany and Europe from what was coming? Was some dynamic now forcing events to run out of the control of even the statesmen and spy masters? Truly the road to hell appeared paved with good intentions. Canaris' subtle mind would no doubt explore every theme and variation that evening, but however he looked at it, one conclusion was inescapable: Kleist's mission to London had been a mistake. From an intelligence point of view, he had misread London's intentions, an unforgivable error. The admiral excused himself from his section chiefs and went early to bed.

CHAPTER EIGHT

LINES OF COMMUNICATION

A Europe divided is a common house at odds with itself.
LORD HALIFAX [1]

Chamberlain's visit to Berchtesgaden not only deprived Germany of the chance of an 'internal solution', it also stiffened those around Hitler who believed England would never fight for the cause of central Europe. If Canaris had misread the intentions of London, Ribbentrop had been proved all too accurate. The parvenu wine merchant, whose distorted views of England, invested with the prejudices of his wife and his own unhappy time there as ambassador, moved swiftly to reassert himself in his guise as the Führer's only 'England expert'. Canaris, however, with his naval background of respect for England's power and strategy, was convinced that war over Czechoslovakia was inevitable.

On 28 September, Canaris outlined his fears of a conflict with France and Britain to Keitel[2] but once again Chamberlain announced his intention to fly to Germany to negotiate. It is important to remember that Chamberlain's actions had the unreserved support of the entire cabinet, including Duff Cooper. [3] The Munich agreement that followed was the natural and logical outcome of a British government determined to avoid war. Could a prime minister, responsible for his country's survival and aware of its weakness and lack of preparation, have chosen to risk an immediate war?

As Czechoslovakia was dismembered with the connivance of Britain and France, the Czech leader Benes could rightly say: 'I would happily sacrifice my country for world peace but you have only made inevitable world war.' However, the German occupation of Prague had not caused a war. France, which together with the Soviet Union was a guarantor of Czechoslovak independence, acquiesced; Hungary, despite Canaris' warnings to Admiral Horthy, and Poland both joined the undignified scramble for Czechoslovak territory. Hitler not unnaturally hoped that these spoils would have a positive effect on the Polish government. With the fate of Czechoslovakia before it, Poland would see that its interests lay in alliance with Germany. After all, only four years earlier, Germany had proposed a joint German–Polish army to be commanded by Marshal Pilsudski to partition western Russia. [4]

But the scales had fallen from Chamberlain's eyes in March 1939. With the occupation of Prague, a complete betrayal of the Munich agreement, the idea of doing a deal with Hitler was no longer a publicly acceptable strategy, although in private it remained the British government's priority. Public opinion was incensed, and as Hitler ratcheted up the pressure on the Poles over Danzig and the Polish Corridor, Chamberlain panicked and the government agreed to what would in modern diplomatic parlance be called a 'line in the sand', offering Poland a historic and, given England's traditional reluctance to become embroiled in continental affairs, unprecedented guarantee to Warsaw in the event of her being attacked. As anyone familiar with the Polish mentality would know, this guarantee would be vigorously interpreted and amounted in Warsaw's eyes to a blank cheque. Such a move was unlikely to encourage the Poles to compromise. In turn a new momentum began to invest German diplomacy.

For some months, the Abwehr had been pursuing a 'forward' policy in sub-Carpathian Ukraine, or Ruthenia. Ruthenia was seen by some members of Canaris' staff as the 'Piedmont' of the Ukraine which could be encouraged to unite a larger nation then partly in Polish hands. This view was, needless to say, encouraged by officers of the Abwehr with an imperial Austrian background, notably Colonel Eugen Konowalez, a former *k.und k. uhlan* officer. Canaris himself was, at the best of times, no great enthusiast for the Ukraine, though he realised its value as an adjunct to the mobilisation of German minorities. However, in the early spring of 1939, he became aware of another check to his department's Ruthenian enterprise, namely the sudden deference being displayed towards the interests of the Soviet Union.

In the February of 1939, Churchill was invited to lunch at his friend Leo Amery's house at 112 Eaton Square. It was a lunch *à quartre*, the other two present being Leo's son, Julian, and Count Richard Coudenhove-Kalergi, the founder of the Pan-Europa movement dedicated to the cause of European unity. Coudenhove-Kalergi was one of the most remarkable men of his time. The son of an Austrian diplomat who had married a Japanese lady-in-waiting while *en poste* in Tokyo, he was, according to Julian [5] someone who knew the 'strings in the background' pulling the forces of history.

Leo had to leave the lunch early. As he got up from the table at the back of the house, he whispered to Julian: 'Make sure Winston has enough to drink.' As the conversation over cigars and brandy in the darkened dining room ranged across the European situation, the mood was intense as Churchill expanded on his close relationship with the Soviet ambassador, Maisky. Through a rapidly thickening fug of Cuban tobacco-smoke, Coudenhove-Kalergi listened attentively before asking a question which stopped Churchill in his tracks.

'You do realise, Mr Churchill, that Hitler and Stalin are just about to conclude an agreement?'

'What?', a startled Churchill exclaimed: 'Impossible ... I see the Soviet ambassador Maisky every week. I would have known. Who told you such a thing?'

Here Coudenhove-Kalergi paused before, with a conspiratorial smile, he replied: 'A source in the Vatican.'

This silenced Churchill. Not many things silenced him. After a few moments staring into the cigar smoke he quietly remarked: 'The Vatican? Then it must be true.' [6]

As all those around the table knew, the Vatican had and always would have a habit of being very well informed. The news was all the more surprising given the fact that Moscow was at that time in negotiations with London. In fact Coudenhove-Kalergi's source in the Vatican had been tipped off by an Abwehr contact, an Austrian, possibly even via Lahousen.[7] Canaris knew of Coudenhove-Kalergi's connections with the Vatican and his relationship with Amery.[8] At the same time he was keen to continue the 'conversation' with Churchill initiated via Kleist during the summer of 1938. As 1939 progressed, contacts with the Vatican were developed by Canaris even more extensively; assisted by the traditional contacts of the South German Catholic aristocracy, several members of which (for example Marogna von Redewitz) had been or were being drafted into the Abwehr in a substantial recruitment drive.

Though negotiations between Hilter and Stalin were not to be concluded until 24 August there was no doubt that the traditional German 'eastern policy' of cooperation with Moscow was a painful and disturbing anxiety for those like Churchill whose links and interests with Russia went back many decades.[9] In the coming conflict, the British Empire would need the help of the Soviet Union. Moreover, a German–Soviet rapprochement could only be directed against the West and in particular British overseas imperial interests.

If these thoughts ran through Churchill's mind that sunny but cold afternoon in Belgravia, in the Tirpitzufer on an even colder day, Canaris noted that the Abwehr's Ukrainian operations would have to be scaled down in deference to Soviet–German negotiations.

However, if the Abwehr was playing down the Ukranian card at this stage for a brief interlude, it was in every other way preparing for the conflict which all felt was now near impossible to avoid. Its budget and manpower were dramatically increased. Its finances would grow to an annual budget, the equivalent of £2,600,000 pounds (current value £5 billion) and there would be more than 30,000 personnel on its books, of whom 8,000 were Abwehr officers.[10] At the same time, as 1939 wore on, Canaris continued to send emissaries to London. Count Schwerin lunched with Menzies and Godfrey, the Naval Intelligence director. Both men asked to be remembered warmly to the admiral.

Intelligence operations against Britain, which had been banned by Hitler in the wake of the Anglo-German naval agreement of 1935[11] were now stepped up. Abwehr agents began to spring up all over the English social scene. One of the most engaging was Baron Robert Treeck. He bought a house and a small estate and was soon riding with the Beaufort Hunt, most of whose members were landed, wealthy and formed an almost honorary network of agents for the future head of the secret service, Sir Stewart Menzies, who was himself an MFH with the Beaufort.[12]

There is some evidence to suggest that Treeck was known to Menzies as an Abwehr agent.[13] There is also some sign that in certain areas of Eastern Europe, notably the Ukraine, SIS and the Abwehr had been cooperating against the Soviets.[14] This cooperation, though formally broken off, was to survive the outbreak of hostilities, notably in Finland where the British forces sent to help the Finns against the Soviets in 1940 were actually assisted in their passage by the Germans. German air and land forces were instructed not to interfere with the progress of these British forces.[15]

Meanwhile, operations against the United States had been in full flow since 1937 when developments in American military aviation technology had become a priority target for the Abwehr. These operations had been successful, notably the Abwehr's covert acquisition of the Norden bombsight in late 1937.

Another priority target for the Abwehr in the UK was the secret development of radar by the RAF. This work was conducted in the greatest secrecy and yet the Abwehr was fully informed. When Luftwaffe General Milch arrived in England for a tour of Fighter Command in early 1939, he took his hosts by surprise when he asked them 'how we were getting on with our development of radar'. Milch caught his hosts 'completely off balance'. As one British intelligence agent ruefully noted: 'What I had seen of their intelligence work showed it to be marginally cleverer than ours.' [16]

As the Abwehr stepped up its operations in England, these were accompanied – as is so often the case between countries facing imminent hostilities – by increased cooperation on the defence and financial fronts. As Britain rearmed, various weapons were ordered from Germany in return for significant sums of money. These deals were brokered on the German side by Abwehr agents and were to culminate with the offer of a substantial loan to Germany in the late spring of 1939. According to several German and Soviet sources, [17] the loan which was negotiated between members of the Reichsbank and officials of the Bank of England was seen by many observers as an incentive to encourage Germany to wage war against the Soviet Union.

As late as 29 June, Halifax addressed an audience at Chatham House with, at least for any Germans present, the following soothing words: 'European minds will meet across political frontiers. Truly is a divided Europe a house divided against itself. Our foreign policy must bear in mind ... the more distant future.' [18]

The speech began with a classic formulation of Britain's policy: 'In the past we have always stood out against the attempts by any single power to dominate Europe at the expense of the liberty of other nations. British policy is therefore only following the inevitable line of its history.' But it went on to hint at compromise: 'If we could once be satisfied that the intentions of others were the same as our own – then I say here definitely

– we could discuss the problems. In such a new atmosphere we could examine the colonial past, raw materials ... ' No experienced diplomat could fail to read the subtext of Anglo–German issues here.

Gordon Etherington-Smith, then a newly-posted third secretary at the embassy in Berlin, recalled having to go to the foreign ministry with a telegram from London in the summer of 1939 asking why certain German arms which had been paid for by London had still not arrived in England. It was barely six weeks before war broke out. 'My impeccably mannered opposite number at the German foreign ministry wryly and half-jokingly observed: "My dear fellow ... you will be very lucky if you get these now: at least in the form you're expecting them."' [19]

Another aspect of this twin-track approach by both London and Berlin to the looming Polish crisis was continued contacts between British intelligence and the German navy. The links Patzig had forged at five days of parties at the Coronation Review of 1937, where he had met everyone from King George VI downwards, continued to be developed.* The old pre-1914 camaraderie of the German and British navies once again showed itself remarkably resilient to international tensions, no doubt assisted by the fact that both services contained officers whose families had served their navy for successive generations.

As the British agent Frederick Winterbotham put it when he encountered the German navy on a visit to Lübeck, the officers' wardroom was comprised of 'pleasant mannered' kindred spirits far removed from the officers of the German army: 'These young men were mainly sons and grandsons of German naval officers of the old regime, an entirely different type from the army types on deck.' [20]

In this context, it is worth recalling that both the British security service and SIS were dominated almost exclusively by philo-German elements who felt the main enemy to be Communism. With the exception of the

---

*Patzig had been presented in a 'moving ceremony' with a relic of the German fleet scuttled at Scapa Flow after internment in 1918.

Comintern agents who had only begun their penetration of both services in the thirties and had been largely recruited from Cambridge and Oxford, the senior officers were, in Churchill's words, 'terrific anti-Bolsheviks.' [21] It was only after Churchill sacked Vernon Kell, the head of MI5, that the services began to reorientate themselves seriously into organisations with an anti-German ethos.[22] Even then the head of the Naval Intelligence Division, Admiral Godfrey, who had been in contact with Canaris since the days of the Spanish Civil War, remained far from intellectually closed to German aspirations.

Unsurprisingly, as German penetration of England continued, Canaris noted that his job was made easier by the low pay and conditions agents of British intelligence endured. He had already broken British ciphers and penetrated British intelligence 'here and there.' [23] His views on British intelligence were mixed. Canaris once told an officer: 'If it is a matter of money, let me tell you, they do not reward services well, and if they have the least suspicion, they will not hesitate to betray you.'

In particular, Holland, the traditional no-man's land between German and British interests, offered the Abwehr scope for infiltration. Holland had long served as a key listening post and operations centre for British intelligence activities in Germany. It was targeted with particular success by the Abwehr. An underpaid British employee inside the MI6 Station in the Hague began supplying the Abwehr with daily reports of British intelligence activities within Germany.

Nevertheless, if the Abwehr was stepping up activities, Canaris was still taken aback when, on 17 August, he received requests for his department to procure 'Polish uniforms' for Heydrich. Canaris' response was immediate. He went to Keitel and asked what the uniforms were needed for. Keitel explained that he assumed it was for an imminent operation behind Polish lines but was also clearly exercised by the request. The conversation is recorded in one of the few pages of Canaris' diary to have survived as it had been copied by Lahousen. Keitel, according to Canaris, was defensive about the request and insisted that he did not care for 'such operations' but that the request came directly through the Führer and that it was not for Keitel to question such orders. Keitel even urged Canaris to tell the SS that the 'Abwehr have no Polish uniforms.'

The uniforms, irrespective of their provenance, were put to sinister use. Convicts were dressed in them and told to storm the German radio station on the Polish frontier at Gleiwitz as a provocation. The convicts were all shot as they attacked the radio station. Canaris was in no position to stop Heydrich's operation but as the diary fragment notes, he once again emphasised to Keitel that if it came to bloodshed, Britain would 'fight with all means in their powers.' Keitel was equally certain, however, that Britain would not intervene.[24] Given the conflicting signals coming out of London, both men could be forgiven their opposing conclusions. Three weeks earlier, despite the undertaking to Poland in March, the German trade official Wohltat could cable Berlin after talks with Sir Horace Wilson that a 'proper Anglo–German non-aggression treaty would enable Britain to rid herself of commitments vis-à-vis Poland.'[25] The Swedish businessman Dahlerus, a friend of Goering's, was also being deployed by both sides, to the intense irritation of the diplomats, to explore a peaceful solution. So seriously did Lord Halifax take this emissary that he sanctioned a prolonged and irregular correspondence which duplicated and muddied the already prolix negotiations going on through official channels.[26]

On 22 August, Hitler summoned his senior officers to Berchtesgaden to discuss the invasion of Poland and the ruthless measures to be deployed against the Polish intelligentsia, aristocracy, Jews and clerics. Though forbidden by Schmundt, the duty adjutant, to take notes, Canaris stood in the background against a stone column and began taking down details on a pad. Hitler's intentions were against all the norms of civilised warfare. Fired up by the imminent signature of the Pact with Stalin, Hitler refused to rein in his extreme feelings with regard to the Poles.

Canaris did not hesitate to ensure the drift of these remarks was communicated to the British. Kleist was in Stockholm and once again was in touch with British diplomats. But this intelligence, and the signing of the Molotov-Ribbentrop pact two days later, only forced the pace of appeasement and Halifax on 25 August called in the Polish ambassador to insist that 'there must be a modification of the status of Danzig.'

The Poles, however, having secured British support – however wobbly – had no intention of backing down: especially with yet another partition of their country staring at them in the smiling faces of the German and Soviet foreign ministers. When, a few days later, Hitler demanded a Polish plenipotentiary to arrive in Berlin and the Swedish businessman Dahlerus appeared to have been, according to his own account, on the point of brokering a compromise based on a non-violent modification of Danzig's status, Henderson found his Polish colleague packing his bags. With the *suffisante* confidence which has always been one of the Polish elite's most endearing qualities, Lipski, who had been instructed by Warsaw 'not to enter into concrete negotiations' told Henderson that 'he had no interest in any German proposals because if war was declared the Nazis would be overthrown and the Polish Army would probably soon arrive in Berlin in triumph.'[27]

In this charged atmosphere, jitters expressed themselves in strange ways. On 2 September, an Abwehr source warned Colonel Denis Daly at the British embassy in Berlin that a blitz daylight attack was scheduled for the following morning on London. A report was accordingly sent in cipher to London. 'I am convinced that there was no intention to deceive us in this matter,' Colonel Daly later recalled. 'The man who came to bring me that message was certainly taking considerable risks.'[28] It is said that Halder dissuaded Hitler from this curious isolated attack, but by then the British could not be advised that the attack had been cancelled and the sirens were famously sounded just after Chamberlain's sombre speech in the House of Commons.

Meanwhile, at the Tirpitzufer, the admiral, who had read out extracts of Hitler's speech on the Poles to Lahousen, declared that if a defeat for Germany would be a calamity, a German victory would be an even greater catastrophe. No effort should be spared to shorten the war and the Abwehr would continue to eschew all methods which offended the ethics of war.[29] To another colleague, a few days later, on hearing that the German invasion of Poland had begun, he confided grimly: 'It is the end of Germany.'

The Abwehr in September 1939, however, was rather more aggressive than its opponents. It began infiltrating Poland with units prepared for hostilities at key points. It also now began ruthlessly preparing sabotage operations against the UK mainland. If Canaris hoped for peace he was under no illusion that war with England was imminent and that his duty involved planning attacks against British interests. Lahousen, who had had some contact with the Irish Republican Army, noted that the IRA was successfully blowing up high profile targets, including Hammersmith Bridge, early in 1939. Could the Irish be persuaded to attack military targets and munitions dumps in the event of hostilities?[30]

Lahousen's attempts to bribe and cajole the IRA taxed even his improvisation skills and Byzantine training in the old *k. und k.* Evidenzbüro. His first problem was a religious one. Several senior IRA members were appalled at the thought of an imminent German attack on Catholic Poland. In common with Catholics throughout Europe, they saw the main enemy as godless Moscow. They would, however, now that hostilities had begun, nevertheless swallow these qualms and detonate explosives at an important arms factory in Waltham Abbey in January 1940, an act of sabotage which badly dented MI5's reputation and that of Vernon Kell, whose office had had warning of the attack.

This spectacular coup, following hard on the heels of the daring U-boat raid at Scapa Flow which sank the Royal Navy's *Royal Oak*, showed all too vividly that the Abwehr's agents were alive and kicking and that

MI5's undoubted successes in rounding up German agents were not as comprehensive as they might have wished.

Nor was the Abwehr absent from those traditional recruiting grounds, the diplomatic and military circuits. From March 1938 until May 1941, Canaris had the services of a Sandhurst graduate, the Iraqi officer Mahomet Salman, who on account of his background and training had some access to senior British officers and was highly informed about developments in British armour. Captain Salman was studying armoured warfare at Sandhurst and other British camps with the full cooperation of the British army.[31] Salman not only had access to highly classified technical information through being attached to the top secret Mechanised Warfare Experimental Establishment, he was in constant social contact with senior British officers.

Moreover, he communicated his information to the Abwehr through the diplomatic bag in the guise of letters addressed to his brother Major General Ahmed Salman, another Abwehr agent and commander of the Iraqi air force. As the Abwehr had a resident officer in Baghdad, it was not too difficult to get the information back to the Tirpitzufer. Thanks to this information, the German panzer command was fully informed about the capabilities of British tanks and such information may have played a role in the rout of Anglo–French forces in the spring of 1940. Later, Field Marshal Rommel would also benefit from Salman's classified reports during his tank battles with the British.

Another English windfall for Canaris was Tyler Kent, a cipher clerk in the American embassy who made copies of Churchill's and Roosevelt's correspondence via the State Department's 'grey code' from October 1939. This correspondence was highly secret, as it included details of the 'destroyers for bases' deal whereby Churchill would offer 99 year leases on several British bases in return for 50 US navy destroyers. The telegrams also gave insights into Churchill's strategic concerns and his desires to get the US Navy to help the Royal Navy deal with German surface raiders. Kent showed some fifty of these telegrams to an attractive Russian woman called Anna Wolkoff who passed them onto the Abwehr via the Italian embassy in London.

These cables gave Canaris every detail of the strength and disposition of British forces in France as well as thoughts on future military strategy, Anglo-American cooperation and statistics of American aid. Not without reason could it be said, 'it was almost as if the Abwehr had an agent sitting in the War Cabinet.' By the time Kent was rumbled in May 1940, British and French forces had been routed in France and there was barely a week to go before the British Expeditionary Force was evacuated from Dunkirk.

Within a few months of Britain declaring war with Germany, the Abwehr had links to many important parts of the British establishment, assisted not least by the many English right wing organisations such as the Link and the Right Club, and unwittingly by a clutch of sincere, well-meaning pro-German Tory peers who were in close contact with Halifax and represented a highly influential part of the Conservative party (Brocket, Darnley, Londonderry, Buccleuch, etc.) and powerful 'money interests'.[32]

In addition to this intelligence network permeating the highest levels of British society, it had scored notable successes in sensitive areas. It was better informed on the progress of US–British negotiations than most of the British government. It was privy to top secret technology being developed in Britain, including radar, and was fully apprised of every political, military and strategic move London was taking with regard to getting US support. It had even shown itself capable of such striking acts of sabotage as sinking Royal naval ships in the most secure of British naval ports and blowing up well-guarded munition factories. Its web of agents had truly, at this critical moment in England's fortunes, fought its opponents to a standstill. Yet this was the same organisation which the distinguished historian, the late Hugh Trevor-Roper, would acidly describe as 'incontestably inefficient'.[33]

As if this was not enough, there was a further debacle for the British at Venlo in Holland when two British intelligence operatives, Best and Stevens, one an MI6 officer, the other a businessman, the latter monocled and trench-coated in the best *Thirty-Nine Steps* style, were kidnapped by the SD under the command of Walter Schellenberg.

Best and Stevens had been in contact through SD agents with what they believed were influential German circles planning a move against Hitler. Richard Protze was monitoring the two Englishmen for the Abwehr and supposedly watching their every move. However, when on 9 November the curious figure of Georg Elser,* a watchmaker, made an attempt on Hitler's life with a home-made bomb in the Munich Brauhaus, the SS saw an easy option for linking the attack with the British by capturing Best and the philo-German Stevens.

Canaris, according to contemporary accounts, was not kept informed of this plot by the SD and mischievously asked Protze the following day, after he had heard the news: 'What are your friends Stevens and Best up to at the moment?' When Protze replied that they were still 'under constant surveillance in Holland,' Canaris looked daggers and angrily told Protze that they were under interrogation in the SD offices.

The SD had hijacked a straightforward Abwehr surveillance operation and used it to try to tempt from the British officers the names of German conspirators. Best, who spoke German well and had many friends among the German aristocracy, had misgivings about the calibre of the men he was dealing with and tried to warn Stewart Menzies, then SIS deputy chief who was overseeing the operation, but he was overruled by the serving intelligence officer, Stevens, who understandably monopolised the lines of communication to SIS headquarters in Broadway.

The Abwehr, which had already suffered the embarrassment of the German ambasssador's secretary, von Putlitz, defecting to the British after a tip-off from his ambassador, was wary of Dutch operations. Von Putlitz

---

*Elser is one of the most mysterious figures of the Second World War. The simple watchmaker was accused by the British of being in the SD's service, but the accusation of agent provocateur does not entirely ring true on closer examination of Elser's background and training (see Stern: *Der Wahre Gegner*).

was successfully blackmailed by SIS, on account of his homosexual tendencies, into spying on his ambassador who nevertheless, on account of Putlitz's old family lineage, then as now a bond in the German service, gave the errant attaché a chance to escape. When travelling together in the ambassadorial car he languidly observed to Putlitz: 'I'm told that there is a spy in my office.' Putlitz disappeared in twenty-four hours.

Venlo was powerful proof – if Canaris needed it – that the SD was still trying to occupy Abwehr territory: 'This *schweinerei* is Heydrich's doing!' he shouted. It also made him realise that Schellenberg was an up and coming man, with designs on the Abwehr.

'He left us in no doubt that Schellenberg was a person we should be wary of having contacts with,' one of Canaris' secretaries noted. [34]

Whatever the machinations behind Venlo, Best and Stevens were a huge propaganda coup for the Germans and another nail in the British intelligence coffin. There is little doubt that under interrogation, until the end of the war, despite their best efforts, they supplied considerable titbits of useful material on the British intelligence community. Schellenberg's notorious list of English citizens to be rounded up in the event of a British invasion may have been partly compiled with information gleaned from these two. Not for nothing would a well-connected politician of those times observe: 'You cannot know what pessimism is unless you had been through 1940.'

Hand in glove with this professional penetration of the UK, the Abwehr had already begun operating behind Polish lines. Deploying members of the Brandenburg division commando units assigned to Abwehr II, preparations had been made to seize key bridges and installations. Though Poland had mobilised promptly, her forces were no match for the overwhelming strength of Guderian's armour and the Luftwaffe. Not that the campaign was uncontested. The Poles fought well and among later battle-hardened German troops the campaign was seen as short but tough.[35]

Canaris arrived in Silesia on 12 September to hear first-hand reports of the fighting from Keitel. It was on this occasion that he remonstrated with Keitel on the question of the systematic liquidation of the Polish intelligentsia, Jews and Catholic priests. Again a fragment of the diary has come to us via Lahousen: 'I told Keitel I was aware of extensive executions planned in Poland and that the nobility and clergy particularly were to be exterminated. The Wehrmacht would in the final reckoning be held responsible for these atrocities carried out under their very noses.' Keitel was unmoved.

Canaris found the Polish experience deeply unsettling. Von Hassell, the diplomat and former ambassador in Rome, who saw him after he returned noted in his diary: 'Canaris has come back from Poland completely broken after he had seen the results of our brutal conduct of the war.' [36]

Canaris, however, had further reasons for his distress. The Abwehr was being forced to play a role in the roundups by the SD. The war had pushed the two organisations closer together. The military field police who were under Abwehr command worked hand in glove with the SD to winkle out those on Heydrich's list, and while it is clear that they did not participate, on the whole, in mass executions they were undoubtedly prepared to play a strong supporting role. Lahousen noted that a new directive was added to those Canaris had issued earlier concerning the methods to be deployed in dealing with operations involving the SD: 'Passive conduct of Abwehr II work with apparent great show of activity,' he noted was of especial relevance now. This would still not prevent the Abwehr working hand in glove with the SD on Polish security issues.

In several cases, however, the Abwehr would actively try to undermine Gestapo activity in Poland. Paul Metternich intervened with Canaris to save a relative who was in the Polish underground. The Abwehr told the man the SD were closing in on him but the relative, a patriotic Pole, refused to take the Abwehr's offer of escape and was rounded up and executed. [37]

Canaris began to compile a file on the executions, even losing his temper with his officers if they failed to bring back exact numbers and details.[38] It was the details of these atrocities that would lead Canaris and Oster to have many an emotional outburst over the need to remove Hitler, by violence if necessary. Canaris was a changed man. Whereas before Oster had been the motor of German military conspiracy against Hitler, the generals now noticed that Canaris was taking more and more of a leading role. 'He was whipping the whole thing up these days,' noted Halder. [39]

Indeed, Canaris went from general to general with the simple message: 'Hitler must be got rid of.' As before the war, many of the generals sympathised but, significantly, not all. Paulus, for example, later to be promoted Field Marshal on the eve of his surrender at Stalingrad, replied to Canaris: 'The special operations, executions and roundups are absolutely necessary to deal with the military exigencies of the Polish campaign.' It was also noticeable that younger officers, who had been trained entirely during the Nazi period, were far less susceptible to the qualms of the older officers.

Canaris worked feverishly to intervene where he could to save lives. On his return to Berlin he began to arrange help for several beleaguered Poles, including – at the request of the US consul general in Berlin – a prominent Jewish rabbi of Warsaw. He enlisted everyone he could to help, including foreign military attachés such as the Spaniard, Juan Luis Rocamora.

One day in September, Canaris went to the Spanish Embassy and told Rocamora that he was needed to help evacuate half a dozen refugees from close to the Polish front. Canaris knew that all the military attachés *en poste* in Berlin were going to be invited to Poland the following week. Rocamora was to be with two cars at a particular hour at a particular place, where he would find five people with false papers to take back to Berlin. He was then to hide them in his flat. Two other attachés had been asked but had baulked. Rocamora, characteristically, agreed immediately. Canaris never told him who the refugees were but that they 'belonged to the elite of the country' and that one was very ill. 'The Gestapo were not to get their hands on them.' [40]

Another person Canaris was to smuggle out was to have more lasting consequences for the Abwehr. Canaris was in Poznan (Posen) when a pale and distressed woman he had known from Berlin days before the war was presented to him. Madame Szymanska had been married to the Polish military attaché, Colonel Szymanski, who had grown up speaking German in Posen, had trained in the Imperial German army before the war and was a well-known and philo-German figure on the pre-war Berlin diplomatic circuit. He was well-known to the British attachés, including Captain Troubridge, who met him several times, even learning during their last meeting finally how to spell the Pole's name correctly.

Madame Szymanska had mentioned Canaris' name while being interrogated and the effect had worked like a magic charm. She later wrote: 'I noticed that the German officer found it hard to conceal his astonishment when I uttered this name. His whole tone and bearing altered. He told me that he could not give me a pass to go westwards but he ordered a military vehicle to take me on its way to Poznan.' [41]

When she arrived at Poznan, she was quickly taken to a carriage of a train under Abwehr command. Canaris gave word for her to be invited into his railway carriage but she, a proud Pole, remarked to one of the officers: 'Can he not come here to me to identify me?' The astonished junior officer gently replied: 'It will be difficult for him to talk to you among all these people.'

Chivalry and gallantry were second nature to anyone of Canaris' training. He comforted Madame Szymanska who, like any Pole in such a situation, was keen to know how her country's army had fought. At the back of his mind, however, was an idea whereby he could not only save this Polish lady but also use her to open up another line of communication with London at a time when so many of the channels established before the war were now being closed.

When she asked to be helped to go to her family in Warsaw, Canaris advised against it. Then, realising that she was fluent in different languages and a lady of some attraction and culture, the admiral suggested neutral Switzerland. His choice of Berne, however, showed how rapidly his mind worked. The Swiss capital would be significant, for there was not only a Free Polish Mission in the city, but also an exceptionally important British intelligence station. As Nicholas Elliot, a young MI6 officer who would have quite a bit to do with the Abwehr later on in the war, noted: 'Canaris knew that anything he told this Polish lady would be reported, she being a patriotic Pole, straight to Polish intelligence who would of course pass it onto us.' [42]

After the war, Ian Colvin asked her whether Canaris had ever attempted to draw her into espionage work, but she denied this: 'The admiral never asked me to find out anything for him about the Allies, although he must have known that I was in touch with my own countrymen in Berne and through them with the British.' [43]

Canaris visited Berne several times during the winter of 1939 and told the British, via Madame Szymanska, that Germany would 'certainly make war on her treaty partner Russia sooner or later.' He also hinted strongly that the German opposition was keen to end the war against Britain by deposing Hitler. For the next few years, British intelligence would have an insight into the mind of one of the shrewdest observers of the activities of the German High Command. 'All his talk was of high politics but you could sense from them what was imminent. He would not have told me of purely military matters – small treason such as agents deal in. When he spoke it was of the Reich and Russia and Great Britain and America.'

The Szymanska connection showed that SIS and the Abwehr could communicate with each other and even cooperate. Madame Szymanska's husband had been captured by the Soviets. Thanks to an exceptional intervention by the British, he was released and handed over to the West, an almost unheard of event for a Polish officer in Soviet hands.[44]

As the Germans strengthened their grip on Europe and rolled back the French and British Expeditionary Army the following spring, this link would preserve a source of sound intelligence about German intentions which would be of great help to an increasingly beleaguered enemy.

Throughout the war this link was never discovered and significantly, it was entirely one way, for as Madame Szymanska pointed out: 'He never once tried to find out anything about the Allies through me.' Canaris, thanks to the Abwehr penetration of Britain, needed no help to know what was going on in London. He knew, perhaps better than most – even in England – that Britain was facing a supreme crisis, and that if she failed to rise to the challenge the civilised world would come to an end. It is this twin-track philosophy, permitting on the one hand a committed attack on the intelligence structures of the enemy, while ensuring that the subsequent victory does not destroy the enemy, which places Canaris far above the agents and spies of earlier generations. Here was a spymaster who believed that a total victory for Nazi Germany would spell disaster for the world and that a balancing act of supreme dexterity would somehow enable him to help his opponents while at the same time saving his country from the jaws of utter ruin.

Later, as Churchill experienced the dark moments of 1940 – a defeated army, an imminent invasion, a broken France, no allies, a defeatist cabinet – no one could sense the desperation of the moment as acutely as Canaris, informed by both sides of the overwhelming strength of the German forces and the pathetic weakness of the British. The Abwehr would know all too well of the peace-feelers coming out of London the following spring.

When an officer gloomily remarked to Canaris that 'I think you will find the British will not go on,' Canaris snapped back: 'Of course they will go on!' If there was one thread that went through his conversations that winter with his Polish friend in Berne, it was that Britain would be poorly advised to come to an agreement with Hitler. Even if Britain had no powerful allies as yet, she still had the friendship of those good Germans who would not wish to see London go down to a Nazi victory. In the person of Canaris they had someone who would now deploy all the skill and deception that only an experienced spy chief in wartime can muster to buy time for an otherwise all but vanquished foe. London did not have an agent in Canaris, but they had, incontestably, an ally. They may have hoped, as any case officer might, that one day Canaris would become an agent, but Canaris would avoid British control as much as he would German.

Canaris busied himself on two main fronts. Internally, he stepped up his support for the plans of the conspirators against Hitler, where possible drawing up evidence that would reveal the entire naked evil of the entire Nazi edifice.

Externally, he set about constructing as many avenues of communication as possible with the British. If Madame Szymanska was one of the more exotic, she was only one of several channels opened up in neutral capitals. As Fortress Europe was built by the Germans on the back of Guderian's panzers, Canaris constructed a rabbit warren of secret communications with the enemy. In Switzerland, at the Vatican, in Spain, in Finland, the Abwehr officers were instructed to pursue a dual policy of seemingly blind obedience to the Führer while maintaining contacts – if necessary through third parties – with Britain.

As the drama of 1940 unfolded and Britain's 'finest hour' began, the Abwehr was going to play the role of a most unlikely 'guardian angel' to the British Empire.

CHAPTER NINE

KEEPING THE EMPIRE AFLOAT

I would rather have three or four teeth extracted
than go through that again.
HITLER [1]

On 19 September 1939, Churchill had recommended to the cabinet that British forces mine Norwegian waters and examine ways of cutting off Narvik harbour, with its supplies of vital raw materials for the Germans, and occupying the area with troops. Within hours, the Abwehr was assessing these statements which, of course, infringed Norway's neutral status. Canaris immediately saw the significance of Churchill's suggestion and, most unusually, gave a lecture to the naval staff on the intelligence: something which gave it added weight in Admiral Raeder's eyes.[2]

Hitler, however, was most reluctant to think of invading Norway. The general staff had never contemplated Norway as a target. The search for military intelligence material on Norway produced only a dusty 1907 guide to Norway's armed forces. Preoccupied with the plans for an offensive in the West, Hitler remained lukewarm on the idea, telling the leader of the Norwegian Fascists, Vidkun Quisling, that all he wanted was for Norway to remain neutral.[3] But Quisling gave convincing news that the British were planning to take Narvik and this, together with the successes of the Royal Navy in tracking down German pocket raiders, may have given Hitler pause for thought.

In any event, by 10 October 1939 Hitler began talking of invading Norway. With the successful conclusion of the Polish campaign, the need to secure the northern territories began to figure in Hitler's calculations. Russia was clearly preparing to invade Finland. The possibility of British aid to Finland through Narvik, even if it did not exist at that precise moment, was only a question of time. More importantly, Narvik lay astride the key routes whereby iron reached the German Reich from the iron-ore fields of Kiruna-Gallivare in Sweden. The German navy was also keen to pre-empt the Royal Navy by seizing the Norwegian bases. By 14 December, Hitler had decided to initiate the offensive, to be called Operation Weserübung, and had earmarked eight divisions for it.

'It was a terribly weighty decision to occupy Norway,' Jodl would write. 'It meant gambling with the entire German fleet.' [4] According to Jodl, the decision to finalise the invasion plans was taken on 2 April on the basis of 'Canaris' reports that British troops and transports were lying in a state of readiness on the north-east coast of England.' The British cabinet's decision on 12 March to revive plans previously discussed for the occupation of Narvik and the sealing off of Germany's northern approaches were, like the discussions earlier in September, swiftly known to the Abwehr.

It has been said that Canaris was hoping for a German setback in the Skagerrak which would make Hitler vulnerable to a renewed coup. There is no doubt that the generals reckoned with the possibility of exploiting a blow to Hitler's prestige, but there is no evidence to suggest that Canaris actively betrayed details of the Narvik operation to the British.[5] Canaris wanted to avoid further hostilities. What he had seen in Poland had sickened him. His deputy, Oster, on the other hand, was more clinical. He hoped a German reverse would damage Hitler enough to give the generals the chance they needed to act. Canaris appears at this stage to have had increasingly little faith in the generals, refusing at one stage to see any of them on account of their moral 'cowardice'.

However, he took no steps to prevent Oster making his way to the

Dutch military attaché, Colonel Gilbert Jacob Sas, to inform him that the invasion of Norway was imminent. This act of treason, for to give information to a country which could incur the loss of fellow soldiers' lives was an act of treachery, shows how desperate the conspirators had become. There is no evidence that Canaris sanctioned this move. Sas passed the warning onto the Norwegian legation in Berlin, where the diplomat who received it found it so incredible that he did not forward it to Oslo. But the German shipping activity which preceded the operation was clue enough for British consuls and other agents. 'We had all the movements of shipping as they occurred. But they [in London] did not know what to make of them,' a British intelligence official is quoted as saying.[6]

By the afternoon of 8 April the interrogation of survivors, mostly soldiers in battledress, from the *Rio de Janeiro*, torpedoed the previous day by HMS *Trident*, left the Norwegian government in no doubt that they were facing invasion. However, there was still doubt as to whether the Germans were going to try to occupy the whole country, or simply Narvik. Canaris may have wanted to help the allies, but the Abwehr nevertheless put up a very professional job of confusing the enemy. The Norwegian fleet was totally unprepared and Chamberlain would defend himself in the House of Commons by referring to the 'bewildering diversity' of reports.

Much of the credit for the success of the Norwegian campaign would shine on Canaris, even though the German navy would suffer severe losses when the Royal Navy sank no fewer than ten destroyers, carrying many of General Dietl's mountain troops. Despite this, and the loss of the *Blücher* in the Bay of Oslo, the campaign was brought to a successful conclusion, not least on account of the brilliance with which Dietl fought a dazzling defensive campaign with his outnumbered troops when the Norwegians counter-attacked. A critical role had been played by the Abwehr in the preparations for the German invasion of Oslo. An Abwehr officer by the name of Pruck had arrived on 30 January, charged with preparing nothing less than a forward military intelligence station in Oslo, giving comprehensive details of the disposition of the Norwegian forces several months before the attack. Pruck's office was so speedily effective that on the basis of all the intelligence he sent, a detailed invasion plan could be drawn up within weeks by the staff. This infiltration of forward intelligence centres behind potential enemy lines, ahead of an imminent conflict, was to become an Abwehr speciality. Now a standard procedure in advance of hostilities, though often as recent events in the Middle East show, varyingly successful, it was then an innovative and highly effective form of assisting an imminent attack.

Pruck's outfit was hugely helpful to the airborne troops who finally took Oslo. A few weeks later, Pruck's wife tried to bring to the attention of the SD her suspicions that the Abwehr was plotting against Hitler. Canaris, in a rare recorded act of ruthless expediency, arranged through Himmler to have her consigned to a mental institution.[7]

Canaris, already gazetted for advancement on account of Pruck's preparatory work, was promoted to the rank of full admiral. Norway had vividly shown the limits of British intelligence and the skill of its opponents. Once again, the Abwehr had proved its worth.*As the campaign for Norway wound down, Canaris was visited by some officials of the German foreign ministry keen to acquire from Canaris' agents and officers, in advance of the planned invasion of France, 'Case Yellow', evidence that Holland and Belgium had been abusing their neutrality status. They were compiling a document that would be officially printed as a diplomatic 'white book' and would provide justification for the forthcoming invasion to any sceptics at home or abroad. Such a book would list the 'sins' of the Dutch and Belgians and provide a justification for the war in the guise of an official document detailing the intelligence assessment of the threat posed to Germany by these 'violations' of neutrality.

*Ironically, while not denting Hitler's prestige as Oster had hoped, Narvik was the final nail in the coffin of Chamberlain's career and paved the way for Churchill to assume the premiership. In that aspect, at least, Narvik achieved all that the enemies of Hitler could have hoped.

Despite the fact that Canaris had many friends in the foreign ministry, and despite the fact that Germany was a totalitarian state, it is surely to the admiral's credit that he refused to have anything to do with this project and instructed his section chiefs to withhold information which he feared might be manipulated and misrepresented or exaggerated.*

Canaris was not immune to pressure or impervious to threat but he was adamant that as head of the Abwehr he owed a duty to an authority higher than political expedience. He refused to help the officials ginger up the document they were preparing and the disappointed diplomats had to leave unsatisfied.

Several months before Norway, Canaris had opened new lines of contact with London in the hope of being able to head off the coming conflict. He was not prepared to compromise at a time when there were still a few unbroken reeds of hope that the coming invasion of Holland, France and Belgium could be avoided and that untold bloodshed could be saved and peace brought back to Europe.

In these hopes he had a willing ally in the form of the Vatican. Canaris had already, towards the end of 1939, initiated new contacts with Pius XII, who was personally known to him from his days as Nuncio in Berlin. Traditionally, the Pope, in Europe, as a temporal leader with a powerful, spiritual component enjoyed for centuries the role of adjudicator in disputes between states, and was their hierarchical superior. The treaties of Tordesilla and Saragossa, which divided the world between Spain and Portugal, were a late exercise of this role. Even today, a legacy of this can be seen in the protocol whereby in many countries the papal Nuncio is still given precedence over the diplomatic representatives of other countries.[8]

Was the Pope prepared to mediate between opposition circles in Germany and London to avoid the war spreading? The Pope never hesitated, though he found the role of secret mediator intensely to his dislike, and,

*The comparison with more contemporary events (2003–4) in the UK is of course vivid and underlines Nicolai's oft-quoted maxim, which implies the need for the highest standards of integrity in the second oldest profession.

while he refused to meet Abwehr agents, he read their proposals and passed them onto the British minister at the Holy See, Sir Francis d'Arcy Osborne. He was acutely aware of the dangers to the Vatican, Catholics in Germany and Austria and above all to the German Jesuits if any inkling of his mediation was revealed to Nazi circles in Berlin.

An Abwehr agent by the name of Mueller sought, through Pius XII's German advisor Cardinal Kaas, to use the good offices of the Vatican to mediate.[9] Detailed proposals were drafted. Again, Beck and the generals were involved and again Britain was offered a chance to do a deal with a conservative Germany, minus Hitler, committed to restoring Poland's and Czechoslovakia's (though not Austria's) territorial integrity.

Canaris was sceptical, however, that these talks would yield very much. He probably knew from his sources in London that these negotiations were being withheld from a number of key figures in Britain. Apart from the King, the foreign secretary and the prime minister, at that time still Chamberlain, very few people knew of these discussions. Neither Churchill nor Vansittart were shown the papers, though Cadogan, Orme Sargent and Strang, the top professionals at the Foreign Office did see them, together with their immediate juniors, Kirkpatrick, Makins and Frank Roberts. These latter three worked vigorously and consistently against German peace-feelers. Makins was long suspected of having strong sympathies with Moscow, Roberts famously put down the phone on a compromise-seeking Goering on the eve of war being declared, and Kirkpatrick was described by one German who defected to London as being 'an adherent of the Morgenthau Plan* or some other scheme for the eternal humiliation of Germany.'

Even without these elements there were plenty of forces keen to sabotage such moves. Moscow appears to have been kept abreast of the developments, as were the SD, who had an agent who, melancholy to

---

* The Morgenthau Plan was conceived in 1944 by the Secretary to the Treasury in Roosevelt's wartime administration, Henry Morgenthau, and proposed the complete post-war removal of Germany's industrial capacity. He had also advocated the sterilisation of all German males under the age of forty.

relate, was a Benedictine monk. His presence was skilfully leaked to the British by someone in the SD to cramp Osborne's style, which began to suffer the interference of paranoid telegrams from London telling him to watch out for German seminarists. Osborne scornfully replied: 'The German seminarists are dressed from head to foot in the brightest possible scarlet which does not conduce to the work of secret agents.'[10] But the report was true and it made London, still reeling from the unpleasant taste of the Venlo incident, suspicious.

In addition, the Vatican ciphers had been broken by German signals intelligence. Though Pius XII was careful to leave no paper trail, his meetings with d'Arcy Osborne did not go unnoticed (least of all by the French, who were ever wary of some deal being hatched at their expense by *Albion Perfide*).

With the benefit of hindsight, these moves stood less chance than those taken in September 1938 to avert the bloodbath that was coming. Once hostilities had commenced, the factor of the West taking military advantage of a putsch in Germany severely dampened the generals' enthusiasm for action. But the men who tried to broker peace cannot be faulted. As Owen Chadwick has written, 'The British lost a chance. In a dictatorship like Hitler's they could hardly expect that conspirators should come out of their anonymity and give their ranks and dates of birth ... To get rid of obsessive anti-Semites from a government and to restore Poland to independence would have averted the Final Solution.'[11]

However, if these talks faltered, the Abwehr was able to do the West one last good turn. With Beck, Oster and Canaris agreed to send Mueller to Rome to warn the West of the imminent attack planned for 10 May. Mueller did not stay long in Rome, but he met a senior Belgian diplomat and gave him the date. Before leaving Italy and returning to Berlin, Mueller took the precaution of asking the Italian frontier official to insert an omitted entry stamp in his passport. The Italian complied, giving the date as 1 May, and point of entry Venice.

This was, in retrospect, a wise precaution. When Mueller visited Canaris the admiral handed him a telegram that Hitler was 'foaming' over. It read:

'From HE The Belgian Minister The Holy See

To Foreign Ministry Brussels

May 1st 1940

An officer of the German General Staff visiting Rome today reports that invasion of Belgium and Holland may be expected with certainty on or soon after May 10th.'

Mueller realised that the Belgian diplomatic code had been broken and that he was staring more or less at his death warrant. Fortunately for Mueller, the stamp in his passport, combined with the conscious disguise of his rank, spared him interrogation at the hands of the SD, though as he later recalled he had experienced in those moments the whiff of the firing squad. Unfortunately for Canaris, however, one of his own officers – Rohleder, a Pomeranian of remarkable thoroughness in his investigations of the betrayal – soon found that all the evidence pointed to Mueller.[12] Only with the greatest difficulty could Canaris ensure the investigation led to no dramatic consequences. Oster, however, was ordered to break off all contact with the Vatican and Mueller.

Irrespective of the warning, the Wehrmacht cut through the Western defences with sensational ease. The invasion of the West, thanks partly to General Manstein's brilliant imagination, was a dazzling success. The French army, which had fought so gallantly in the First World War, was vanquished in weeks. 'C'est la dislocation,' a demoralised Weygand told a dumbstruck Churchill, who had never imagined the army he had seen fight so gallantly at Verdun would simply melt away.

The Brandenburg units of the Abwehr were everywhere in the vanguard of the attack, seizing vital points ahead of Guderian's panzers. Canaris, on the one hand staggered at the disintegration of the French and British armies, on the other hand intoxicated at the clink of champagne glasses everywhere on the Tirpitzufer, could not but be infected with a sense of pride that his organisation had contributed brilliantly to the operation at every level. At the same time, German army officers exulting in their easy victories had some difficulty in getting Canaris to join in wholeheartedly with the celebrations. But beneath such superficial sentiments, there rested the vexing question of whether Britain would continue the struggle and how London could hope to withstand the forces of the most success-ful army the twentieth century had ever known.

As a naval officer Canaris was, of course, by the standards of his time an educated man. He therefore knew that the key to Britain's future lay not only in events taking place along the northern coast of France but also in the one area that Hitler consistently underestimated: the Mediterranean. In both theatres he would play a role, but as the remnants of the British Expeditionary Force made their way to Dunkirk, it was the English Channel rather than the Mediterranean which appeared to be the most pressing challenge. The Battle for France was ending and the Battle of Britain was about to begin.

In the strange spring days of May, the British government came close to throwing in the towel. Several members of the cabinet were for peace negotiations. One of them, Rab Butler, was so defeatist that memory of his pessimism in those days would blight his career and chances of leading the Conservative party decades later.[13] Through the British embassy in Madrid and again through the Vatican the peace-feelers came and went. The Vatican wanted Britain to seek peace terms. They could see the danger of Germany invading Britain and winning, and into that horrible specula-tion came the awareness of a similar fate awaiting them. Above all, they feared the end of European civilisation if Britain fought and lost. Churchill's response to all this, however, was characteristic: he ordered Admiral Somerville to destroy the French fleet. Whatever the cost in life, in this case nearly 1,200 French sailors, however shocking to the Royal Navy to have to train its guns on its former comrades in arms, however damaging for the future relationship between the Royal and French navies, no action could signal to the world more vividly that Britain meant to continue the struggle, whatever the consequences. In Rome, the Cardinals examined the despatches of their nuncios and resigned themselves to a long war.

Two weeks before Churchill took the fateful decision to sink the French fleet at Oran, a strange link had been established with the Abwehr that would give the beleaguered British leader some grounds for optimism. He would later write that: 'Our excellent intelligence confirmed that Operation Sealion had been definitely ordered by Hitler.'[14] But he also noted that, 'already in June, I had some inkling' of the German navy plan. Given that the outline plan only went forward to Keitel for detailed planning on 2 July, this was remarkable. There had, of course, been an invasion paper prepared by Admiral Raeder in November 1939, but this was long before Hitler expressed an interest in such planning. Churchill knew that the plan envisaged an attack along a front which he described as 'altogether different from or additional to the east coast on which the Chiefs of Staff, the Admiralty and I in full agreement still laid the major emphasis.' [15]

As has been noted before,[16] this intelligence could not have come from air reconnaissance or ground observers. Nor was it possible at that stage for it to have come from Ultra decrypts. It was only on 22 May that Ultra began breaking any significant codes and its 'golden eggs' were confined for several weeks to the Luftwaffe operational key, useful perhaps for picking up intended Luftwaffe targets such as Coventry or London, but unable to cast much light on strategic decisions.[17] Churchill's 'inkling' could only have come from someone in close contact with the German naval staff or the chiefs of the High Command. Barely a dozen senior officers in Germany knew what Churchill knew. Of these, Canaris was one. Operation Sealion, when circulated among these few officers, offered the strategy of 'a surprise crossing on a broad front extending approximately from Ramsgate to a point west of the Isle of Wight.' As Ian Colvin noted: 'The hand of Mr Churchill seems to have been guided at this time by somebody to whom the innermost counsels of Hitler were revealed.' [18]

By acting in this way Canaris appears to have stepped further along the route of treason. Communication to an enemy of details of the invasion plan might cost the lives of many German sailors. But Canaris appears to have been motivated by the belief that armed with such information the British would take the necessary steps and Operation Sealion would be stillborn.

It would seem that not only the details of the German invasion plan were being given to Churchill. With this intelligence came a strange ray of hope, illuminating the dark landscape of defeat and despair. The source of this intelligence might offer more insights and by extension more support for Churchill to overrule his cabinet colleagues bent on a compromise peace. As Churchill's speeches resounded with all their oratorical splendour across the ether, Canaris took home copies of the Abwehr monitorings of the forbidden texts and read them to his wife.[19] According to Erika Canaris, the Admiral remarked after reading out one of the speeches: 'The English are lucky to have a statesman to lead them.' Canaris saw in Churchill's messages something he and Beck and the other opponents had long sought in England: backbone and resistance.

Richard Protze later recalled: 'Canaris admired Churchill. He had the same initials and would refer to him as the great 'W. C.' When some big stroke of British statesmanship turned the screw a little harder on Germany, he would say, " What can I do against the great W. C.? I am only the little W. C."' [20]

After the war, when Michael Soltikow asked Churchill how it was possible that he had been so well-informed about Sealion, Churchill merely pointed to Colvin's book on Canaris.[21] How the intelligence reached Churchill remains a subject for speculation. Some evidence points to Mueller being sent to Rome and passing it through the Vatican.[22] Other evidence suggests Spain; however, the fragments of evidence are not conclusive.

The useful details of the operation that were reaching London were not the only ways in which the Abwehr assisted Churchill. Canaris was helping Churchill on several other fronts with regard to Sealion. He was acutely aware that Hitler was himself riddled with reservations about the plan, not least as he knew the business of a contested occupation of Britain would make a compromise agreement leading to an alliance far more difficult. Why, in any event, stage an invasion if a pro-German fifth column might seize power in London, the seed of an idea which Churchill himself may have allowed to be conveyed to German circles to delay the invasion? Certainly, Canaris' advice to the High Command seems to have supported those arguing for caution on 'Sealion'.

Canaris, having played a role in leaking the details of the plan to London, now seems to have enjoyed relaying reports of British preparations which he said indicated that a strong defence could be expected. Canaris' reports from England were consistently supportive of the idea of a well-planned British defence in depth. As the German navy and army wrangled over the pros and cons of a landing on a narrow or broad front, the invasion was repeatedly postponed. With each postponement came a report from Canaris estimating British strength in the region of thirty-nine divisions, though in fact there were no more than sixteen to defend the invasion area.

One Abwehr report, dated 5 September, has an especially picturesque flavour:

'The area Tunbridge Wells to Beachy Head (especially the small town of Rye, where there are large sandhills) and also St. Leonard's is distinguished by a special labyrinth of defences. These defences, however, are so well camouflaged that a superficial observer on the sandhills, bathing spots and fields would not discover anything extraordinary.' [23]

The report went on to give a martial picture of St Leonard's and its nearby golf courses bristling with armoured cars, a landscape which the good burghers of Sussex, even in those days, would have found very difficult to reconcile with reality.

As the Luftwaffe failed to destroy the RAF, reinforced by Polish and Czech pilots, the long-wished-for prerequisite of air superiority demanded in Keitel's and Raeder's directives of 2 July failed to materialise. Canaris' reports reinforced the mood that the invasion of the British Isles would be an expensive undertaking. Subsequently, the Abwehr's failure to report the chronic weakness of British forces in southern England would be noted and analysed in London. Sir Stewart Menzies, who remembered Canaris from joint days in Spain in the First World War, began to study his opposite number more carefully. So assiduously did he begin to examine Canaris that one of his subordinates observed: 'He really understood the character of Canaris better than he understood himself.' [24]

Menzies had heard from his counterpart in Spain that the admiral was sceptical of Germany invading Britain. [25] Menzies was also analysing the messages passed via Madame Szymanska in Switzerland with intense scrutiny.

The events of the next few months would deepen this interest, not least as it would focus on the country both men knew well, Spain. As has been noted earlier, Canaris knew that the key to Britain's imperial power was the Mediterranean. And the key to the Mediterranean was Gibraltar. If the Germans could occupy Gibraltar, the entire position of the British forces in the Mediterranean would become untenable. Rommel's later campaigns might well have prospered if the Strait of Gibraltar had been closed by German siege guns. All this was transparently clear to any naval officer of any country's service.

Plans for a German entry into Spain, with an ensuing attack on Gibraltar, existed and had even been worked out in some detail. It only remained to procure the support of the Spanish. When, on 23 October, Hitler met Franco at the border railway station of Hendaye, the German conqueror imagined there would be little obstacle to his plans from the man he had helped build into a political force. Franco, after all, would never have held Spain against the Soviet-backed Republicans without German arms and men. He owed Hitler almost everything.

Contrary to many later reports, [26] Franco was actually the first to arrive at Hendaye. The German diplomat, Stille, was detailed by his ambassador, Canaris' old friend von Stohrer, to accompany Franco on the train and he noted that it arrived 'a minute early'. [27] But if Franco was determined to show no discourtesy to Hitler by being unpunctual, he was not particularly accommodating in any other way.

He was well prepared for the encounter. He knew what Hitler would want and had formulated careful arguments to counter him. He knew that Hitler would try to overawe him with a sense of Germany's military superiority, in particular her plans for the invasion and occupation of Britain. Again, Franco was forewarned and forearmed. Canaris had told Serrano Suñer, Franco's foreign minister and brother-in-law what to expect in some detail. More than that, he had briefed Suñer with several pieces of information which would give Franco the edge once the conversation turned, as it inevitably would, to the concrete plans for taking Gibraltar. First Canaris warned Suñer against any operation in alliance with Germany, against Britain. When Suñer asked Canaris about the imminent invasion of England, Canaris briskly replied, 'Tell Franco that no German soldier will ever set foot in England.' [28]

Canaris and General von Rintelen had both been heavily involved in drawing up the siege plans for Gibraltar. They both knew the type of siege artillery that would be required and they also knew whether it was available at that time in the German Reich. According to depositions in the Institute of Contemporary History in Munich,[29] Canaris then briefed the Spanish chief of staff, General Martinez Campos, to advise Franco to ask for a particular type of heavy artillery to be deployed in the siege of Gibraltar, knowing full well that there were no weapons of this calibre available in

Germany owing to a sudden interruption in production. The admiral insisted that Franco must describe, in detail, the impoverished state of Spain after the terrible ravages of the previous years of conflict.

Franco was in any event unwilling to be compliant. His sense of dignity and sovereignty was being almost daily offended by the activities of the SD in Spain. Setting to work with their usual zeal, they were spreading rumours that plans for a partition of Spain were being drawn up in Berlin, a speculation bound to draw Spaniards together and strengthen Franco. [30]

Moreover, to add insult, the SD set up its own station in the Spanish post office centre, issuing Nazi censor stamps so that the correspondence of Allied embassies not travelling by diplomatic bag would be franked with the censor's stamp, complete with swastika. This was a huge irritant to the Spanish leadership, to whose attention this unhappy and impertinent intrusion was almost daily pointed out by neutral and Allied ambassadors – a chorus of complaint which culminated in some heated exchanges when Franco discovered that even some of his own mail was being franked in this way.

The SD then completed its near total demolition of amicable German–Spanish relations by importing 220 agents and attempting to assassinate one of Franco's more pro-Allied generals by a clumsily staged air crash. This was followed by an equally crude attempt to blow up General Varega. All this was accompanied by relentless pressure on the political front. Himmler even obliged Franco to remove his old comrade-in-arms Beigbeder, a former military attaché in Berlin and old friend of Canaris. This the *Caudillo* deeply resented.

The official accounts of the Hendaye conference remain sparse on details of the conversations. Serrano Suñer, who replaced Beigbeder as foreign minister, was forbidden by Franco from referring to them in his memoirs, while the official German documents later published in the US in 1946 break off with the laconic observation that 'the record of this conversation is incomplete.'

Paul Schmidt, Hitler's genial and brilliant interpreter, gives perhaps the most lucid account of the talks, which he rightly describes as a 'fiasco'. They show that in every detail, Franco followed Canaris' briefing. When Hitler came to the subject of Gibraltar and made Franco the offer of an alliance with Germany which would deliver the Rock to Spain 'once and for all', his 'trump card' in Schmidt's words, Franco said nothing. As Schmidt later wrote, 'I really could not tell from his face whether he found the idea a complete surprise or whether he was just considering his reply.' [31]

Franco then gave a long lecture on the food and agricultural difficulties Spain found herself in after the years of civil war. When Hitler promised food supplies, Franco countered knowingly, with a wary smile, that he did not feel Germany was in a position to make such generous promises. Then Franco delivered the demand for at least a dozen of the heavy calibre howitzers. Hitler was dimly aware that there was a shortage of these and was taken aback by the suggestion. When Hitler suggested bomber aircraft instead, Franco went into a long monologue on the need for artillery to defend his coast against counter-attack. When Hitler questioned the English ability to launch such attacks, Franco went into another long lecture on American support for the British and how he had reliable intelligence that the Royal Navy would even be prepared, *in extremis*, to operate out of Canada. All this information came to Franco via Canaris, who had briefed General Martinez Campos on these issues.

As one close to these talks noted: 'Canaris put nothing down on paper: no telegrams, no notes. He simply briefed Martinez Campos who passed everything onto Franco.' [32] Canaris also suggested to Campos that he keep the roads of Spain in poor repair as they were a barometer of Spanish war readiness for the SD agents in Spain.

Canaris repeated the same message to Vigon, Franco's intelligence chief. If Franco held firm on artillery and grain deliveries for Spain he would call Hitler's bluff.

Above all, Canaris repeated again to Vigon, he should assure the

Caudillo that 'not a single German soldier will ever set foot in England'. Unsurprisingly, as one German noted, 'Franco's position at Hendaye was totally influenced by Canaris.' [33]*

When Hitler talked of a date in January for both the German and Spanish armies to take Gibraltar, Franco went into another detailed and historical discourse on the exclusive right of Spain to reclaim Gibraltar and avenge the hundreds of years of humiliation.

As Schmidt noticed, the more serene, soft and gentle (though persistent) Franco's voice became, the more emotional and impatient Hitler's arguments waxed. Eventually, Hitler withdrew, uttering the much quoted remark that it was like having teeth pulled. He left the negotiation to be continued by Ribbentrop and Suñer. But Ribbentrop, acting under the pressure of his master for an agreement, behaved less like a diplomat and more like a schoolmaster dissatisfied with his pupil's work: 'We need an agreement on paper as a joint statement by eight o'clock tomorrow morning. Do you understand? Eight o'clock!,' he shouted at Suñer, as if giving him a detention, adding importantly 'I have to be in France with Pétain tomorrow.' [34]

Suñer, like all Spaniards of his class, knew perfectly well how to deal with such types. The following morning when the sun rose, it rose without Serrano Suñer. The pupil, with or without his homework, chose not to appear. Instead, he sent his under state secretary, the ever genial Espinosa de los Monteros, whose character had been enriched by a somewhat epicurean upbringing in Vienna, whose broad and friendly dialect he spoke perfectly without a trace of Spanish accent.

Ribbentrop stared in disbelief as the friendly Spaniard apologised in his *gemütlich*, flowing, Viennese German for the delay and equally genially, as if discussing something of little more importance than a choice of menu for lunch at Sachers, promised to get the document to Germany as

---

*Not all Franco's generals were pro the allied cause. One of them, General Munoz Grande, told the SD in Berlin that Canaris was responsible for keeping Franco out of the war.

soon as the *Caudillo* had come to a decision on it.[35] The combination of this old Austrian charm and slow Spanish etiquette, both impervious, indeed indifferent, to Ribbentrop's mood was too much even for the German foreign minister's temper. Echoing Hitler's remarks about 'Jesuit swine', he turned and slammed the door of his train.

Suñer would be summoned a month later to Berchtesgaden for more pressure to be applied by the Reichminister, but once again Spanish tenacity would see the Germans off, this time with claims that though Spain agreed in principle, Spain's preparations would take time. Franco knew from December, courtesy of Canaris, that if he spun the delay out to March he would be saved by simple dint of the Führer's eyes looking east: there would be no weapons available to take Gibraltar once Barbarossa reached the final planning stage.

Tempting though it might be to ascribe these remarkable exchanges entirely to Canaris, these curious events at the foot of the Pyrenees, rightly described as one of the major turning points of the war, were also invested with other factors. Canaris may well have known that Churchill, deploying a tactic long used in such circumstances, had ordered ten million dollars to be deposited in an account of the Swiss Bank Corporation in New York to the benefit of Franco and a number of his generals to 'persuade them of the sweets of neutrality.'[36]

To administer the transfer of this munificence, Churchill had entrusted the colourful Commander Alan Hillgarth with this most sensitive of tasks. A former naval officer, wounded at the Dardanelles, Hillgarth had been appointed vice-consul in Majorca in 1933, where on the eve of Franco's rebellion, Churchill had met him. It seems more than likely that Churchill may have met Hillgarth's best contact on the island, Juan March, though no evidence to support this has yet come to light. March of course knew Canaris of old, and Hillgarth would also have had reason through March to know of Canaris. Once again, the name long forgotten from the First World War telegrams concerning the elusive *Dresden* would reappear in

Churchill's mind, as he discussed in Majorca the formidable activities of the German naval intelligence in the area, past and present.

In any event, Hillgarth used March as a crucial intermediary with the Spanish generals, despite Treasury and other strongly voiced objections. Churchill wrote to Admiral Godfrey 'The fact that ... he made money by devious means in no way affects his value to us at present.' [37] Moreover, Hillgarth would become Churchill's most trusted intelligence adviser, to the chagrin of his other advisers, such as Cadogan, who regarded Hillgarth with great suspicion. 'I am finding Hillgarth a great prop,' Churchill would tell Hoare after a barrage of complaints about the former naval officer. [38]

Such bribes are not an unknown practice, even in peacetime, when the senior politicians of smaller countries often need to be suborned in the interests of their larger neighbours. Those who pretend otherwise have an unrealistic grip on the vagaries of human nature and are therefore unsuitable for a career at the more exalted levels of public service. In war, the practice was inevitably stepped up on both sides and the Abwehr, with its huge budget, was certainly not averse to such moves and would, of course, have anticipated similar steps being taken by its opponents.

Yet here in Spain one senses a cooperation between two sides. London had noticed that the Abwehr withheld much useful information from the OKW. Any talk among senior intelligence officers that Canaris might be an ally of the British was stamped on. A convenient rumour was started to blame the strange assessments of British defences on the 'Abwehr losing its touch'. Yet there is plenty of evidence to suggest that important circles began to take a much more profound view of these developments and see the possibilities such cooperation opened up.

At one level, it would be reflected by the activities of Don Daniel de Araos, Baron de Sacrelirio, a shipping magnate and a retired officer of the Spanish fleet. The baron's wife was well known in Spain for her Anglophile sentiments, but both were also personal friends of Canaris. It was noticed that the baron's shipping interests flourished with British support, even though he was well known as a friend of the admiral.

But this was an exchange of information via a third party at a relatively junior level. Above these encounters there seemed to hover a higher community of interest. Churchill's personal interest in Spain, and his use of Hillgarth, who after the war would remain one of his most trusted advisers, point to events on the Iberian peninsula being seen as absolutely critical.

It was noticed in many capitals. Above all, it was perceived with misgiving in Moscow, where the events on the Iberian peninsula were being reported by a man well aware of Canaris' influence. Kim Philby, soon to be an officer in the SIS, was keeping Moscow abreast of developments in Spain in the guise of a *Times* correspondent. It was not a coincidence that the brightest of Moscow's English recruits was focussed on events in the western Mediterranean.

Between them, Churchill and Canaris had played their respective parts in preserving Spain from the ravages of war in the years to come. Both men had sought the same aim, Spanish neutrality. Both men had used whatever weapons they had in their armament to work for the same end. Might there be other shared objectives?

With the western Mediterranean no longer a possible destination for the Wehrmacht, and with the British Isles 'robustly fortified and defended,' the dynamic of war would now turn Hitler unavoidably in other directions. The fire that had spared Spain was still a force of terrible danger, and the spy chiefs of every country watched closely for some clue as to its direction. Blocked to the west and the north it appeared, now more than ever, to be turning towards the vast imponderable expanses of the Soviet Union.

CHAPTER TEN

TOTAL WAR

War has a way of leading to unexpected consequences.
JULIAN AMERY [1]

While the diplomatic game of cat and mouse was played out at one end of the Mediterranean with Castilian dignity, at the other end of the sea it was mirrored by a more subtle and strange, but increasingly relevant, drama. In the Hagia Sophia, the great mosque of Istanbul, under the vast shields imploring the faithful to remember 'Allah is Great', a young Englishman in blazer and flannels gazed up, Baedeker in hand, at the broad shafts of light cutting across the sombre corners of Stygian Byzantium.

A few tourists wandered around and there were plenty of the faithful sitting cross-legged and lost in prayer. None seemed to notice a slight, wiry figure with high cheek bones catch the Englishman's eye and nod towards a rather disreputable and shabby looking man of thick-set features in a large overcoat. The shabby man looked at the Englishman. For a second their eyes met and across the vast hushed space of blackened Byzantine masonry, a keen observer might have noticed the rather scruffy man turn towards the Englishman and bow. Ever cautious and ever suspicious, Soviet military intelligence, still in late 1940 nominally allied to Germany, was nevertheless establishing, for the first time since hostilities broke out, eye-contact with Britain's secret service.[2]

Julian Amery, the young man in flannels – then a young attaché at the embassy in Istanbul – recalled these tentative steps: 'One day in September a strange thing happened.' Over lunch in Regence,* a Russian restaurant much frequented by diplomats and their agents, a Czech intelligence officer who was in Istanbul organising the sabotage of essential supplies to the Germans through the Balkans, said he had been approached by an official of the Soviet consulate-general.

'The official had asked him for advice about how to organize similar Soviet sabotage operations against the Germans.' The Czech was used as an intermediary by the British and the Soviets, still wary of meeting each other directly, though, thanks to the mosques of Istanbul, the young Amery was able to keep the discreet contact and see its implications for the future direction of the war.[3] In January 1941, at another secret meeting between the Czech and a senior officer of Soviet military intelligence (GRU) it was agreed that a Czech officer would be sent to Moscow, although the candidate for the post, Colonel Pika, was not eventually sent until April.[4]

As these events played out in the former Ottoman capital, there occurred, at more or less the same time, a strange counterpoint in Berlin. It contained a bold theme and its outlines were easily recognisable. On 7 September 1940, the head of the Abwehr's Section III (counter-espionage) received a sealed envelope from Hitler's headquarters marked 'Most Secret'. It read:

> Our Eastern territories will be occupied by stronger military effectives in the next four weeks. At the end of October the dispositions shown on the attached map will have been made. These dispositions must not give Russia the impression that we intend to attack in the East. On the other hand Russia will realise that strong and well-trained German formations in Poland and Bohemia-Moravia indicate that we

---

*Regence still plies its powerful lemon vodka to spies at semi-secluded tables between dark panelling and remains a favourite haunt of diplomats, mostly consuls whose names are engraved on brass plaques at their tables.

are able at any moment and with strong forces, to defend our interests against a Russian attack, especially in the Balkans. [5]

This memorandum, signed by General Jodl, reflected well the anxieties of the German High Command towards the Soviets. There was the fear of an imminent Russian attack on Romanian oil fields, which were vital to the German war effort. In August there had been two movements of German troops to eastern Poland in readiness for contingencies arising from a Russian attack on the oil fields. There was not, however, a formal plan to attack the Soviet Union at this stage, though of course it had been discussed countless times before the war and had been the subject of loan negotiations with London as late as the summer of 1939. Nor was Stalin in the least bit interested in taking on the Wehrmacht simply to relieve pressure on a beleaguered Britain.

But both German and Soviet intelligence officers noted the developments and began taking precautions. Moreover, the geo-political interests of both sides were forcing the dynamic of war in their direction. The Wehrmacht's need for oil and raw materials, German interests in the Ukraine, Russian interests in Finland, all were factors in cooling relations between the two countries. As noted earlier, British aid to Finland's struggle against the Soviet Union had been transported with little interference from the Germans. Moscow's suspicions were intense.

Above all, the Balkans, as Jodl's memorandum explicitly underlined, were part of the map where respective spheres of influence had still not been agreed between Germany and the Soviet Union. This was a factor of huge potential for disrupting German–Soviet relations. Just as in the run-up to the First World War, the Pan-Slav agitation, strongly supported by Britain and France, had provided the sparks to ignite the tinderbox of clashing Austrian and Russian interests, so now the British would play a decisive role in harnessing the Yugoslavs to drive a formidable wedge between Moscow and Berlin.

With the fall of France, German influence in Belgrade rapidly grew. The German legation became the most powerful foreign influence in the capital, dictating key positions in the Yugoslav media and consolidating its already formidable commercial interests. Under its pressure, the Anglophile regent Prince Paul reined in anti-German propaganda and closed down the lodges and other centres of Yugoslav patriotism. Astutely, though, he opened negotiations with Moscow by appointing an ambassador to the Soviets.

As the German legation was all too aware, the former anti-Allied leaflets of the communists in Belgrade had become, with the fall of France, increasingly anti-German. The Germans in Belgrade heard the slogans calling for the first time against 'Fascist infiltration' of key positions.[6] This pattern was repeated in other countries, notably Bulgaria, where the Communist party – again on instruction from Moscow – had dropped its propaganda against British imperialism and was working in parallel with other opposition parties to resist German influence.

As the leader of the Bulgarian Peasant party, Obov, noted, there could be no doubt that Moscow was 'dismayed and alarmed' at the prospect of a German occupation of the Balkans.

Significantly, at their summit in Florence in October, both Ciano and Mussolini had expressed reservations about the Soviet Union's penetration of Europe, and Hitler had reassured both men that he would not tolerate any Soviet incursion in the Balkans which might threaten Italian interests, notably the eastern Adriatic, including Albania and parts of Yugoslavia.[7]

By the time Molotov arrived in Berlin on 10 November, relations between Germany and the Soviet Union, while still publicly cordial, were cooling rapidly. When Ribbentrop asked whether Moscow would like to join the tripartite pact, Molotov made cautious soundings about Finland. Ribbentrop refused to accept Russian annexation in its entirety. Ribbentrop also notified his opposite number that as a result of the difficulties the Italians were facing in Greece and the eastern Mediterranean, Germany would have to occupy Greece. Molotov seemingly accepted this; the Greeks were after all not Slavs, but he then mentioned the difficult issue of the other parts of the Balkans and asked that Germany accept Russia's interests in Bulgaria. Bulgaria, ruled by a monarch, in this case Boris, who was a German, was even more open to German pressure than Belgrade. Ribbentrop made expansive gestures and referred to expanding Moscow's interests in the direction of the Persian Gulf. Molotov's scepticism cut the air with surgical clarity: 'Precision,' he noted, 'was necessary in a delimitation of spheres of influence.' [8]

According to papers in the Munich Institute of Contemporary History, the issue of a joint German–Russian attack on Turkey was mentioned.[9] Molotov, in this context, also demanded Bulgaria's alliance with Moscow. Once again the Balkans were seemingly and unavoidably proving thorny ground.

As Keitel told Canaris the following day, briefing him on the conversations and Molotov's views: 'They want to extend their influence in the Balkans and the Dardanelles. The Führer sees these projects as the beginnings of a grand plan to encircle Germany.' [10]At meetings with Hitler, Molotov's sharp manner and unyielding line on the Balkans began to confirm Keitel's misgivings. 'The fates of Bulgaria and Romania were also of interest to the Soviet Union,' Molotov growled. Once again Yugoslavia was a topic for clarification: 'It would further interest the Soviet Union to learn what the Axis contemplated with regard to Yugoslavia.' The tone of these comments reflected what Moscow's spies in the Balkans had been telling the Kremlin for months, namely that Germany had no desire to allow Moscow to play any significant role in Europe.

The interview with Molotov confirmed Hitler's worst suspicions that Stalin was a blackmailer and that the best way to deal with Moscow and Britain's resistance was, in the words of his Directive Number 21 of 18 December, 'to crush Soviet Russia in a quick campaign.' It is said that at one of these meetings, shortly after Molotov had heard a long lecture on the 'beaten and defeated British', an RAF raid began on Berlin and the diplomats had to adjourn to a bunker. Molotov is said to have dryly remarked to his German hosts, 'Why, if Britain is defeated, are we holding our meeting in an air raid shelter?'

The British were not the only service to make use of Czechs. The Abwehr also made use of a man with Czech connections in Istanbul and the Balkans, Paul Thummel. Thummel, a long-standing friend of Himmler's, later to be the Abwehr chief in Prague, was working for Czech Intelligence and was, like Canaris, committed to preventing where possible a Nazi domination of Europe.

It is highly unlikely that Thummel, whose British intelligence code symbol was A-54, was carrying out his activities without Canaris' knowledge. Far more likely is it that Thummel was being used by Canaris as yet another of his routes into London. Thummel also was in contact with the Soviet consulate in Prague and was therefore a slender but increasingly important link between British and Soviet intelligence.

A list of all the peace-feelers London had received from Germany between the outbreak of war and April 1941 was compiled by the Foreign Office.* They do not, understandably, include several of the clandestine contacts outlined here above.

In any event, Thummel arrived in Canaris' office on 19 December, shortly after the Directive for the invasion of Russia was issued. Thummel found the chief preoccupied but all Canaris said was, 'I am going to Turkey and I will take you with me.' It is not known what Canaris and Thummel were up to in Turkey together but it seems likely that it was in connection with Hitler's Directive[11] and a sudden urgent need to acquaint themselves with the activities of Soviet and British intentions in the Balkans. The German High Command certainly believed that London was pinning its hopes on Moscow entering the war.[12] At the same time, however, on the ground in Istanbul, as Amery testifies, the Russians and British still regarded each other with intense suspicion. Canaris, the sworn enemy of

*See PRO FO 371 26542, C4216/324/18.

Communism, would have seen the greatest peril in any rapprochement between Britain and the Soviet Union. Part of him may have yearned for a German annihilation of the Communist hordes, but the stronger part of him knew all too well what a war on two fronts would mean. Germany's destruction would come sooner, as Canaris was fully aware. What had defeated the military genius of Napoleon could not but succeed against the Wehrmacht led by an Austrian corporal.

For Canaris, the only advantage in a conflict with the Soviet Union would be the possibility it opened to resurrect with London the old policy of a coalition against Communism. But events in the Balkans began to move with unerring swiftness to undermine such a development.

Prince Paul, the Oxford-educated and most Anglophile of European sovereigns, certainly enjoyed the best of relations with the British embassy in Belgrade. He forbade his security service to monitor the embassy's telephones and he personally warned the British ambassador that his traffic was being read by the Italians in Rome, who had broken a number of Foreign Office ciphers.[13] Such extravagant generosity was not to be reciprocated.

As Moscow saw the need to cooperate with elements of the British secret service against Paul, a plot was laid that would appeal to many dissatisfied circles in the Yugoslav military and church. The young Julian Amery had been on holiday on the Dalmatian coast when war broke out. Thanks to his father's influence, he was able to proceed to Belgrade and become an honorary attaché at the British legation.

In the early months of 1940 he immersed himself in the problems of the region and developed close ties with leading figures in the Yugoslav opposition. His mentor, a brilliant Marxist by the name of Jakob Altmeier, sometime correspondent of the *Manchester Guardian* and the *Frankfurter Allgemeine Zeitung*, opened every door he could for him. Amery soon heard from many sources, but especially from members of the patriotic societies, the Orthodox Church and the military, that Britain was wrong to put its faith in Prince Paul. Paul was neither a soldier nor a Serb. He was a white

Russian and an intellectual. Serbia's honour was more valuable than peace or economic prosperity. What value was material prosperity if the country lost its honour?

The official British view, as articulated by the Foreign Office and to a certain extent by SIS, was unmoved by such sentiments. Prince Paul was a friend and a very useful one at that. However, for the newly created SOE, with which young Amery was in touch, such considerations were outweighed by the harsh realities of war.

From Amery's and SOE's point of view there was little to be lost by inveigling the Serbs into rebellion. If Yugoslavia was seen to stand up to Germany, some pressure might be relieved from the preparations to invade Britain. Moreover, as anyone with a sense of history and knowledge of the Balkans would realise, it would inevitably provoke a strong reaction from Berlin which would decisively rupture relations between Russia and Germany. As Amery noted, 'There was just a chance Russia might be drawn into the war. At the very worst it meant that the Germans would have to fight for the Balkans, instead of picking them up for nothing; and war has a way of leading to unexpected consequences.' [14]

Canaris and the Abwehr were not blind to the danger some of these officers in Belgrade posed, but they were heavily reliant on information from Croatia and few Germans possessed the mental elasticity to imagine that Prince Paul, an Oxford graduate and relation of the British royal family, and the most Anglophile monarch in the Balkans, could be undermined by factions within the British secret service. SIS policy under Menzies, who never reconciled himself to SOE, which he regarded as 'crassly amateur', making the life of his agents more rather than less difficult, was not in favour of the coup. Canaris, therefore, would have found little intelligence from his sources in that quarter to warn him of impending events.

It seems more than likely that Canaris was, for once, taken by surprise that a country could commit what would amount to collective suicide rather than submit to increasing pressure from Germany. Von Hassell's diary for 27 March, the day of the coup, notes quizzically: 'The affair is still obscure. A plot with the English?' The question mark suggests that Von Hassell, who had seen Paul only a few days before staunchly defending British morale, simply could not imagine he could be deposed by the British, [15] not least as Paul was in such close touch with London.

The Abwehr diary[16] shows an increasing focus on Yugoslavia from February 1941 and notes on 4 March that key strategic positions were being given increased protection; but otherwise there is no reference to any dissent among the Yugoslav officer corps to Belgrade's compliance with Berlin's demands.

While the young Julian Amery had worked hard to build a coalition of forces to move against the Prince, he had had the full backing of his father, a former *Times* correspondent in the Balkans. Though now stationed in Istanbul, (the British ambassador in Belgrade had correctly divined his motives and banned him from returning), the young Amery continued to encourage from afar the forces of 'progress' in the Yugoslav capital. At the same time he involved his father in the plans for a coup. A number of documents in the Amery archive point to his father's involvement with senior intelligence advisers with regard to the events of 26 March.[17]

On the evening of 26 March, the day after the Yugoslav government had signed the Tripartite Pact, Leo Amery broadcast a strong and impassioned plea to the Yugoslavs to remember that on the field of Kosovo King Lazar had chosen the heavenly crown rather than the earthly one of subjection to Ottoman rule. It was as if a long awaited signal had been given. A *coup d'état* spearheaded by a group of air force and army officers, many with links with Moscow as well as certain sections of the British embassy, deposed Prince Paul within hours. Leo Amery wrote in his diary the following day: 'Various other people like Rab Butler ... good humouredly attributed [the coup] to my broadcast. It is at any rate possible that my appeal may have influenced some waverers ... I imagine Julian's share in originally working up the Opposition movement months ago was really greater ... Home to celebrate Julian's birthday.' [18]

Between them, the two Amerys had helped to throw perhaps the most spectacular political hand grenade of the war into the already charged powder keg of German–Soviet relations. It would almost certainly guarantee an arctic frost descending over the few flickers of well-intentioned activity, notably by the German ambassador in Moscow, von der Schulenburg, trying to avoid a war between Moscow and Berlin. More, while achieving this fundamental purpose it would at the same time, in the event of such aggression taking place, delay it significantly until Yugoslavia was subdued. As Karl Ritter, the German foreign office liaison officer with the OKW, later summed up the consequences of the postponement of Barbarossa by five weeks: 'The delay cost the Germans the winter battle for Moscow and it was there the war was lost.' [19]

The Belgrade coup, however, had a further effect which, perhaps, was only apparent to a few men in England and Germany, but certainly would not have been lost on Canaris. Prince Paul, as von Hassell's diaries make clear, was actively trying to help peace-feelers that were still emanating from certain circles in London,[20] and of which von Hassell himself was apprised.[21] These particular feelers (not listed in the foreign office document quoted above) involved Hitler's deputy Hess, Sir Samuel Hoare, then British ambassador to Spain, and Canaris' old family friend Prince Hohenlohe, and it seems were issued with Hitler's blessing.[22]

Canaris had long used the Lufthansa agent, Otto John, as a go-between with Samuel Hoare[23,] and as the month of March gathered momentum it saw rumours of Hess imminently visiting Spain and Churchill being replaced 'by some appeaser like Hoare'.[24] On 5 March Hoare had met Hohenlohe and the conversation, according to the Italian ambassador, ranged over Hoare becoming Prime Minister instead of Churchill and Rab Butler replacing Eden at the Foreign Office.[25]

'In this connection,' wrote von Hassell in his diary, 'the idea was broached that perhaps a German conflict with Russia might constitute a bridge towards an understanding with the West.' Such thinking would, of course, strike a chord of sympathy with Canaris in touch with the 'terrific anti-bolsheviks' around Menzies in the British Secret Service. But such thinking would also provoke a reaction, especially when it became known.[26] Of course, von Hassell, who was in contact with senior members of the British aristocracy and members of the royal family, was articulating a view commonly held in influential circles in both Germany and England and which had indeed been British policy before the war.[27]

The news of the coup falling out of a clear blue sky was shattering. Though the Tripartite Pact which the Yugoslav government had been pressured into signing on 25 March at the Belvedere Palace in Vienna (built for Prinz Eugen who 'boldly by battery besieged Belgrade') had caused the Abwehr to begin to note some signs of discontent in the Serbian military, even the rough treatment accorded to the returning Yugoslavs in Belgrade, where an angry crowd jeered and spat at them, seemed to have passed more or less unnoticed by the High Command. No one in Berlin was expecting any dramatic developments. After a while the lazy, temperamental Serbs would settle down, for as a Bulgarian diplomat had observed a few weeks earlier: 'I should like to know which country in the Balkans would risk an encounter with the best equipped and best led army in the world.'[28]

Hitler was incensed. On 28 March, barely hours after the coup, he noted that the 'clique' which organized it was 'lunatic in its analysis of the military situation' which was correct in as far as the Yugoslav military equation was concerned.

But those like Amery who had gambled on it being a decisive inter-vention, destined to destroy the ever more plausible chances of a flawed compromise peace, gambled correctly. Hitler's temper and lust for revenge now moved inexorably eastwards.

Less than a month later, as Russia offered support in the form of a pact to Belgrade, Hitler began to register, in a conversation with his ambassador to Moscow, von der Schulenburg, the full significance of what was happening. To this day the heat and passion of Hitler's feelings leap off the page of the rather formal minutes taken by the ambassador:

> Hitler asked me what devil the Russians were riding by agreeing to support Yugoslavia ... I said this was to register Russian interest in the Balkans. It was also an attempt to organize a peace.
>
> Hitler was still not clear who was the organising genius behind the putsch but he believed England rather than Russia was responsible, though the Balkan people felt that Russia was to blame ... I told him there was no shred of evidence to suggest official Russian involvement. [29]

Here the ambassador is drawing a distinction similar to that much analysed point in the diplomatic 'books' following the First World War, as to whether the Serbian secret service through the 'Black Hand' organized the assassination of the Austrian Archduke in 1914 without the knowledge of the Serbian cabinet. Schulenburg is implying a difference between governments and their secret services. As Stalin, toasting the British secret service, remarked to a protesting Churchill after the British prime minister had denied British government involvement in luring Hess to Britain: 'The Russian intelligence service often did not inform the Soviet government of their intentions until their work was completed.' [30]

That Hitler was discussing a month later the possible causes of the coup is evidence of his bewildered anger. It implies moreover the fact that the Abwehr and Canaris were clearly caught napping and that there had been hopes of Prince Paul acting as a bridge between Germany and Britain. Canaris, it appears from these minutes, had come up with either an unwelcome or an incoherent answer.

During the rest of the conversation Hitler dwelt on the Russians' 'unreliability', noting the concentration of Russian divisions building up in the Balkans. Significantly, however, he repeated on two separate occasions his conviction that Russia would not attack Germany, though he noted: 'there are powerful hateful emotions there.'

But Hitler's most acid words are for England and here the sense of betrayal is even more vivid than in his words about Moscow. It is as if he had still been hoping for peace with England along the lines von Hassell was discussing with British circles through Burckhardt of the Red Cross and Prince Paul. It is difficult to dispel the impression that Canaris, a confidant of von Hassell, was not also briefing Hitler about these moves with their potential for that deal with some circles in London which Hitler always appeared to long for. Given the involvement of Hess and Hoare in Spain, it has been persuasively argued by recent research that these peace-feelers had been carefully constructed with the Führer's blessing.[31]

These terms, which it is implied by some authors were actually set down on paper and brought to Britain by Hess in May 1941,[32] are likely to have included the following, to which London, according to von Hassell, was interested in agreeing:*

1. Holland and Belgium to be restored.

2. Poland minus German provinces to be restored.

3. Otherwise no special interest in the east 'not even for Czechoslovakia'.

4. Former German colonies to be restored to Germany.

5. 'The British Empire otherwise to remain unshorn.' [33]

The coup in Belgrade shattered these hopes at a stroke, threatening to derail all peace-feelers and reminding Hitler that he was dealing with some elements in England that were a formidable and ruthless enemy. As von der Schulenburg coolly noted: 'Hitler observed that he was surprised

*Some authors also note that there may have been provisions concerning the fate of European Jewry (see Padfield, *Hess*; Picknett, et al, *Double Standards*).

at England's ability to mislead countries and show that money and hate are more powerful than intelligence and logic.'

Hitler continued: 'Through English promises and lies, first Poland which was offered the best conditions, then France, which never wanted a war, then Holland, Belgium, Norway and now Greece and Yugoslavia were being forced into tragedy.' [34]

But Hitler, apparently basing some of his comments on Ribbentrop's conversations with Filoff, the Bulgarian prime minister, noted confidently that Stalin would never ally himself with London.[35] Filoff had reiterated to Ribbentrop that Stalin 'could not work with Britain or France.'

This was a view shared by certain circles in London. It is significant in the context of Anglo-German dialogue preceding the March coup that Britain was gathering intelligence on the Soviet order of battle with particular intensity at this time. The SIS representative in Helsinki was supplying radio equipment to the Finns to monitor Soviet military signals.

As the Germans began their advanced planning for Barbarossa in early March 1941, British intelligence was acquiring a great deal of information on the Soviet order of battle from Finland, where it was cooperating on sigint with the Finns. Three months earlier the Russian section in Bletchley Park was receiving as many as 800 Russian naval messages and 500 Soviet military and air intercepts a day.[36]

The immediate priority for Canaris was to discharge the Abwehr's duties in preparing for the attack on Yugoslavia, Operation Marita. Once again, Canaris played both tracks, exploiting the Abwehr's formidable Jupiter network in Croatia to prepare for the German invasion while at the same time warning the senior officers of the Yugoslav general staff that Belgrade would be subject to a devastating aerial attack and that it should be evacuated.

According to the pre-war Polish ambassador to Berlin, Lipski,[37] a written warning was given to senior Yugoslav officers, giving the date of the attack as Palm Sunday. This has not survived. In any event, the plea to evacuate the city appears to have been ignored, though on 3 April the Yugoslav government declared Belgrade an 'open city'. Three days later, on 6 April, between 10,000 and 17,000 civilians, depending on varying estimates, were killed or maimed in the attack.*

The dynamic of war was seemingly almost capable of sustaining itself. Canaris, arriving with Pieckenbrock and Lahousen at a ruined Belgrade, felt helpless and sickened by the destruction. The ruins were still smoking and the air was heavy with the smell of burning and putrefaction. To complete the picture of dislocation, the gruesome corpses and bloodied bodies were joined by hundreds of animals, escaped from the city zoo. Canaris saw death at every street corner as they wandered along the fortifications overlooking the great confluence of the Danube and the Save.

He could do nothing to slow down the spiral of destruction. It was obvious that a terrible war was going to be unleashed against Russia. Yugoslavia would be neutralised within a few weeks and then the planning for Barbarossa would resume. The invasion of Russia, projected for April, would be postponed until June, although curiously most of Hitler's generals would observe, after the war, that they were only brought into the picture at the last moment and won over by claims of Russian preparations to attack Germany. These claims bore no relation to reality, as von Rundstedt, the most ardent opponent of the attack, soon realised once his forces totally overran unprepared Soviet positions.[38]

Collapsing at the end of the day in his chair in Zemlin, a suburb of Belgrade along the Danube, Canaris simply said: 'I can stand no more of this. We will leave tomorrow for Spain.' Some writers have seen this as the comment of a weary man, tired of life and eager to find solace in the cobbled streets of Seville or in the great cathedral of Cordoba. But the timing of the visit is significant, for at precisely the same time as Canaris reached Spain, the second week in April, Sir Samuel Hoare, the British ambassador in Madrid and 'arch appeaser', in strict contravention of

---

*For a good account of the bombing see Andreas Graf Razoumousky, *Kampf um Belgrad* (Munich 1982).

Foreign Office instructions, absented himself for a week, travelling to Seville and Gibraltar.

Hoare, the man Harold Nicolson feared might even one day replace Churchill, was at large unchaperoned in a country crawling with German agents, several of whom, such as Otto John, the Lufthansa agent, were links between Hoare and Canaris.

A clearly suspicious Roger Makins minuted: 'It should be set on record that the ambassador went to Gibraltar in spite of categorical instructions that he was not to do so. He did not inform us of his movements, nor has he given any explanation why it was necessary for him to spend a week at Gibraltar.' [39] The governor of Gibraltar at that time, General Mason-Macfarlane, had been military attaché in Berlin before the war and had at least a passing acquaintance with Canaris. (Hoare's discreet movements around Gibraltar at a time when Canaris was in nearby Algeciras would be echoed a year later by Menzies. See Chapter 12.)

There is of course no evidence to suggest that the two men met but it seems likely they were in touch, not least given Hohenlohe's meeting with Hoare a few weeks earlier in which an Anglo-German rapprochement was discussed. Three days later, around the weekend of the 19–20 April, a flurry of reports suggested that Hess himself would be in Spain, ostensibly (though implausibly) to attempt to browbeat Franco into submission.

After Spain would come Switzerland and another encounter with Madame Szymanka, who asked: 'Will Germany attack Turkey?' To which Canaris replied: 'No we won't attack Turkey. Russia perhaps.' Once again Canaris was giving the British advance knowledge of what was imminent, partly, one suspects, in the hope that it would stiffen the 'terrific anti-Bolsheviks' in London. It has been said by Colonel Viktor von Schweinitz that Canaris was able to fly around so freely and without comment largely because 'nobody in the German government had any idea how an intelligence service works.' However, Canaris, it should be remembered, was simply keeping the lines of communication with London open, something Hitler himself required of him, for it was Canaris' connections with London which were the key to his position in the Nazi hierarchy.[40]

Canaris, however, had a further link with his opposite number in London, which would leave London in little doubt as to German intentions.

The arrangements agreed by London with the Finns to monitor Russian intercepts involved the supply of funds and equipment to Helsinki, even though by the middle of January 1941 Menzies knew that there were 1,500 Wehrmacht personnel, including an Abwehr unit, stationed in Finland.

On 6 June, sixteen days before Barbarossa fell on the Russians, Menzies, after some reflection on 'information we have lately received which points to increasing collaboration between the Finnish General Staff and the Germans,' sanctioned the dispatch of more radio intercept equipment to Finland.[41] Menzies must have been confident by this stage that either the Finns would be able to conceal their sigint relationship with London from the Germans or, more likely, that he could trust Canaris not to disrupt it for the simple reason that the Wermacht would also benefit from the SIS equipment. The idea of the entire Soviet order of battle being delivered to the Abwehr thanks to equipment supplied by Menzies is piquant, to say the least.

The chance of a common front with England against Bolshevism was appealing. However, it appears that Canaris was enough of a realist to see that such a move would require a gesture from Churchill, and that was unlikely to happen. When Hess flew to Britain in May, it appears now with Hitler's blessing, Canaris would have seen it for what it was: a gamble which Churchill, at that stage of the war with defeat in North Africa staring him in the face, could not have hazarded, if he was to survive politically.

Canaris' well documented admiration for Churchill would have prevented him seeing much scope for an agreement between the 'great W. C.' and Hitler. Moreover, Canaris would have wanted little to do with any agreement with London which left the Nazi grip on Germany intact. But both Canaris and his foreign ministry colleague Weiszäcker knew that Churchill would be delighted for Germany to turn eastwards, if only because it would relieve the pressure on the British Empire. Moreover, Churchill was confident that Russia posed a formidable obstacle even for the most successful army of the twentieth century.

Like Churchill, Canaris was sceptical that Germany would ever be able to win a war against the Soviet Union. He would have agreed with Weiszäcker who tartly commented : 'Would one burning Russian village help sink a British destroyer?' [42]

'I am convinced that this campaign against Russia which the Führer sees as the answer to all his difficulties will only overburden Germany and destroy the few remaining chances of peace,' Canaris noted in a memorandum to the OKW.[43] Keitel patronisingly replied: 'My dear Canaris, you may know your way about the field of intelligence but you are a sailor. Don't try to give the army lessons in military strategy.' [44]

Barbarossa burst like a thunderbolt on the Soviet Union. Thanks to the Abwehr, Hitler's generals had the entire Soviet order of battle and complete surprise. Churchill's repeated warnings to Stalin were ignored, thanks to well laid deception plans by the Abwehr. Within weeks more than half a million prisoners had been taken and Manstein's tanks had reached the Dneiper.

Thanks to his files on Poland, Canaris was under no illusions as to the fate in store for the Russian population. He had, in any case, been acquainted with Hitler's decree of 31 March providing for the administration of conquered Eastern territories whereby all Communist leaders and Russian political commissars were to be 'physically liquidated'. In the event of no SD units being available, army sections would carry out summary executions. Canaris was fully aware that it was Himmler and Heydrich's policy to involve the army where possible in these criminal acts which were of course in flagrant breach of all civilised norms of war.

Despite protests by Canaris, who noted that executions *en masse* were not only affecting army morale but were also deterring any uprising against the Russians by Ukrainians, or even small Moslem communities, whose menfolk were being wiped out by SS units mistakenly convinced they were Jews on account of their being circumcised,[45] the 'cleansing' operations proceeded.

As Lahousen noted, the arguments 'had no effect whatsoever'. Keitel minuted: 'These objections are the consequence of a chivalrous idea of war. We are concerned here with the destruction of an ideology.'

A few days before Barbarossa was unleashed there occurred a poignant event which underlined to Canaris the unhappy circumstance that the old values of Germany were passing away. On 4 June the old Kaiser died. Despite stringent efforts by the regime to play the death down, many officers attended the solemn if low key funeral. Canaris went, accompanied by Oster. Both men, according to von Hassell, were deeply moved.[46]

CHAPTER ELEVEN

DUEL TO THE DEATH

Have you heard the news? Heydrich has been murdered.
CANARIS TO SPITZY [1]

On 8 September 1941, General Reinicke issued the following instructions for dealing with Soviet combatant personnel:

> The Bolshevik soldier has lost all right to be treated as an honourable adversary in accordance with the Geneva Convention. Orders must be given to react pitilessly and energetically to the least sign of insubordination ... Whoever carries out these orders ... with insufficient energy is liable to punishment. [2]

Canaris felt compelled to protest and with the help of the Abwehr's legal department drew up a memorandum which, while accepting that the Geneva Convention concerning prisoners of war might on account of legal arguments not apply, nevertheless underlined that the 'fundamental provisions of international law demanded it was 'inadmissible to kill or maim prisoners. Every belligerent has moreover the interest of ensuring that his own troops are protected from bad treatment if they are made prisoners-of-war.'

With the onslaught against the Soviet Union, the role of the SS liquidation squads once more became very prominent and with it, the designs on the territory of the Abwehr again became topical. Canaris' 'squeamishness' was noted and the file on the Abwehr's political unreliability that Heydrich was compiling grew thicker.

The Abwehr had, by any objective analysis of its activities, discharged its duties to the highest level of professionalism. Moscow refused to believe Churchill's personal warnings to Stalin that Hitler was planning to attack. The Abwehr's disinformation campaign, focussing on such obvious red herrings as an attack on Spain, had wrong-footed the Soviets and indeed nearly everyone else. As Harold Nicolson had noted in his diary 'everybody' regarded the idea of an attack on Russia as 'fantastic'.[3]

But the Abwehr once again now found itself fighting a war on the home front against Heydrich's organisation. In August 1941, Schellenberg, together with Dr Walther Huppenkothen, the SS lawyer, lunched with Canaris at Horchers. Huppenkothen noted that Canaris was definitely 'not the Prussian officer type'. Canaris, however, had some powerful weapons in his armoury. He knew that Heydrich was, by strict application of the Nuremberg race laws, partly of Jewish origin, an inconvenient fact for someone of Heydrich's towering ambition. Ventilating the details of Heydrich's family tree could at any moment be used by Heydrich's many enemies in and outside the Gestapo to destroy his career.[4] As one of his contemporaries noted: 'Heydrich had a complex about his alleged Jewish origins. He always wanted to be more Nordic than anyone else.'

Some writers on Heydrich dispute the Jewish element in his background, noting that Heydrich's grandfather 'Süss' had married his grandmother after his father, Bruno, had been born.[5] This may not necessarily be conclusive, as Süss may have been Bruno Heydrich's biological father. The argument that Süss was not Jewish but Catholic would not have cut much ice with the grotesque racial theorists who framed the Nuremberg Laws, and it recalls the rhetoric of the anti-Semite Karl Lueger, pre-Great War Mayor of Vienna, who declared: 'I decide who is a Jew in this city.'

Irrespective of all this, as one resident of Halle observed of Heydrich's father, Bruno: 'Most of the inhabitants had not the slightest doubt about his Jewish origins.' [6]

Heydrich had gone to extraordinary lengths to keep rumours of his Jewish origins – true or false – at bay. Between 1935 and 1937 he had three times used lawyers to disprove allegations of Jewish origin. In one of these cases one of the witnesses had disappeared without trace. A family tombstone inscribed 'Sarah Heydrich' also disappeared, to be replaced with one bearing simply the words 'S. Heydrich'. Among the details in the Abwehr's Heydrich file, which Patzig had handed over to Canaris in 1934, were the details of the court cases and the bill from the Leipzig stonemason who had altered the tomb.[7]

As the campaign in the east unfolded, relations between Heydrich and Canaris, though outwardly cordial, began to cool. The more the SS and units of the army and even units of the Abwehr's Brandenburg Division proceeded against Russian prisoners and civilians, the more determined Canaris became to keep the Abwehr's reputation intact. The few operations involving blackmail (usually of Irish operatives, to little effect)[8] were wound down and colleagues noticed that anyone suggesting 'camps' or the rounding up of civilians was likely to be transferred rapidly away from the Abwehr: for example, Langendorf in Paris, who proposed putting Spanish refugees into detention centres.

Nevertheless, despite the sharp contrast between the methods and beliefs of the two men, they continued to socialise. Both men were neighbours in the wooded Schlachtensee suburb of Berlin. Canaris' house, a modest establishment with wooden eaves on the today renamed Waldsängerpfad, was linked by a common garden to the more imposing Heydrich residence with its twin gables in the classic alpine Nazi style. The different houses reflected the two mens' personalities. Where the interior of the Canaris villa was soft wooden panelled walls lined with books, heavy metal doors and iron sculptures in the best totalitarian style adorned the Heydrich villa. The proximity of the two houses gave rise to many encounters after office hours when Heydrich would play the violin accompanied by Canaris' wife on the piano. Canaris himself would cook, often a dish of Spanish inspiration.

However, Heydrich continued to watch Canaris and the Abwehr like a hawk. By the time of the attack on the Soviet Union he was already investigating the Abwehr for treason in connection with the attack on Belgrade. The young Schellenberg, the 'hero' of the Venlo incident, following the German occupation of Belgrade had found a copy of a telegram which the British military attaché had failed to destroy in an abandoned part of the British embassy. It read simply: 'The Luftwaffe will commence attack with overwhelming bombardment of the capital, according to our faithful friend 'Franz-Joseph'. Inform the Yugoslav government.'

The telegram came from London but Schellenberg soon established through other files that the 'Franz Josef' warnings were based on secret operational files deposited in the safe of the Abwehr office in Prague. Repeated Gestapo investigations yielded little that was conclusive, but for Heydrich they were grist to the mill of his complaints that the authorities in Prague were too soft under the Reichsprotektor von Neurath, former foreign minister and a well-known anti-Nazi.

The administration of Bohemia and Moravia was too gentle. The Czechs were seething with resentment and conspiracy against the Germans which they only thinly cloaked with the veil of humorous indifference. However, despite a number of attempts by the SS to unseat von Neurath, Hitler had kept him in place, promising a showdown with the 'damn Czechs' after the war.[9]

It was only with the compilation of lengthy reports listing supposedly large scale resistance movements planning to 'sabotage and destroy harvests' that Hitler began to listen more attentively to Heydrich and Himmler. With the help of the police commander in Prague, Karl Böhme, the SD began to draw up evidence that the security situation in Prague was deteriorating rapidly under von Neurath and that a new viceroy would be needed who, unlike Neurath, would not wish to 'work with and through the Czechs' in running the province. Thanks to Böhme, Heydrich was fully informed of every detail of the situation in Prague and could impress Hitler at a lunch on 21 September with his grasp of the situation. Heydrich demolished Neurath's record and said the integrity of the Reich was threatened. Hitler was incensed by the Czechs, whom he despised with all the vehemence of a provincial Austrian. Without consulting Neurath he appointed Heydrich 'acting protector' and promoted him to SS Obergruppenführer.

As always, the decision was supported by senior figures for their own reasons. For Himmler, the move meant the SS could virtually take control of an entire state within the Reich. For Martin Bormann, Hitler's enigmatic link with Moscow,[10] it shunted Heydrich sideways into the administrative distractions of state bureaucracy.

For Canaris, however, the move was far from unalloyed good news. First, Heydrich was not giving up his position of chief of Reich security. He would remain a dagger pointed at the heart of Abwehr activities. Second, Heydrich's appointment gave him ministerial status and therefore greater access to Hitler. Those who have worked in organisations belonging to one personality will know that access to the owner equates more than any other factor to power. Heydrich was still only thirty-seven. He had come a long way since being cashiered by the German navy.

For his part, Heydrich lost no time in pursuing his twin objectives of building his reputation as the coming man in the Reich by subduing the Czechs, while at the same time using his newly appointed powers to leave nothing unchecked in his ceaseless search for incriminating material on the Abwehr. The Gestapo, whose activities had been circumscribed by the 'old gentleman' Neurath, now sprang into life without the faintest moral constraint. The Czech prime minister, General Alois Elias, was arrested and tortured, thousands of suspects were rounded up and hundreds executed after summary trials. This campaign of massive intimidation was initiated so that in Heydrich's own words, 'We will try using the old methods to Germanise these Czech vermin.' The Jews in particular came to fear the 'Butcher of Prague', and even before the Wannsee Conference had sealed the fate of European Jewry, the Jews in the Czech lands were herded into newly established ghettoes at Theresienstadt before being deported to the death camps. Of the 93,942 Jews deported from the Protectorate, only 3,371 survived the war.[11]

As well as the suppression of any subversive activity on the part of the Czechs, Heydrich also ensured that there were measures in place to turn the screw on the Abwehr. A Gestapo raid on a secret transmitter on 3 October yielded a number of uncoded messages which the unfortunate wireless operator had not had time to destroy before committing suicide. The messages referred this time not to 'Franz Josef' but to 'René'. According to Abendschön, the Gestapo police chief: 'The information attributed to René appeared to me of such particular secrecy that it could only be known to a very few people in Prague, such as Frank, the Protector's adjutant, Geschek, head of the Gestapo and Dr Holm, alias Paul Thummel of the Abwehr.'[12] To Canaris' dismay, Heydrich proceeded to move against Thummel, thus threatening one of the Abwehr's links with SIS.

When Thummel was arrested a cascade of protest descended on the Gestapo from Canaris, Bormann and even Himmler, who had known Thummel for many years. The tension between the Abwehr and the SD was escalating rapidly now. Canaris sensed a new aggression in Heydrich and during his morning rides with Schellenberg, the younger man was at pains to point out to the admiral that only a new agreement between Canaris and Heydrich could defuse the situation.[13]

In November, Canaris travelled to Prague and according to Schellenberg, a very frank conversation was held in which Heydrich used Thummel's arrest to browbeat Canaris about 'treason' in the Abwehr.[14] Heydrich, however, overplayed his hand and the following dialogue, taken down by Schellenberg, shows the admiral was not easily intimidated.

'In proposing negotiations to you admiral,' Heydrich stiffly began, 'I will not conceal from you that after the war the SS will take over everything in the Abwehr's field.'

'After the war, my dear Heydrich?' said Canaris, smiling, adding: 'You know very well that nobody will touch the Abwehr as long as I am alive.'

'Nobody, Herr admiral? Not even the Führer?' answered Heydrich.

Canaris parried the thrust: 'Do not imply what I have not said. The Führer is not concerned in this as you very well know. It is you and I. That is very different and very clear.' [15]

It was agreed that Thummel would be released but kept under close surveillance. But to achieve this, the admiral had had to compromise. He explicitly admitted that the time had come for certain 'questions between the Abwehr and the SD' be examined 'in depth'. A *modus vivendi* would be established which would aim to remove the unfortunate friction of the last few months. Schellenberg noticed that Heydrich went pale during the meeting, sensing that the admiral had somehow outwitted him. Canaris gave away territory very rarely. What, the ever-suspicious Heydrich must have thought, was the reason for this strategic withdrawal?

Thummel, meanwhile, continued his official Abwehr duties, which included monitoring the activities of three Czech officers in the resistance, Colonel Balaban, Colonel Masin and Captain Vaclav Moravec. The first two were quickly found by the Gestapo, the third, Moravec, appeared more elusive and when, after the Gestapo lost patience with him, Thummel was rearrested, continuing to deny treason, he offered to help the Gestapo search for Moravec as a gesture of loyalty.

But Thummel tried to warn Moravec and as the case continued to mount against Thummel, Heydrich used it to blackmail Canaris into more and more concessions.

Was not the Thummel case the greatest act of treason in the history of the Third Reich? Did the Führer need any further proof that the Abwehr was a nest of defeatist traitors? The questions rained down on the Abwehr chief from Heydrich's office, the most sinister being: why did the Abwehr allow Thummel to establish links with British intelligence?

While the investigations of Paul Thummel continued, it was impossible for Menzies not to be aware of what was happening, not just to his network in Prague but also to the Abwehr. Menzies was fully informed about the rivalry between Heydrich's SD and the Abwehr. As Paul Thummel was arrested for the second time, Canaris made a sudden visit to Spain. The SD report on his activities in Spain at that time includes material which shows that the Abwehr chief was under close surveillance by his own side. Frequently, however, they lost him as his own Abwehr officers helped him disappear for a few hours. The SD were able to note, nevertheless, that he had arrived in Madrid with four heavy suitcases and had left without them. Given Canaris' frequent use of Spain as a conduit for information to London, it is difficult to imagine some hints of his predicament not being transmitted.

Through his various channels to British intelligence, Canaris would have been perfectly capable of conveying the pressure he was under. The line of communication through Halina Szymanska[16] still functioned through the German vice consul, Hans Bernd Gisevius. Information about Canaris was being distributed among a close circle of Menzies colleagues. One recalled: 'It was about this time that we definitely registered that the baddies, that is the SD, were gunning for Canaris.' [17]

On 20 March Thummel was arrested for the third time. He had tried to warn Moravec but without success. The following day Moravec, on the basis of Thummel's information, was ambushed by the Gestapo at a planned rendezvous with Thummel and wounded in a gun battle lasting several minutes. Moravec had fired over fifty shots at his assailants before committing suicide. He was found with two automatics and nine empty clips of ammunition. Canaris appears to have intervened with Himmler to save Thummel's life, no doubt stressing Thummel's links with SIS, something which would eventually be of interest to Himmler.[18] Thummel, like Canaris and so many other enigmatic links with London, including Georg Elser, would be executed two weeks before the war ended.

By April 1942, therefore, Canaris knew that his organisation was facing a virtual total takeover by Heydrich. Not only that, Heydrich was making a play for the intelligence functions of the Wehrmacht in France. These demands would neutralise all Canaris' work, not least making the Abwehr's connections with the British intelligence service far more risky as the unfortunate case of Paul Thummel had shown.

In London, the thought of Heydrich taking over the Abwehr's principal functions in Europe, including possibly France and the Balkans, filled Menzies with gloom. He knew better than anyone else what Canaris was dealing with. Had he not studied every aspect of his opponent's psychological make-up? Had he not also been accused by his colleagues of knowing Canaris better than himself? [19]

As Canaris fenced with Heydrich, the relationship between the two became more and more charged. When, after agreeing to all Heydrich's points at one meeting, Canaris then drafted a document that omitted the key concessions, Heydrich flew into a rage, refusing to see the Abwehr chief and keeping Canaris cooling his heels for two hours outside his office. Only after Keitel intervened on Canaris' behalf did Heydrich yield to see him. As one cynic in British intelligence observed at the time: 'It was a bit like a lovers' tiff.' [20]

The series of agreements that emerged, governing relations between the two agencies, was to be known again as the Ten Commandments and was to be finalised at a meeting in Prague on 18 May. This conference was to be the final negotiation preceding what Heydrich hoped would be the surrender of the Abwehr to the authority of the SD.

It began at 10.30 a.m. in the magnificent German hall in the Hradčany castle, not far from the spot where the defenestration of the Holy Roman Emperor's two councillors had marked the beginning of the terrible Thirty

Years War. On the agenda was the 'reorganisation of cooperation between the Abwehr, the Gestapo and the SD.' Present were Canaris, Heydrich, two Gestapo chiefs, Nebe and Mueller, and the increasingly ubiquitous SD intelligence boss Schellenberg. Supporting Canaris were his lieutenants, Bentivegni and Pieckenbrock.

According to Schellenberg, Heydrich came quickly to the point: 'The security of the Reich demands a reorganisation of the secret services on a centralised basis.' The Abwehr had displayed its 'incapacity' and needed to be replaced by new men trained in SS centres who would be responsible to Heydrich. This démarche evinced no reaction from Canaris, who was calm and relaxed throughout the meeting as he conceded point after point, until all the agreement appeared to leave him was the chance of retaining his staff, with whom he could over the following weeks work out the new structures for incorporating the Abwehr into unified service under SD leadership. Meanwhile, over the following weeks, Heydrich would put down on paper a proposal listing the points agreed and send it to Hitler. Heydrich, having seemingly won the contest, was in no hurry to rush things. He had sent a report on the Thummel case to Hitler's HQ on the Eastern Front two days before. In accordance with standard protocol he would obviously wait for the Führer's reply before forwarding the next document with its detailed description of the agreement he had reached with the Abwehr for extending the influence of the SD.

The details of the Prague conference were kept secret, but despite the disruption caused by Thummel's arrest, the news that Canaris would be visiting Prague appears to have been known in circles close to Menzies several weeks before the meeting took place.[21]

Some might attribute Menzies' concern to what one writer has referred to as his ingrained sense of Edwardian chivalry – he was after all rumoured to have been an illegitimate son of Edward VII. It will be recalled that Menzies had sent his warmest regards to Canaris in 1939 via Count Schwerin.[22] More likely, Menzies, a ruthless operator, would have seen the

DUEL TO THE DEATH

possibility of the SD and Heydrich taking over the Abwehr as a negative development for Anglo-German intelligence relations.

Just over a year earlier, in December 1940, Menzies had opened up a new channel of communication with Canaris through the double agent Dusko Popov, a Dalmatian banker with all the charm, sexual energy and vigour which is the hallmark still of a true Ragusan squire. Popov had been recruited by the Abwehr to operate in London.

Menzies invited Popov to his house in the country for the weekend, ensuring a beautiful and vivacious Austrian girl was in the party to keep him happy. Popov recalled in his memoirs: 'Menzies took me into a small study. Deep armchairs, a fireplace where the flames were miraculously steady, book-lined wall ... ' After issuing the usual mild put-down, noting that Popov had 'too many devices' on his 'banner' for his liking, Menzies came to the point: 'We already have a fair amount of information about many officers of the Abwehr, including Canaris, but I want to know much more about everyone who is intimately connected with Canaris.'

By way of explanation Menzies continued: 'It may be helpful if I explain the reasons behind this request. We know that Canaris, Dohnanyi and Oster are not dyed in the wool Nazis. They are what might be termed loyal officers or patriotic Germans. In 1938 Churchill had a conversation with Canaris ... Churchill came to the opinion that Canaris is a sort of catalyst for the anti-Hitler elements in Germany. That's why I want to know more about the people he attracts. Eventually I may want to resume the conversation Churchill initiated.'

It is generally assumed that Menzies was referring to the Kleist visit, though the reference to the conversation Churchill 'initiated' suggests that a separate meeting between Canaris and Churchill cannot entirely be ruled out, perhaps through Hillgarth in Spain.

Menzies, the 'terrific anti-Bolshevik', would for a host of operational reasons no doubt have wanted Canaris to survive. But in the first months of 1942, there seemed very little even the head of the British secret service could do to help keep Canaris 'in play'. If Britain was ever to break with Soviet Russia it would need Canaris and the German opposition as an ally. Menzies' views on this were quoted, unattributably, by Colvin at the beginning of the Cold War: 'The understanding which he (Canaris) sought in Europe against one tyranny may be achieved against another.' [24]

The idea of assassinating Heydrich was first bruited in October 1941 but not by SIS. According to Colonel Frantisek Moravets, the Czech head of military intelligence (and no relation to Captain Vaclav Moravec) who worked closely with SIS, there were patriotic reasons enough to justify such an action but political considerations dominated. The exiled President Benes was barely recognised by London, who it will be recalled from von Hassell's discussions with the British a few months earlier[25] had no interest in reconstituting Czechoslovakia. Foreign Office policy still recognised the territorial 'adjustments' made at Munich, more than two years into the war.

Moravets also noted how the British never ceased to reproach the Czechs with passivity under the German occupation: 'It was alas partly true the Germans had not behaved in Czechoslovakia with the same ferocity and cruelty as in Poland, Greece and in Soviet Russia.' [26] The idea of assassinating Heydrich was the solution to all these doubts. It would inject ginger into the Czech resistance, show the world that the Czechs were prepared to fight and finally perhaps help a beleaguered Benes curry favour with the Olympian mandarins at the Foreign Office. As Moravets later pointed out he could not 'imagine' that reprisals would result in the terrible massacre at Lidice. [27]

Moravets worked very closely with Menzies but the planning and training of the assassination party was handled by SOE in the autumn of 1941. It was their mission, and attempts to claim that it was SIS inspired are partly undermined by the chronology. However, as we shall see, Menzies did play a role in the mission at a critical moment in May, at the height of the Abwehr's troubles with Heydrich in Prague.

The assassination team, codenamed 'Anthropoid', had already been infiltrated into Prague but at a heated meeting between them and local resistance leaders it was agreed that the head of the parachute group, Alfed Bartos, send an urgent plea to Moravets in London imploring him to call off the mission. [28]

Bartos, on reflection, considered the plan to be wilfully blind to local conditions, liable to provoke harsh reprisals in the ensuing *ratissage* and bound to impede the activities of Czech intelligence, on which London placed such high value. Through an agent, a signal was sent to London protesting against the operation:

> This assassination would not be of the least value to the Allies and for our nation it would have unforeseeable consequences. It would threaten not only hostages and political prisoners but also thousands of other lives. The nation would be the subject of unheard-of reprisal ... Therefore we beg you to give the order through SILVER A for the assassination not to take place. Danger in delay. Give the order at once. [29]

The signal went on to say that if for reasons of foreign policy an assassination was necessary, another target should be chosen.

According to one account, by Prokop Drtina, Benes' secretary, Benes ordered Moravets to bow to the opinion of the home resistance whose views 'had to be respected and that no action should be taken without the agreement of the home organisation.' [30] Another account notes that Benes ordered that there be no reply to the signal.

Moravets, however, as well as showing the message to Benes, also showed it to Menzies, 'who said nothing' and while there is no evidence (and indeed given the sensitivities towards assassination even in wartime this is hardly surprising) that Menzies pressured Moravets into disregarding the fears of the home resistance, it is clear that pressure was applied. The mission was not cancelled. In Moravets' words: 'I learned after the war that the British not only did not cancel the operation but continued to insist on it being carried out, though without telling me.' [31]

When André Brissaud asked Moravets why this had happened, he received the curious reply: 'I cannot say. I have been told that Heydrich was on the track of important British agents and that to protect them it was necessary that Heydrich should die'.[32]

The most important British agent in Prague, Paul Thummel, was safely incarcerated in Theresienstadt. Though the reader must make up his own mind, this writer does not subscribe to the belief that Canaris was a British agent. The term 'agent' implies control, and though some British circles may have hoped to convert Canaris from an ally to an agent, Canaris was a difficult candidate to control, though that did not prevent US intelligence, as we shall see, from giving Canaris the code symbol 659, implying a high level of control, or at least intimacy. Nevertheless, the destruction of Heydrich in order to 'protect important British agents' is plausible if the all-important dialogue between Menzies and Canaris was to continue. That dialogue was important not only for the strategic insights it gave London. It was essential if the chance of that Anglo-German 'understanding', which Menzies hinted was the motivation for Canaris' actions, and which Menzies, too, may have hoped for, was ever to take place. Canaris and his Abwehr needed to be preserved. As Menzies' decision to supply new wireless interception equipment to the Finns, knowing there was a certainty they would pass on to Canaris the intercepts of the Soviet order of battle, days before the German invasion, illustrated, the search for an 'understanding' may not have been entirely one-sided.

When, on 27 May, the Czechs pulled off the only assassination of a high-ranking German official of the war by ambushing Heydrich in his Mercedes on the way to his office, (in fact Heydrich was only wounded, but died in hospital of his wounds on 4 June) they struck a blow for the Abwehr as much as they did for Czech freedom.

The fateful attack on Heydrich's car was carried out with a sophisticated bomb and it was only after Heydrich had leapt from the car, firing at his assailants for a few minutes, that he realised that splinters from the bomb had penetrated his stomach and he was rushed to hospital.

There is no evidence that Canaris either wanted or called for Heydrich's death. He may have imagined, perhaps, that he could still salvage something of his Abwehr and that in some way the lines of communication with London could remain open. London, however, was unlikely to take such a sanguine view. Menzies knew Canaris' dilemma and he was, according to those who knew him well at this time, someone who would not shrink from ruthless, decisive action to help his opposite number, as well as, more importantly, further his own service's interests.[33] 'Anthropoid' had not been an SIS mission but it is significant that at the moment of crisis over the future of the mission it was Menzies who Moravets sees on the British side and, if Moravets is to be believed, ensured that the mission was not called off.

For his part, Canaris may well have been surprised at the swiftness with which his prayers may have been answered, but his emotions were clearly mixed. He was certainly genuinely moved at Heydrich's funeral, where several witnesses commented on his tears. But at the same time, Canaris had indeed lost his most powerful opponent. The Ten Commandments were stillborn with Heydrich's death.

He had, however, also lost someone he had undoubtedly once loved as a protégé. His thoughts would no doubt have touched on the strange fate which had brought the two together and on the terrible war which was now devouring its progenitors.

He may also have harboured in that complex mind the thought that he was indeed responsible for Heydrich's death. This would have caused him considerable personal grief even if, from a professional point of view, he could only sense relief.

When the day after Heydrich's death, the young officer and former secretary of Ribbentrop's, Reinhard Spitzy, encountered the admiral and seeing a chance to curry favour with Heydrich's old opponent made some disparaging remark about Heydrich, Canaris gave him the dressing down of his career: 'I bumped,' Spitzy recalled, 'into Canaris, who said, "Have you heard the news about Heydrich? He has been murdered!"

"Good," I replied, "thank God that swine is out of the way." At this Canaris immediately put on his official hat and ordered me to report to his office. He stared at me sadly for a while before saying: "I don't like people using expressions like that. In the first place we are dealing here with a human being, and a dead one at that, and secondly, that is no way to address an admiral."' [34]

Canaris would have wanted to put Spitzy in his place, but the intensity of the response was indicative of the emotions Heydrich's death had unleashed. His greatest protégé, linked to him over so many years, at one stage by the closest of platonic bonds, was dead.

Whether London, in the form of Menzies, felt at the last moment the need to keep the Czechs 'on track' lest Heydrich destroy the Abwehr, will never be proved. The Foreign Office regarded the attack on Heydrich as 'an internal Czech affair' and played down the British involvement.

What can be said with certainty, however, is that the only positive strategic result from Menzies' point of view of the assassination was that the Abwehr and Canaris continued to function for another year and a half with more or less unfettered authority, something that looked highly unlikely after 18 May. This was the only instantly positive consequence. No Czech resistance movement rose up inspired by the acts of the parachutists. Neither the great arms factories of Skoda in Pilsen to the south, nor the granaries of Olomouc to the north, were 'set ablaze'.

The other consequences, the terrible reprisals: the razing to the ground of the village of Lidice where the parachutists took refuge, the virtual destruction of the Czech intelligence networks, are all better known. All 199 men from Lidice were summarily shot. All 184 women of the village were deported to Ravensbruck and all of the village's 88 children were also deported, ostensibly for a 'better upbringing'. Eighty-one of these children would be gassed in the concentration camp of Chelmno.[35]

The long-term unquestionable benefit to Benes and the Czechs was the gradual upgrading of relations with the Foreign Office and the subsequent British government decision to repudiate Munich and agree to support the post-war expulsion of a million and a half Germans from Bohemia and Moravia, but this was hardly a concern at that time of SIS.

As 1943 approached, the question of that 'understanding' which Canaris sought within Europe began to become acute. It would take up the remainder of his energies and lead to more serious peace-feelers between the Allies and Berlin than at any time during the war.

CHAPTER TWELVE

THE SEARCH FOR PEACE

There is a lot of talk about peace in 1940 but it seems
to me that we came even closer to it in 1943.
JULIAN AMERY [1]

A few months before the dramatic and violent events in Prague, a curious encounter had taken place one windy day in London at SIS headquarters.

Broadway Buildings in the autumn of 1941 was a dreary place, despite its relative proximity to St James's Park and Buckingham Palace. The bronze grill of the lift slammed squeakily shut. The small lift operator in a dark suit pressed the button for his two passengers, both men of medium height, one young and bright eyed, the other rather older and smarter but graver of mien. When the latter, acknowledging the former's glance with a brief smile, got out on the fourth floor, the remaining passenger asked the liftman who he was. 'Why, sir that's the chief'. Kim Philby had had his first glimpse of his boss, the head of MI6, Colonel Stewart Menzies.

Philby had left the *Times* in the summer of 1940 and had gone seamlessly into Section D of the secret service, which was at that time being incorporated into SOE, the secret organisation that Churchill famously hoped would 'Set Europe ablaze'. Philby's knowledge of the Gestapo and Sicherheitsdienst made him a popular lecturer for the SOE agents being trained at Beaulieu, in the New Forest, for infiltration into enemy-occupied

Europe. The majority of these, in November 1940, were Dutch, who six months later, after leaving Beaulieu, would be transported to the beach by British motor torpedo boat. Fifty-five of them were caught by the Germans, who exploited them to penetrate the Dutch underground. Most were then arrested with their contacts and executed. Of the 144 Allied agents sent to Holland between May 1940 and September 1944, 116 were killed.[2]

According to recently released CIA reports,[3] Philby was involved in an operation against the Dutch resistance codenamed 'North Pole', which involved attacking any attempts to prepare for a return of the House of Orange. When the prime minister designate to the Dutch government, Herman B. W. Beckman, waited at night on the beach at Schevingen for a British boat to pick him up and convey him to Queen Wilhelmina in London, Beckman was arrested by the Germans and a number of Beckman's associates were also captured, one of whom was known to Menzies because he 'had established a secret contact between him and his German counterpart Admiral Canaris.'[4] No details exist of this contact but in the light of the preceding pages it is certainly an explanation.

It was certainly not in the Soviets' interest to have a royalist underground established in Holland but it was also, as we have seen, a key priority to ensure that links between Canaris and 'C' were cut.[5] If 'C' was using Holland as one of his links with Canaris, which would be logical given the geography and recent history of the country, that would be enough to cause Philby to betray the SOE cause in Holland.

The events surrounding the tragedy of SOE's agents in Holland still remain obscure, but according to the recent research produced by William E. Henhoeffer, a former CIA Soviet analyst,[6] Philby was 'inextricably involved' in the events of 1940–1941. According to Henhoeffer, Philby had passed details of the SOE missions to his Soviet control in London, who forwarded it to Moscow, who in turn under the terms of the intelligence-sharing agreement established by the Nazi–Soviet Pact of August 1939, passed it on to Berlin.

Menzies was fully apprised of Philby's communist past and indeed may have exploited it once Hitler attacked the Soviet Union. One of Philby's duties was 'maintaining liaison with the Soviets'. Menzies would certainly have entertained the possibility of the Soviets even being fed some false information. If it were fed through Philby it would have a whiff of authenticity. But as Menzies later wrote to a subordinate: 'One could not have thought him an out-and-out traitor.' [7]

It is certainly unlikely that Menzies imagined he had recruited a fully committed Soviet intelligence agent who would do his best to destroy any chance of an understanding between Britain and Germany during the war. Moreover, given the importance 'C' attached to his contact with Canaris, it is inconceivable that Menzies would have allowed the intelligence from the Abwehr and Canaris to be examined by Philby if he had thought the evaluations were going straight to Moscow, as indeed they were. Experienced intelligence officers may ask themselves whether Menzies was not deliberately leaking information to the Soviets on contacts with Canaris to keep pressure on Moscow to stay in the war on the British side. There is some evidence that Menzies' mental elasticity extended to such subterfuge.

Moscow, as Menzies must have suspected, had no illusions about Canaris. The Soviets regarded him as a deadly opponent. According to the Soviet file on the admiral he was, 'The most dangerous intelligence man in the world; capable of manipulating international industrial and capital interests.' [8]

But by the second half of 1942 Menzies felt sufficiently confident of Philby's fundamental reliability to appoint him to evaluate, with a young Oxford historian, Hugh Trevor-Roper, the information coming via various sources to 'C' from intercepts of the Abwehr signals, whose ciphers began to be comprehensively broken from December 1942 and

THE SEARCH FOR PEACE

forwarded in a series of ISOS (Intelligence Service Oliver Strachey) reports.

The two young officers had many things in common. They were both united by their keen intellects and powerful anti-German convictions, but even Trevor-Roper's unremitting hostility to the teuton world was tempered by some intellectual integrity. One day towards the end of 1942, Trevor-Roper was surprised at Philby's reaction to an evaluation report on Canaris he was penning.

As Trevor-Roper recalled many years later, 'Late in 1942 my office had come to certain conclusions – which time proved to be correct – about the struggle between the Nazi party and German General Staff, as it was being fought out in the field of secret intelligence. The German Secret Service ... and its leader, Admiral Canaris, were suspected by the Party not only of inefficiency but also of disloyalty, and attempts were being made by Himmler to oust the admiral and to take over his whole organisation.' [9]

Trevor-Roper is about a year behind events if Menzies' conversation with Popov the previous December is to be believed.[10] Nevertheless, the date is important, for as Trevor-Roper continued:

'Admiral Canaris, himself, at that time, was making repeated journeys to Spain and had indicated a willingness to treat with us; he would even welcome a meeting with his opposite number 'C'.

'These conclusions were duly formulated and the final document was submitted for security clearance to Philby.' [11]

Philby, who had so ruthlessly severed Canaris' Dutch connection with Menzies was, of course, hardly likely to collaborate in any further link between the two spy chiefs. December 1942, as we shall see, was the crucial month for such a link. The very thought of a meeting between Menzies and Canaris would have certainly put the fear of God even into the Godless Communists.

According to Trevor-Roper, Philby's reaction was to discount the material entirely. 'Philby absolutely forbade' the circulation of the report, insisting that it was 'mere speculation'. Trevor-Roper, however, need not have been so concerned: the report had certainly been seen by 'C', though it would only have confirmed what Menzies already knew about Canaris.

A year later, another report suggesting a German plot to assassinate Hitler was also blocked by Philby, though this time Trevor-Roper risked a court-martial to bring it to his superior's attention. With some difficulty Trevor-Roper was transferred. Menzies saved him from dismissal and a ruined career.[12]

Nor were these the only signs of Canaris' readiness to talk. It will be recalled that Canaris' emissary Schwerin had, before the war, lunched with Menzies and Admiral Godfrey, the Director of Naval Intelligence.[13] There is evidence to suggest that at first, Canaris was hoping to exploit the naval connection and establish contact with Godfrey, who was in that rare but valued tradition of being an intellectual naval officer, just as Menzies was the embodiment of the glamour of the Household Cavalry. Moreover, Godfrey was a great protégé of the legendary Admiral Hall, whose personality had long impressed Canaris.

The British Naval attaché in Madrid, Commander Don Gomez-Beare, noted: 'At that time it seemed as though Canaris was practically inviting the Naval Intelligence Division to open secret negotiations with him.' Gomez-Beare, according to one source, was actually in contact with Canaris through, needless to say, their mutual acquaintance Juan March.[14] He observed how Canaris 'dropped hints that he might have talks with a certain naval person.' Gomez-Beare felt that the certain naval person was Ian Fleming, an assistant to Admiral Godfrey, the DNI, who was fluent in German and had long been interested in Canaris.

But these possibilities came to an abrupt end when suddenly in August 1942, for no real apparent reason, Churchill decided to sack Godfrey as DNI and move him to take command of the Royal Indian Navy (a mutiny occurred not long after he took it over). Godfrey would be the only naval officer of his rank not to be decorated at the end of the war and was dismissed for reasons which even today remain strangely obscure.

The lack of knighthood on relinquishing the post of DNI was a very public act of colossal official disapproval. Godfrey was a highly intelligent officer who had transformed the Naval Intelligence Division into a formidable machine. It is hard not to suspect that his connection with Canaris may have in some way played a role in this unprecedented and puzzling event.

Canaris, when he heard the news was, according to sources quoting Juan March who was with him at the time, visibly annoyed. 'The Naval Intelligence Division is not as circumspect as it was in Admiral Hall's day,' Canaris said, adding curiously, 'How can you deal with an organisation which changes its directors so frequently?' [15]

With Godfrey no longer available it was logical for Canaris to turn his focus onto Menzies, the other member of the Schwerin lunch party.

Despite the immense precautions after Venlo, and the atmosphere of suspicion and distrust that Canaris' feelers would inevitably arouse in SIS, Menzies appears not to have ruled out grounds for exploring further contacts.

Part of the reason for this might have been that some months earlier Menzies had received yet more evidence that his German opposite number was someone he could cooperate with. Early in 1942, 'C' had come to the conclusion that 'the horse' to back in France was not necessarily De Gaulle, or Admiral Darlan, whom the Americans were wooing, but General Henri Giraud, who had commanded with distinction the French Seventh Army during the battle for France in 1940.

Giraud, however, had not only been captured by the Germans and incarcerated in the castle of Königstein in Saxony, Hitler had given orders to Canaris, presumably on account of Allied interest in the general, to have him murdered in captivity. Even if Giraud could escape, the odds were not stacked in the general's favour: he was sixty-three, six foot three inches tall, had only one arm and was barely able to speak two words of German.

Hitler's orders to Canaris to have Giraud murdered somehow found their way to London, though it is not clear how. Political assassination, even in the Third Reich, was not usually the subject of wireless traffic. It was noted, however, that despite Hitler's orders no action was taken against the general.

Menzies, it has been suggested, had ordered MI9, his section specialising in exfiltration of agents from Fortress Europe, to organize Giraud's escape in March 1942, discussing it with Cadogan on the 25th, who noted in his diary: 'Interesting talk with 'C' about LUCAS (codename for Giraud) and future plans.' [16]

Somehow – it is still not clear how – the general escaped and despite his appearance and a huge reward (carefully monitored in London through SD intercepts), against rather high odds, he made it to Switzerland more or less in time to reach North Africa by the end of 1942 and take over from Admiral Darlan, who was a thorn in the side of British interests and who, it seems, with some British encouragement, was assassinated on Christmas Eve by a young French 'idealist'.

Canaris had undoubtedly played a role in the organisation of the escape, according to Lahousen. The admiral subsequently skilfully deflected the criticism directed at him by blaming his 'failure' to liquidate Giraud on his having given the 'job' to Heydrich in Prague a few days before the Reichsprotektor was himself liquidated.

Once again it would seem a common interest between Menzies and Canaris could be registered by the discerning eye. If Menzies had wanted proof that Canaris would not exploit contacts with him to Britain's disadvantage, the escape of Giraud was a textbook example of 'good faith'.

If Menzies, with his legendary intuition, sensed that his links with the admiral were those between two kindred spirits he appears to have been sometimes strangely indifferent to the fact that it would incur the unwelcome interest of certain circles within his own organisation.

Throughout his career he seems to have consistently underestimated the sheer ruthlessness of the Communist intelligence machine and its extensive penetration of the British establishment. Canaris, however, was fully aware of the risks he was running in his contacts with Menzies. Already before the war, he had told his friend Juan March that 'I have penetrated the Naval Intelligence Division and MI6. So if any German, however important and discreet, felt tempted to work with the British Secret Service, be sure I should find out about it.'

The admiral went further in his advice to March, hinting that he knew how parts of the British service might work against his secret communications with London: 'Now in that service there are conflicting minds and it could well happen that one section of the secret service would keep faith, but that the other would not hesitate to betray any such Germans either to me or someone else in the Abwehr.' [17]

The need for caution would have no doubt been confirmed later through exchanges of information with the Russian service between September 1939 and January 1941. Canaris would with his skill and experience hardly have failed to appreciate the extent of Soviet penetration of British institutions.

By the end of 1942, the Allied landings in North Africa had taken place thanks to Operation Torch. Most sources note that the complete surprise of the attacks was evidence of the Abwehr being caught off guard. Other sources suggest Canaris deliberately did not pass the evidence of his agents to the High Command.[18]

However, according to documents in the Institute of Contemporary History in Munich, the landings had been accurately predicted by the Abwehr. The Algeciras station could hardly have failed to note the build-up of vessels across the strait and even its opponents admitted the Algeciras station was one of the Abwehr's best. According to the documents deposited in Munich this intelligence had been overruled by Ribbentrop, ever jealous of the Abwehr, who relied on his intelligence service within the embassy in Spain. The view from the chancery in Madrid, robustly expressed, extensively discounted the Allies landing before the end of the year and the Abwehr's reports were ignored.[19]

Irrespective of the causes of the intelligence lapse, the landings had a number of interesting and possibly unpredicted side-effects. One, completely unforeseen by the Allies, was that Panzer Army Africa was saved from imminent extinction by the swift arrival of German reinforcements provoked by Vichy's sudden switch of sides.

Another was that with the landings in North Africa 'Menzies was now in a position to open direct negotiations' [20]if he wished with Canaris and accept the invitations which Trevor-Roper and Gomez-Beare had encountered.

The question of whether such a meeting ever took place must now be addressed. At first glance it would appear no such encounter occurred. Menzies, when asked after the war about Canaris, simply said that any such meeting 'had been blocked by the Foreign Office' for fear of 'offending Russia'.[21] But for the Foreign Office to have 'blocked' or even 'advised against' such a meeting, a case for such an encounter would have had to have been made. Therefore if the meeting were to be 'blocked', a proposal, however brief, should have had to have been prepared.

Unsurprisingly, given the sensitivity of the subject matter, there are no documents pointing to such a proposal. Therefore, officially, the meeting, though clearly discussed at a high level, if Menzies' words are to be taken at face value, did not take place. In fact, the only trace is Colvin relating an exchange with a senior intelligence officer late in 1942, who asked him 'Would you like to meet Canaris?' A question that implies some preliminary planning of a meeting.[22]

Another version suggests that Eden refused Menzies permission for the meeting.[23] Again there are no documents, though this is certainly plausible given Eden's determination to keep the Russians happy in the face of huge tensions between Moscow and London, not least over Soviet territorial demands. Eden more than Churchill took the classic Napoleonic line that Russia was Britain's natural ally. Churchill, with America now embroiled in the war, was far less sympathetic to the Soviet demands. As the travails of London's ambassador to Moscow at this time, Sir Stafford Cripps, reveal all too vividly, December 1942 was a low point in Anglo–Soviet relations.[24]

In the absence of any documents directly referring to the proposed meeting, it is surely a fair question to ask where the two spy chiefs were in the weeks following Canaris' 'invitation' to Menzies in the 'late autumn' as referenced above by Trevor-Roper and Gomez-Beare. If Eden had been consulted and proved to be a sticking point, it is interesting to note that from 7 December until the end of the month, Eden was travelling to and visiting Moscow and not therefore personally accessible. From the moment Eden left Euston for Scotland on the morning of the 7th, Menzies needed to fear no direct interference from that quarter.

According to Abshagen, Canaris was in Spain late December 1942 and arrived in Algeciras a few days before New Year's Eve, where his staff found him in the highest of spirits, joking and cooking for his staff, even appearing wearing a chef's tall hat and apron while he prepared a German Christmas turkey. Canaris had put some thought into the party, securing the services of a Spanish cook that he knew and could work with. Several writers have observed how optimistic the admiral appeared, notwithstanding the criticism for failures over 'Torch'. 'For a few hours Canaris gave up his worries ... and was once again the avuncular friend of his staff.'[25]

That Canaris would be in Spain is hardly surprising. He was a virtual nomad and had complete licence as to where he could travel, although Christmas and New Year's Eve are traditionally times when most Germans, if they could, would celebrate with their families.

Far more intriguing is the fact that Menzies, 'the man who never went anywhere beyond St James's unless in the imperial interest,'[26] had spent the previous few days, while Canaris was preparing his 'Sylvester' dinner, secretly in nearby Algiers and Gibraltar. On Christmas Eve, according to Frederick Winterbotham in his book *The Ultra Secret*, Menzies had 'a splendid lunch on the sun-drenched roof of a little house in Algiers.'

Menzies only twice set foot outside England during the war and on this particular occasion he was now suddenly within virtual spitting distance of Algeciras and Canaris.

Menzies, according to Winterbotham, had flown out when he had heard the 'news in London' that Colonel Rivet, the head of the French secret service, had managed to get out of France and had arrived in Algiers. Yet this does not tally with either the date or the suddenness of Menzies' secret departure from London.

'C''s personal assistant, Patrick Reilly, after the war, told Anthony Cave Brown the following curious tale: 'This was the strangest episode of my term as 'C''s personal assistant. At the beginning of December 1942 'C' asked me whether I would like to take a short leave.' Reilly left the office some time in the third week in December with 'C' still working at his desk. Reilly recalled: 'When I got back 'C' was still at his desk'. Reilly did not know that Menzies had been away until forty years later.

'I am now inclined to the view that he gave me leave at that time because he wanted me out of the way while he was abroad,' Reilly stated.

It has been suggested that Menzies was in Algiers to 'plan' the assassination of Admiral Darlan.[27] But this also does not ring true. Darlan's murder, though wished by many in Churchill's circle, could never have been an SIS mission. As in Prague earlier in the year, the immediate fingerprints of assassination, if they pointed in any British direction, were those of SOE, not an organisation Menzies had a great deal of time for. The events surrounding the murder of Admiral Darlan, whose negotiations with the Americans provoked Cadogan into minuting 'We shall do no good until we have killed Darlan,' remain controversial.[28]

Unlike Prague, Darlan's assassination had major political implications that would logically involve the secret service chief, especially as

Darlan's successor would be Giraud, whom Canaris had helped exfiltrate. But even so it is still surprising that Menzies absented himself from London only for something as banal as the 'immobilisation' of an awkward Frenchman.

However, we know from Churchill's correspondence with Eden a year earlier that SIS was actively involved in evaluating the sincerity of German opposition peace-feelers.[29] But if the purpose of Menzies' *absentia* had been to meet clandestinely with his German counterpart to explore the possibilities of 'an understanding', no evidence survives as to whether the encounter ever took place.

Having examined the geographical proximity of our two protagonists, we should look closely at the motive behind such a possible meeting. It would have been an opportunity, as one writer has suggested, to bring off the biggest coup of the war; two spy chiefs ready to open negotiations for an early end to the conflict.[30]

Certainly, if Britain had ever needed to explore Canaris' offer of an understanding, this would have been the moment. The invitation had been repeatedly extended; the relationship of trust between the two men was tried and tested in the Giraud operation and the dynamic of war was showing both sides, after three years, that uncharted dangers lay ahead.

The 'conversation' initiated by Churchill might have to be reopened, not least because the first disturbing reports were coming through that some circles in Germany were, even as Russians and Germans slaughtered each other by the thousand around Stalingrad in those days, contemplating an accommodation with Stalin.

The secret telegrams of the neutral powers from September 1942, intercepted by Menzies, contained ominous references to 'a separate peace between Germany and Russia'. The Japanese government was involved for several weeks trying to broker a deal.[31] Moreover, as Hitler would himself admit to the Japanese ambassador, Oshima, the following spring, noting that he was imparting 'information of an extremely confidential nature', Germany had only once seriously 'made a peace proposal to Russia towards the end of 1942.' [32]

This proposal had, in Hitler's words, offered to 'return all the conquered territories except the Ukraine.'

At about the same time as the German peace offer, Eden's December mission to Moscow would end, in Churchill's words, 'without any flourish of trumpets', and the future of Anglo–Soviet relations seemed likely to founder on the thorny issue of frontiers, mutual suspicion and ideological conflict. Stalin could never rid himself of the idea that somehow the German attack on Russia had been orchestrated by London in some devious plan, which had at the last moment miscarried, to keep Britain in the war against Germany. At the same time the German army was still mounting a vigorous campaign. The surrender of Stalingrad was several weeks away.

According to the secret state security assessments of public opinion in Germany, rumours of an imminent agreement with Moscow began to circulate in the late autumn of 1942.[33] Canaris himself had instructed agents to keep contact with the Soviets and these instructions would have been read by 'C' in his ISOS intercepts of Abwehr traffic from early December, when the Abwehr ciphers were broken. Moreover, the Swedish security service were monitoring the activities and telephone conversations of the German embassy in Stockholm and noting emissaries arriving from Keitel in Berlin.[34]

From May 1942, Edgar Klaus, a Rigan Jew working for the Red Cross as an Abwehr agent in Stockholm under the control of one of Canaris' officers, Werner Boening, was given standing orders to communicate with the Soviets. The admiral was adamant that Klaus must keep all lines of communication open, notably links with the Soviet ambassador in Sweden, the formidable Madame Alexandra Kolontaj, an old friend of Lenin's with whom Klaus had made contact through a mutual Slovene acquaintance.

Moreover, at the end of November 1942, Menzies would have seen from his German foreign ministry decrypts that Peter Kleist, a friend of Ribbentrop's, had been sent to Stockholm to broach the possibility of a separate peace with Moscow.

According to recent German research, this development appears to have rung alarm bells in London and had curious results. It would provoke another tangible sign of cooperation between Menzies and Canaris, for the foreign ministry in Berlin appears to have gone to some lengths to prevent the Abwehr from knowing of Kleist's mission. According to those who worked with Canaris at this time, the Admiral would be kept abreast of this mission not by the German foreign ministry but by 'sources in London'.[35]

Kleist's mission was in response to a hint from Stalin in a speech delivered on 19 October 1942, interestingly around the time Churchill was voicing his views of expecting the Russians to lose. Moreover, serious differences were opening up at this time between Churchill and Roosevelt on the one side and Stalin on the other with regard to frontier questions.

Moscow continued to believe, with some justification, that while the Allies would do all they could to help prevent Russia being decisively defeated, they would do nothing to help Russia win a decisive victory.[36]

By the time Kleist arrived in Stockholm on 2 December there were also signs that leading figures in the Nazi regime were moving behind the idea that hostilities needed to end. Reinhard Spitzy would recall in a letter to the Soviet journalist Lew Besymin[37] that Himmler approved of peace overtures at this time. Spitzy would later write that 'our view of the Slavs cost us the war.'

Already in November 1942, observers of the Nazi machine both in and outside the country also began to notice a softening in the language of Goebbels' propaganda. There were no longer innumerable references to the 'Jewish–Bolsheviks' and there were noticeably fewer personal attacks on Stalin.[38] Within weeks, Klaus would be reporting his conversations with Kolontaj as taking a positive turn, quoting her saying that 'Russia never wanted war with Germany.' [39]

At the same time, the Turks in Istanbul were picking up strong hints of a possible deal between the Germans and the Russians from the Japanese ambassador. The Japanese were especially engaged in this process. Careful not to be at war with the Soviet Union, they were keen to see an agreement between their German ally and the all-too-near Russians.[40]

It is important to stress that at this stage these were only straws in the wind but it was clear to those who followed these developments that they were harbingers of things to come. By the end of 1942, von der Schulenburg, the former German ambassador to Moscow, would offer to have himself smuggled over the Soviet frontier to make a personal plea to Stalin for peace.

More extensive exploration of an armistice on the Eastern Front would come several weeks later after the disaster at Stalingrad, when the Germans, under Manstein's inspired leadership, had recaptured Karkov early in 1943.[41]

According to Manstein's ADC, the possibility of an armistice was uppermost in Manstein's mind for several months in the run-up to the summer.[42]

Manstein would write in 1968: 'I was far more convinced that after our successful counter-offensive across the Dneiper and at Karkov in March 1943, we still had the possibility under a skilful leadership to fight for, at the very least, an armistice.' [43] By April 1943 many 'well-informed' sources in neutral Sweden would be predicting an 'imminent Russo-German peace.' [44]

Already then, at the beginning of December, sufficient evidence was beginning to build to show that Churchill's semi-permanent neurosis concerning a separate peace between Germany and Moscow was receiving ominous encouragement in the run-up to 1943. Though critical of Stalin and callous of the Russians who would in his words 'have to go on fighting anyway,' [45] Churchill's recurring nightmare was the spectre of that armistice in the east which had cost the West so dearly in 1917.

The question that begs to be asked is whether Churchill, taking advantage of Eden's enforced absence in December 1943, would have authorised Menzies, in the light of these developments, to meet with Canaris and resume the 'conversation'. It is unlikely that Menzies – born and bred to obey orders – would have made such a journey entirely off his own bat. If Menzies met Canaris in December 1942, it seems more than likely it would have been with Churchill's tacit consent. Churchill would certainly have seen the value of a brief parley with Canaris if only to illuminate German intentions towards a separate peace with Moscow. Of these, Canaris was well informed as he had established personal contact with Manstein through Manstein's adjutant Stahlberg.[46]

Churchill, in any case, was now setting off for America. If he had given an encouraging hint to Menzies, he, too, would not be personally accessible to discuss it any further. Should something go wrong, in fact, Churchill would have the perfect alibi, and he would no doubt have heaped opprobrium on Menzies in the grandest of styles, without hesitation finding a new 'C'.

After the war, with Germany vanquished and the full extent of the horrors of the camps in the public domain, neither man would wish to admit that such conversations with the 'inhuman' enemy had taken place. Thus if the meeting had occurred it would in modern parlance have to enjoy 'total deniability' at all levels.

Having established possible motive and geographical proximity, it remains for us only to explore the means whereby the two men could have met. Gibraltar, separated from Algeciras by a short ride in a motor boat, was inevitably the key to this logistical problem.

Algeciras was at this point in the war frequented by countless British officers from Gibraltar. Indeed, on News Year's Eve the Abwehr officers who had eaten Canaris' turkey could be seen after midnight rubbing shoulders with British officers on the lavish dance floor of the Hotel Reina Maria Cristina. It would not have been beyond the wit of Menzies and Canaris to meet somewhere in that town or nearby. After the Venlo experience, however, it must be assumed that Menzies would have wished to take more than just the standard precautions. Another, more remote, rendezvous, a monastery on the Spanish–Portuguese border, has also been suggested.

It also cannot be ruled out that Canaris himself, at great personal risk, would have visited an SIS safe house or even the 'Rock'. He was, as Menzies would recall, 'damn courageous' and would have had only Menzies' word to guarantee his safety, but this in the freemasonry of spy chiefs would have been enough. Later in the war Canaris would pay at least one visit to an SIS safe house in occupied France.

Colvin notes that there was an extensively prepared plot to kidnap Canaris in Algeciras about this time, when Mason Macfarlane, who had been military attaché in Berlin before the war, was governor. It was countermanded by London. The significance of this, however, is also that 'C' would have known very well, had he wished, Canaris' movements and location in the town.

If the meeting had occurred it would go some way to explaining Canaris' optimism on New Year's Eve. Spitzy, who had seen the admiral a few weeks earlier, had been horrified to see him looking so depressed.[47] Now the admiral seemed his old optimistic self.

Perhaps he had also been heartened by intelligence of American intentions, communicated to neutral Turkey, which stressed 'in order to ensure that Germany is not "bolshevised" they are thinking of reaching an agreement with her against Russia before she is completely routed and of saving her economic position.'[48]

It is difficult to speculate on the contents of a meeting that might never have taken place. But it would almost certainly have focussed on the possibility of bringing the war between Germany and the West to an end in 1943. Canaris was under no illusions that Germany was losing the war. He had, from the very first day, refused to believe in a German victory. The question was, at what price could the conflict be brought to a rapid conclusion? Someone who knew Menzies well at this time noted: 'He hoped as we all did that the conflict could be brought to an end.' [49] This would have required British support for an alternative government to Hitler and a deal with the opposition. It would have implied a common front against the Red Army, whose march westwards would have been arrested at Karkov, not just for a few weeks but perhaps for many years as the full force of the Wehrmacht was brought to bear on the Eastern Front and stalemate moved inexorably towards an armistice.

Both men, representatives of an older order, would also have felt an instinctive sympathy with any move which could help bring about a cessation of hostilities before Communism spread across Europe. In addition to these areas, there might also have been discussion of a topic that had preyed much on Canaris' mind since January 1938, when German scientists had announced in *Naturwissenschaft* the discovery of nuclear fission and its implications for the construction of a hugely destructive weapon.

Thanks to the efforts of the physicist Weiszäcker, son of the diplomat, and Hitler's conviction that nuclear physics was 'Jewish alchemy', [50] the German nuclear physics programme which had led the world before the war had, however, been dramatically curtailed. But unlike most of the senior generals in Germany, Canaris had long been convinced that whoever constructed this weapon would be 'lord of the world' and was determined to help any efforts to slow down German research in this direction. He extended the protection of the Abwehr to Weiszäcker and other nuclear physicists at the Kaiser Wilhelm Insitute and shielded them from the SD. It was agreed between Canaris and Weiszäcker that with Abwehr help the nuclear physics weapons programme could be retarded. [51] At the same time, he feared its use against German cities by the Americans should they develop it before the war was over.

No doubt the two men would have also discussed the future of European Jewry, whose fate in the death camps was known to Menzies through wireless intercepts.

But as if to frustrate such a dialogue, there occurred a diplomatic event that would amount to nothing less than, at first glance, a shattering of any hopes of an 'understanding' between Germany and England. Two weeks after the New Year celebrations which Canaris had so lovingly prepared with such good humour, the Casablanca conference opened with Churchill, Roosevelt, their staffs and De Gaulle and the fortunate Giraud in attendance.

At his final press conference on 24 January 1943 Roosevelt announced, 'Peace can only come about with the total elimination of German and Japanese war power (which) ... means unconditional surrender by Germany, Italy and Japan.' [52]

CHAPTER THIRTEEN

UNCONDITIONAL SURRENDER

I believe the other side have now disarmed us of the last
weapon with which we could have ended the war.
ADMIRAL CANARIS [1]

The impact of the words was disastrous from a propaganda point of view as Goebbels used the phrase relentlessly to convince the German people that it was better to continue the war than suffer the horrible privations that would follow unconditional surrender to the Allies, lurid descriptions of which now daily filled the airwaves of state controlled propaganda.

Canaris' reaction, as recounted by his colleagues, bordered on near-petulant fatalism: 'How do they think they can end the war with all this talk of Unconditional Surrender? Our generals will not swallow that.' [2]

Canaris continued: 'The students of history will not need to trouble their heads after this war as they did after the last to determine who was guilty of starting it. The case is however different when we consider guilt for prolonging the war. I believe that the other side have now disarmed us of the last weapon with which we could have ended it.' [3]

Some historians have concluded that the unconditional surrender phrase was a sudden improvisation by Roosevelt. This is far from the truth. The formula is recorded in the Joint Chiefs of Staff minutes of 7 January 1943 and will therefore have been discussed as a serious policy in Washington before Roosevelt left for Casablanca. The idea had been worked out in advance by Roosevelt for a number of reasons. These have been persuasively recounted by the diplomat Frank Roberts who was present at the conference. Roberts put it to Dick Lamb in 1988:

> I think unconditional surrender was originally a Roosevelt idea ... Winston felt he must agree because there were so many other issues on which he and Roosevelt were at variance.
>
> In addition there was a general feeling prevalent that this time Germany must be completely defeated so there would be no repetition of the 1918 legend that the German disaster came from a stab in the back from German socialists and that this time we should just substitute anti-Nazis. [4]

Roberts is implying that Churchill and Roosevelt had clearly discussed the question of doing a deal with the German opposition at some length, but had come to the conclusion that 'this time Germany must be completely defeated'. No doubt Menzies' reports, whether or not he had met Canaris a few weeks before, would have formed some part of Churchill's intelligence assessment of the German opposition.[5]

Roberts continued:

> At that time, rightly or wrongly, there was little confidence in either Churchill's or Eden's mind that any conceivable German opposition who might have been attracted by the prospect of terms other than 'unconditional surrender' either would or could deliver the goods.

If Roberts is to be believed, these words strongly imply that Churchill's assessment of Canaris' ability to use the Abwehr convincingly against the regime in conjunction with the generals was negative. However, Roberts added a further reason which may have outweighed all other considerations:

> Last but not least, the slogan was thought likely to appeal to Stalin as
> proof of our toughness and as removing from his suspicious mind the
> concept that we might want to do a deal with non-Communist Germany
> and so tempt him to do his own deal as in 1939 with Hitler. [6]

Here Roberts candidly reveals Churchill's anxieties that Moscow was
thinking of doing a deal with Hitler and links this fear with the need to
head it off by breaking all links between London and Berlin. As Roosevelt
acknowledged at the time: 'It is just the thing for the Russians ... Uncle
Joe might have made it up himself.' [7]

However, it is surely also possible that an alternative method of heading
off such an armistice between Moscow and Berlin would have been to
consider doing a deal with the Germans.

Roosevelt had received from Allen Dulles, his man and OSS resident
in Switzerland, evidence from Adam Trott, the German diplomat and
former Rhodes scholar with extensive leads to Britain, that 'the German and
Russian peoples could come to some agreement.' [8] Dulles shared Trott's
views, passing them on to Roosevelt before the Casablanca declaration.
Such a possibility was a nightmare for western statesmen. Trott, who had
studied at Oxford before the war, knew what a sensitive nerve such a
prediction would touch in English circles.

William Cavendish-Bentinck, then a senior Foreign Office official,
throws further light on the thoughts then current in the highest quarters
on the alternatives available:

> After the First War, the spirit of the army remained in Germany.
> This would have happened after the Second War had it not been for
> unconditional surrender. If the spirit of the army had remained we
> would soon have found the German General Staff coming to terms
> with the Russians ... I was not keen on the German generals and if
> there had been a Goerdeler government after the 20th July bomb
> plot, the generals would have held the trump cards. [9]

Bentinck's statement strongly implies that some advanced thinking had occurred in certain quarters of Whitehall about doing a deal with a German opposition supported by Canaris and some of the generals who had conspired already, back in 1938, and that this view had unleashed quite a row at the highest levels of state.

However, unconditional or no unconditional surrender, the conversations with the German opposition were not ended. On the contrary, they appear to have resumed with almost redoubled efforts, as if the statement was only for Stalin's consumption and would not affect relations between Germany and the West. Undaunted by the declaration, Canaris, inspired by his contacts with Menzies and recognising that what governments said and what they did were, then as now, often different, worked more feverishly than ever; keeping his lines of contact with Menzies intact and opening up negotiations with the Americans on a number of fronts. In Switzerland, Gisevius was instructed to renew contacts with Madame Szymanska and strengthen contacts with Allen Dulles in Berne. When Gisevius brought Dulles evidence that his ciphers had been broken, the two began to talk more and more frankly.

In London the increased activity did not go unnoticed. Germany may have been losing the war but she still had strong cards to play. At SIS headquarters, Philby saw the threat and decided to take serious action against Canaris. As he himself recorded:

> In 1943, I received (a decrypt) revealing that Canaris was to visit Spain. He was going to drive from Madrid to Seville, stopping overnight at a town called Manzanares. I knew the town well from Spanish Civil War days and I knew that the only place Canaris could stay would be at the Parador.
>
> So I sent Cowgill (Head of Counter Espionage) a memo suggesting that we let SOE know about it in case they wanted to mount an operation against Canaris. From what I knew about the Parador,

it would not have been difficult to have tossed a couple of grenades into his bedroom.

Cowgill approved and sent my memo on up to 'C'. Cowgill showed me a reply a couple of days later. Menzies had written in his official green ink: "I want no action whatsoever taken against the admiral". [10]

As the Casablanca conference was in progress, Hitler, according to several senior German intelligence officers, gave orders to assassinate Churchill.[11] However, as Lahousen's war diary shows, there was at Canaris' insistence a complete ban on all 'such acts of terrorism'. Nevertheless, Keitel passed on an order to have Churchill murdered by nationalist Arabs. On 1 June 1943, Leslie Howard and Alfred Chenfalls – who, smoking a cigar, bore an uncanny resemblance to Churchill – were killed when a BOAC plane was shot down on a return flight to London. It was the only attack on a BOAC flight on that route during the entire war. It would seem Canaris' writ could not influence everything.*

Philby had to limit himself to monitoring for his Soviet masters the admiral's movements and the increased signs of clandestine diplomatic activity he was stimulating, though as Philby soon realised, they were not confined to the Abwehr or opposition.

One part of the peace-feelers involved Reinhard Spitzy, by now working undercover as a salesman with Skoda. Working closely with Schellenberg, and it would seem with Himmler's blessing, in January 1943, within days of Casablanca, Spitzy made contact with the Americans on the Iberian peninsula. By the third week in February, he was travelling to Switzerland for talks with Dulles in Berne.[12] The conversation lasted until three in the morning and ranged over the threat of a Bolshevik Europe and the need for an agreement between Germany and the West. The talks included Canaris' friend and agent Prince Max Hohenlohe.

*Another theory links the crash with the fact that high ranking representatives of an organisation trying to rescue Jews from Germany and resettle them in Palestine were also on board. Howard himself had impeccable old Austrian antecedents . See Colvin, *Flight 777*

The Dulles line at these talks was encouraging. Dulles saw positively a compromise peace that would preserve Germany's integrity, maintain the Anschluss and help provide a *cordon sanitaire* around Russia. Hohenlohe and Spitzy were both left with the impression that while London sought a balance of power in Europe with different spheres of influence, Dulles wanted a single entity of Europe that would create a large and extensive market for US commercial interests. This was encouragement indeed for those Germans seeking an agreement.

About the same time, in February 1943, Canaris received from General Treskow – a key conspirator against Hitler, then stationed in Smolensk – the laconic message: 'It is high time to act'. On 22 February, Canaris met Treskow. The occasion was a conference of intelligence officers; a member of Canaris' staff carried a small package of plastic explosives, intercepted apparently from SOE sources, and a set of time fuses. Dohnanyi, a member of Canaris' staff, went into a meeting with Treskow and Schlabrendorff and it was agreed that an attempt would be made on Hitler's life when he visited the Army Group.

In 1970, in an interview with Professor Deutsch,[13] Spitzy characterised Canaris' attitude to the conspirators: 'The admiral knew everything and said, "It would be good if you succeed and I will protect you but after all these immense crimes it is not possible to deceive history through a small trick. There must be *expiation*." He used the French word.' To another of the conspirators, he observed 'You will be judged only by one thing, your success.'[14]

Canaris, despite his reservations concerning murder, appears by this time to have seen little alternative if an agreement with the West was to be reached.

On 13 March 1943, the explosive device was put into Hitler's aircraft as he left Smolensk. Disguised in a parcel of cognac bottles, the fuse ate its way through the retaining wire but when the wire parted, the intense cold rendered the detonator unserviceable and the bomb failed to explode.

Schlabrendorff flew to Rastenberg and retrieved the parcel before it was opened. [15]

This attempt on Hitler's life appears to have been stimulated in some ways by the conversations with the Americans that had begun more or less at the same time as Casablanca As well as the Hohenlohe-Spitzy-Dulles talks in Switzerland, peace-feelers from the Americans were extended in Istanbul towards the end of January.

These had been predicted by Canaris, who late in 1942, over lunch in his villa close to the Schlachtensee, had asked Paul Leverkuen to set up a new Abwehr office in Istanbul. Leverkuen recalled after the war: 'Canaris did not mention a word to me about peace negotiations but I have no doubt that he posted me to Istanbul to take up whatever threads might be put in my hand.' [16]

Canaris was aware that before the war Leverkuen had known, quite well, General William Donovan, who was later to become Head of the American OSS, the forerunner of the CIA. Leverkuen was soon in touch with the Americans. As he recalled, 'It was about the time of the Stalingrad disaster that the first peace-feelers reached me from the Americans.' [17] These would develop into a dialogue which recently declassified documents from the OSS show was more profound than many have hitherto suspected. Canaris and Gisevius were both known to the OSS by symbols.

Some of these initial peace-feelers came from George Earle, a former governor of Pennsylvania and personal envoy of Roosevelt's, who had accompanied the president to Casablanca before arriving in Istanbul.

Earle's arrival in Istanbul followed a series of colourful incidents with a cabaret artiste called 'Adrienne' in the Bulgarian capital, where he had been minister. Following the German occupation of Bulgaria, Earle returned to the US where Roosevelt thought long and hard for a mission which would be acceptable to the US State Department, who had had enough of Earle's somewhat unconventional diplomatic profile. Although Roosevelt was sceptical of the German opposition, he could not ignore the intelligence coming to him via Dulles in Switzerland. Thus while preparing to comfort Stalin with formal talk of unconditional surrender, Roosevelt also opened up contacts with the Germans informally through trusted mediators.

Earle had made many enemies while minister in Bulgaria. The Soviets were monitoring his movements from the moment he set foot in Istanbul, and it may have been they who placed the bomb in his luggage that exploded in the Parc Hotel the day he arrived. A few weeks later a bomb attack by Soviet agents narrowly missed killing the German ambassador, von Papen. The bomb proved defective and killed the plotter, in whose mangled remains the Turkish police found evidence of Russian complicity.

In Earle's case no one was seriously hurt and within days he was establishing contact with Canaris through the Abwehr's Leverkuen. According to Colvin, these contacts included an 'exploration of the sort of terms of peace that America would be prepared to consider.' [18]

Von Papen not only supported these contacts, he had by February 1943 begun, despite his murky past as one of the worst accomplices of Nazi aggression, to assume an important role among the conspirators. As Leverkuen recalled, 'I told the ambassdor about this approach and Herr von Papen composed a little speech for our war cemetery in February.'

Papen noted in the course of his oration: 'We have always had great esteem for the men who made history across the ocean and created the land of unlimited opportunity through their initiative and dynamism. We bow to Washington, Abraham Lincoln, Monroe and many others. But we would not find it unfitting if the Monroe doctrine were extended to Europe.' [19]

The last sentence, said Leverkuen, was inserted to mollify Ribbentrop, who remained hostile and suspicious. He was not alone. In the Kremlin the thought that Papen was aiming at a separate peace with the West confirmed their most intense suspicions.

The results of von Papen's kite were almost instantaneous. In early

March 1943, the Turkish foreign minister, Numan Menemenjoglu, informed von Papen that Monsignor Spellman, the archbishop of New York, would be visiting Turkey and had expressed a desire to meet with the ambassador.[20] The choice of Spellman as an intermediary showed the important role the Vatican might play in bringing about an end to the hostilities in the West. Ribbentrop, however, prevented this meeting but contacts with the Americans in Istanbul continued. Leverkuen, who had lived for ten years in the States, was optimistic, confiding several times to junior colleagues that a peace agreement was imminent.[21]

By June, Adam Trott, a long-standing opponent of Hitler, arrived in Istanbul to confer with von Papen. Trott had had extensive talks with Dulles in Switzerland, and one of his repeated themes to the American had been British intransigence towards dealings with the German opposition. If Roosevelt was prepared to follow a twin-track policy of formal declaration of unconditional surrender and informal talks, London was backtracking fast from any encouragement of its contacts of late 1942 with Canaris and other members of the German opposition. What debate there had been at the highest levels on this issue had, as we have seen in Roberts' and Bentinck's evidence, been resolved in favour of crushing Germany.

Leverkuen, like his opposite numbers in Istanbul, was monitoring events in the Balkans. From there it was becoming increasingly clear that the British and Americans were unlikely to succeed in keeping the Russians out of central Europe. The British transfer of allegiance from the royalist partisans in Yugoslavia to the Communists under Tito was observed in good time. It implied an understanding with Moscow not only with regard to the conduct of the war but to the future arrangements after the war. All these trends injected urgency into the German contacts with the Americans.

It is important to recall that all this was happening a year before the Allied landings in Normandy. The possibility of cooperating with the Germans against the mortal enemy of capitalism held some attraction for many Americans as well as many Britons. The Americans were placed in a much easier position than the British here, for they had had very little personal grievance against the Germans. America had been neither occupied nor bombed and the conflict in the Atlantic, in North Africa and Italy took the form of ordinary military confrontation. There was not, as yet, any expression on the American side of uncontrollable animosity, though the fate of the Jews rightly disturbed many at every level of American society.

As the talks progressed, von Papen's position became more visible to those on the Allied side. They noted, too, that Hitler kept von Papen in his post, though never allowing all the members of his family to leave Germany at the same time. Both the German opposition and the Nazi leadership were placing hopes on the wily diplomat pulling something off with the Americans. Hitler appears at any rate not to have been displeased with von Papen's efforts. By August the talks were given further impetus by reports in August 1943 from the Turkish foreign minister, who explained to the British ambassador, Sir Hugh Knatchbull-Hugessen, that von Papen had told him that he expected shortly to be summoned to Germany to replace Ribbentrop. Such a development could only have presaged a full-blown diplomatic offensive towards the western Allies to achieve a compromise peace.

Von Papen, according to a later OSS assessment, had told the Turkish foreign minister that: 'his own role and that of Turkey would become clear. With his help Turkey would be asked to intervene in the hope of securing a negotiated peace.' [22] According to this assessment, Papen was not ruling out the possibility that he might even succeed Hitler. As von Papen had cabled to Ribbentrop when the latter had prevented him from meeting Spellman, 'If there is no use talking peace, there is no point in maintaining missions abroad.' [23]

Canaris, by sending Leverkuen to Istanbul, had indeed seen the trend of where peace-feelers might be renewed, but he was becoming increasingly diffident, not least in the face of continual British hostility to an agreement.

Hugessen, in response to the Turkish minister, noted that 'our terms were unconditional surrender', but his telegram draws attention to 'earlier guidance on the subject in May', an admission that the subject matter of the conversation was not new and that the peace-feelers between the Americans and Germans were gathering some momentum.[24]

Indeed, Roberts extensively minutes his thoughts on any modification of the unconditional surrender doctrine under the interesting heading: 'PEACE APPROACH BY VON PAPEN', a title suggesting that the German ambassador's activities with the Americans were generating quite a lot of traffic.

The impact of these talks was now involving London and Churchill. He appears almost to have had a slight change of heart by the summer. For once, he encouragingly minuted: 'There is no need for us to discourage this process by continually uttering the slogan 'Unconditional Surrender'.[25]

Although this is the only official reference by Churchill to a weakening of the Casablanca line, the activities of the previous weeks indicate how far the Allies had travelled away from the formal declaration at Casablanca. Unconditional surrender was perhaps not quite unconditional. This would certainly be the case with Italy in a few months.

In Scandinavia meanwhile, the peace-feelers explored earlier in the war were also being reinvigorated. Here, the principal intermediary was Count Wallenberg, a scion of the most influential family of Sweden with excellent personal links to London and Berlin. Once again, the British documents are silent, but by May 1943 these contacts had clearly assumed a regular aspect. That month a memorandum from Carl Goerdeler, a possible choice for an alternative German leader well-known to the British from before the war, was dispatched via Wallenberg to Churchill.

The memorandum requested: 'Please restrict bombing of cities as this will only make a putsch more difficult by destroying all communications.' The tone, as well as the content, of this fragment suggests that it is only one of several exchanges between two parties working towards a common aim. As we have seen from Bentinck's comments, a Goerdeler government in Germany was being widely discussed in London.

As well as these contacts, the lines of communication between the Abwehr and the West through the Vatican were also reactivated. Josef Mueller and General Beck met and again discussed with Canaris the chance of treating with London through the Vatican and Osborne.[26] It was agreed the attempt should be made and Mueller came to Rome and met advisers to the Pope but the Gestapo were on Mueller's trail and he was promptly arrested.

The British papers unsurprisingly show (so far) nothing of this. But it is clear from Vatican archives and German documents that the plans were again well advanced. The Pope, via one of his staff, asked Osborne the significant question, in this context, of whether, if Hitler were overthrown by Germans, there would be a chance of agreement, or whether the formula of unconditional surrender ruled out such a possibility? Osborne's reply to this question does not appear to be in the British files but it is suggested by subsequent statements by the Vatican that he did not offer outright rejection of the possibility. Significantly, on 6 March, Osborne received a telegram from Orme Sargent inviting him to return to London. Osborne would return to London for extended briefings and, most important of all for secret negotiations, new ciphers.[27]

Vatican documents show that the Pope indicated that after a German coup he would be willing to act as a mediator between the warring parties and send a special envoy to Berlin; an act which would show the world that a new start had come to Germany.[28] So keen was the Pope to assume the historic role of the Vatican as mediator that he was not prepared to compromise it by openly denouncing the horrendous persecution of the Jews.

As Kessel, the German diplomat assisting Weiszäcker in the embassy to the Holy See noted, this fear of burning bridges with the Nazi leadership and therefore losing the chance to broker a peace caused Pius XII daily anguish over the fate of the Jews. The reproaches of Edith Stein, the Jewish convert who became a Carmelite nun, whose letter imploring him to take up the cause of Jewry remains to this day the most eloquent testimony to the challenges facing the Pope's moral leadership, did not go unread. But the Pope was convinced that his public intervention would not save a single Jewish life and that everything had to be sacrificed, in his view, to the greater cause of ending the war and with it the conditions which made the factory slaughter of the innocents possible. His thinly veiled reference to the plight of the Jews in his Christmas speech of 1942 had incensed both Hitler and Mussolini. 'The Vicar of God ... ought never to open his mouth,' Mussolini threatened.[29] Hitler, as we shall see, considered more severe measures against the Pope.

As one who saw the Pope daily at that time commented, Pius XII struggled 'day by day, week by week and month by month' to come up with a solution that could help the Jews, while not compromising the chances of peace.[30] This struggle did not prevent the Pope personally intervening to save most of Rome's Jews when the Germans arrived in September 1943 following the Italian armistice.

On the eve of the Germans taking over Rome after the Italians sued for peace in September, Weiszäcker and the Pope worked into the small hours to get Rome's Jewish population into safe houses inside the Vatican or religious houses outside the perimeter which enjoyed extra-territorial status. While the Pope ordered his religious to open their doors, Weiszäcker travelled along the Vatican's perimeter ensuring every German officer he encountered knew that they must 'as a direct order of the Führer' respect the Vatican's sovereign and neutral status. Thanks to their efforts, 7,000 Roman Jews out of a total population – according to SS figures – of just over 8,000 were saved. The respecting of the Vatican's extra-territorial status also allowed the 'enemy's' diplomats, including Osborne, to continue to work largely uninterrupted – a privilege his opposite number Weiszäcker would not be afforded when the Americans arrived under General Clarke a few months later.

The Pope's role was fraught with danger and the risks run are illuminated by General Karl Wolff who, as commander of all SS troops in Italy, was ordered on 15 September to abduct the Pope to Hitler's field headquarters in Rastenberg. Already on 26 July Goebbels had recorded Hitler's desire to seize the Pope.[31]

Hewel's minutes of his conversation with Hitler noted the following sinister exchange:

> Hewel: 'Should we say the Vatican and its exits will be occupied?'
>
> Hitler: 'That doesn't make any difference. Do you think the Vatican embarrasses me? We'll take that over right away. For one thing the entire diplomatic corps are in there. It's all the same to me. That rabble are in there. We'll get that bunch of swine out of there ... Later we can make apologies.' [32]

Two thousand SS troops surrounded the Vatican and systematically blocked all the roads and several underground tunnels linking the miniature state and the Italian capital.[33] Hitler had shown himself perfectly capable of imprisoning statesmen and holding them as hostages. King Leopold, Marshal Pétain, Schuschnigg and Admiral Horthy were all eloquent testimony to this gruesome pastime of the Führer's.

All that saved the Pope was the belief held by many senior Germans, including Canaris, even Himmler and perhaps eventually Hitler himself, that an unseized Pope could be useful in a negotiated peace. But this protection, as has been pointed out, was 'flimsy'.[34] Wolff took his time, gradually the idea faded away. The Pope was on probation, but as Chadwick points out at any moment he could have been seized. Indeed, it is not beyond probability that part of Pius XII's sensitive and highly intelligent nature may have wished at times for such a fate to liberate him from the appalling choices he now faced.

But if the Germans hoped the Pope could play a role it seemed more and more unlikely as 1943 slipped away. After the strange and still puzzling lull before launching Operation Citadel, during which the Germans had tried to come to an understanding with Stalin, they renewed their offensive against the Russians in July. The threat of a separate German–Russian peace was now slipping away with Manstein's offensive. Mirroring its ebb were also the chances of an Anglo–German understanding. If the Soviet Union no longer felt the need to do a deal with Berlin, London need not become too involved in talking to the opposition. Germany was doomed.

The talks in Istanbul failed to progress. Von Papen was not made foreign minister, though he continued to hold talks with representatives of the Americans throughout the rest of the year and well into 1944.

The impetus was gradually but perceptibly lost. London and Moscow had already come to a broad understanding about the future of post-war Europe as early as 1941, and it was to be constructed on the wreck of a destroyed Germany.

Mr Berle of the State Department had asked Mr Stevenson of the Foreign Office whether proposed arrangements for the reconstitution of Poland, Czechoslovakia and Yugoslavia under 'some kind of federated system but in close relation with Russia did not really mean – to the Russians at least – that they were to dominate that entire area.'

Stevenson gave the candid reply: 'Speaking frankly, the British government had to give a half-promise to that effect. At all events they had permitted the Russians to believe that the British would be favourable.' Mr Berle drily observed: 'This would necessarily bring the Russian system considerably west of Vienna.' [35]

As Canaris had foreseen, *expiation* was Germany's unavoidable destiny.

CHAPTER FOURTEEN

THE END OF THE ABWEHR

It was his particular personal tragedy that Admiral
Canaris with all the knowledge that was at his disposal
was able perhaps before any one else to recognise the
fateful approach of an inexorable doom.

PAUL LEVERKUEHN [1]

While the Abwehr ran with whatever possibilities there were in Istanbul, the Vatican, Scandinavia and Switzerland, it became clear as the autumn of 1943 approached that *pace* Casablanca, whatever obstacles were mounting against an understanding with Germany, conditions were beginning to be negotiated for Italy to cease hostilities.

Inevitably, once again, the Vatican was involved. Osborne, the British minister who had gone on 'leave' and returned to London on 8 April, was to spend nearly three months in intense activity in King Charles Street. Osborne, like most intelligent diplomats of his vintage, found the doctrine of unconditional surrender inimical to the traditions of European diplomacy. His summons to London occurred as the German contacts with the Americans in Istanbul were beginning to yield some movement and the ill-fated bomb intended to kill Hitler was to be placed in the cognac bottles of Smolensk.[2]

In London, Osborne received new instructions, however, on several

274

fronts and on his return to Rome immediately began exploring the possibility of an Italian surrender. By 28 June, Osborne supplied a formal document in English, which compromised the unconditional surrender declaration by stating that it did 'not portend any ill-treatment of the Italian people after surrender or any ill-will towards a future non-Fascist government and state.'[3]

This was an important qualification. In fact it was a notable concession. The reader can probably by now imagine the effect a similar 'easement' might have had on Canaris and the German conspirators. Unfortunately for them, and some would say for many others, no such mercy was to be granted.

The pressure on the Abwehr and Canaris was now being applied from all sides. The Allies who, after the summer, seemed to back-pedal on chances of an agreement; the SD ever- anxious to encroach on the Abwehr's activities; and, most ominously of all, the Gestapo, who were beginning to uncover evidence of Canaris' links with the Allies through the Vatican. In April 1943, the Gestapo searched the anti-Nazi lawyer Dohnanyi's office at Abwehr headquarters. Colonel Oster, the head of section Z, was removed from his position and Dohnanyi was arrested together with the pastor Dietrich Bonhoeffer, who had been exempted from military service by the Abwehr on account of his valuable foreign contacts which included the Bishop of Chichester, whom he had met in Stockholm.[4]

Kaltenbrunner, the Gestapo chief, began to interrogate Canaris, especially about his contacts with Rome and his links with the Hungarian secret service, several of whom were in close contact with London.[5]

The Hungarian intelligence community, then as now, was philo-British. Indeed, the intelligence and diplomatic officers among the Hungarians were so close to the British that they actually signed articles of surrender on board Sir Hugh Knatchbull-Hugessen's yacht off Istanbul in October 1943, eighteen months before surrender was actually possible.[6]

As the Italian forces reeled under the invasion of Sicily in early July, the pressure on Mussolini grew. Canaris, by this time, according to contemporary accounts, was becoming more and more disillusioned and nervous. His confidence was visibly declining and his apparent failure to predict the timing of the Sicily landings again gave fuel to his enemies.

The success of those landings has been attributed to the brilliant deception operation involving 'Major Martin'. The ingenious Operation Mincemeat, described so vividly by Ewen Montague in his book *The Man Who Never Was*, remains a tour-de-force of imaginative deception. What is less widely known is that the British knew that by dumping the body, with its staff plans of invasion off the coast of the Iberian peninsula, it would inevitably reach Canaris for assessment. The Iberian peninsula had become Canaris' fiefdom. If he suspected the 'plant', SIS had good reason to imagine he just might not pass his suspicions on.[7] The 'ally' of the British, now so keen to bring the war to an end, was acting almost as effectively on London's behalf as if he were to all intents and purposes an 'agent' of the British.

Canaris knew from his contacts with the Vatican that Italy was about to defect to the Allied side. When Mussolini was arrested on 25 July, it was a delicate matter for Hitler to decide whether to believe Marshal Badoglio's and King Vittorio Emanuel's professions of loyalty, or suspect treachery. His Austrian instincts, of course, which saw Italians as untrustworthy at all times of chaos made him suspicious. He began to contemplate not only rescuing the recently imprisoned Mussolini but also kidnapping the King and Pope.

The admiral travelled to Venice early in August, officially on a fact-finding mission but, according to Lahousen, in reality to warn his Italian counterpart, Cesare Amé, of his fears of a German occupation and Hitler's intentions towards the Pope. At a large, formal breakfast in the Hotel Danieli attended by Amé and his staff, Canaris, flanked by Lahousen and Freytag-Loringhoven, discussed Italo–German relations at length. He then took Amé by the arm and the two men went to the Lido where they walked together for an hour, Canaris warning Amé of the kidnapping plans.

According to Amé's later testimony, Canaris insisted that Italy was so fortunate to have got rid of her dictator and that now it would be only a question of time before Germany was similarly 'liberated'. As the general recalled: 'He told me to watch the northern frontier of Italy and avoid allowing German troops transit rights.' [8]

Amé's rapport with Canaris was enriched by a present he had prepared for the admiral: 'I told him that we had researched his family tree and that we had proved that his forefathers had been Italians in Lombardy. He seemed moved to tears when I told him this.' [9]

Back at the Danieli the formal party broke up with loud declarations of undying fealty from the Italians. In a long speech, which Canaris heard out with 'great seriousness', Amé assured Canaris that Italy held its 'brotherhood of arms' with Germany as a 'sacred duty'. Canaris duly instructed a member of his staff to take down a note of the proceedings and a memorandum was drawn up emphasising Italy's determination to remain allied to Germany.

Such a move was, of course, unequivocal treason. Amé recalled, 'He loved Germany deeply and seemed convinced after the events of 1943 and his failure to get the Allies to negotiate a peace that every event that could hasten the downfall of the Nazi regime would be of benefit to his country in tending to avoid a total catastrophe.' [10]

Canaris had now stepped irrevocably beyond the frontiers of seeking an understanding with the enemy to actively helping him. The regime had to be undermined as rapidly as possible. Returning to Zossen, he regaled Kaltenbrunner with stories of Amé's undying loyalty to Germany. Unfortunately Schellenberg had an agent who was well placed with regard to Amé's servants and he began to piece together the truth of the Venice conference. Perhaps Canaris was losing his touch. Perhaps he did not care. But it is hard to imagine him normally taking such risks even two months earlier.

However, when Schellenberg presented the dossier to Himmler, the Reichsführer told him to drop his investigations and leave 'the old man in peace'." By this time of course, Himmler too was searching for some way out of the war and needed Canaris' contacts with the West.

In any event, Italy's intentions were to be betrayed by the West. Careless talk by Roosevelt on the scrambler to Churchill about 'arming our prisoners' was intercepted by the Abwehr station in Pas de Calais and as the SD had a man standing behind the Abwehr officer taking down the intercept word for word, the intelligence reached the correct destination with unerring accuracy.

This telephone conversation was beamed by wireless and therefore vulnerable to a variable unscrambling instrument which could be quickly attuned to the same frequency as the PE sets. The presence of an SD official shows how increasingly fragile confidence in the Abwehr was becoming as the failure to negotiate a settlement with the West became more and more apparent.

From this one intercept, it was clear that Italy was about to change sides. Within forty-eight hours the Germans moved divisions rapidly into the peninsula and Operation Alarich proceeded with alarming smoothness to break any optimistic expectations that with Italy knocked out of the war peace might be imminent.

Meanwhile, SIS and Menzies had by September apparently, if not abandoned the lines of communication with 'the enemy', reduced their contacts to the cause of achieving the logical and straightforward war aim of disrupting the Abwehr as decisively as possible in the run up to the Allied invasion of mainland Europe. By this time, the target was indeed a vulnerable one.

In war, the major shifting tide of the conflict has perhaps a more decisive effect on an intelligence organisation than any of the other forces committed. As the fact that Germany could not win the war became daily clearer, the effects were everywhere apparent. Agents recruited from neutral states inevitably began drifting away. Sources once enthusiastic became wary and taciturn. The Abwehr lost its best agents as the protection bought by fear of a German victory was replaced by the expectation of a German defeat.

An opportunity for SIS to disrupt the service spectacularly soon presented itself in Istanbul. This dazzling coup was, however, to be played out largely with both sides engaged superficially at least with the best of intentions.

Early in the summer of 1943, Adam von Trott had asked Leverkuen to help a friend, and opponent of the regime, Erich Vermehren, get a posting in Istanbul. Vermehren was a young lawyer with an impeccable anti-Nazi background who had been prevented from taking up his Rhodes scholarship to Oxford on account of his failure to embrace the Nazi youth movement while at school and his trenchant anti-Hitler views.

He was married to one of the most remarkable and courageous women of his day. Countess Elizabeth Plettenberg was a devout Catholic who had risked imprisonment countless times distributing anti-Nazi leaflets through the Catholic Church and disseminating the banned encyclical of Pius XI 'mit Brennenden Sorge', with its criticism of the pagan Nazis, through the Catholic underground during the years before the war. Vermehren's family was linked by a cousinhood of anti-Nazi lawyers and journalists to many influential figures in the opposition. He was also, through his marriage, a convert to the Catholic faith, therefore linked to the Catholic underground, which was beginning to attract the attention of SIS. He was, moreover, through his marriage to a Plettenberg, a cousin of von Papen's. Already, in 1943, Vermehren had made an attempt to defect to the British in Lisbon.

After a brief course on secret inks and codes at the Abwehr training school, his arrival in Istanbul had been duly noted by SIS's Section V (Counter-Espionage) representative in Istanbul, Nicholas Elliott. Section V had in fact built up quite a file on Vermehren since his first approaches in Lisbon. Indeed the XX Committee had hoped to exploit him as a double agent.[12]

Vermehren's wife had been forbidden to leave Germany by the Gestapo and for several months Vermehren pursued his duties alone. These were very modest and consisted of occasional evaluation reports on British shipping movements in the near East. Later, British propaganda would play his role up but he was barely more than a glorified secretary. He was consumed only by the thought of saving his wife from the Gestapo and their both escaping somehow to the West. In December 1943, Vermehren renewed his contact with the British; contacting an officer by name of Cribb, 'a dead ringer for Colonel Blimp'.[13]

Cribb, under his bluster, carried out the standard procedure for such cases: 'Ah, you, er, want to defect do you? Well why don't we meet in the Parc Hotel for a drink?' Vermehren thought he was mad suggesting a location swarming with SD agents. The Parc Hotel was a well known haunt of almost every spy in town and was consequently closely monitored by Vermehren's 'colleagues'. In fact, Cribb was only following official guidance in testing Vermehren. After Vermehren had told Cribb that he should choose somewhere else, Cribb came back to him with another address, a much more discreet one, which he said was his flat in Pera.

On the appointed evening, Vermehren turned up, to be greeted by Cribb. But after a few moments of questioning, a concealed door opened to reveal a smiling Nicholas Elliot who said, again in strict accordance with procedure to show that he knew with whom he was dealing, 'Erich Vermehren? You were coming up to Oxford I believe?'

At that moment, as Vermehren later recalled, 'I had a sense of tremendous relief. I felt almost as if my feet rested already on English soil.'

Vermehren broke his plan for escape to his wife in late December 1943 and then in the greatest of secrecy, with help in the foreign ministry, secured papers with the assistance of his friend, Adam von Trott, allowing his wife to join him in Istanbul. No one in Istanbul had the faintest idea that, after a short leave in Germany, Vermehren would return with his wife, as it was widely known she was on the Gestapo black list.

It is not the least remarkable event of this escape that the train which took the Vermehrens to Istanbul contained several SD officers, one of whom was in the neighbouring sleeping compartment. This figure maintained his reserve for the first part of the journey. However, when the train reached the Bulgarian frontier, Vermehren's wife was taken off and told her papers were not in order and that she should report to the German embassy in Sofia. Again, friends in the German diplomatic corps helped her avoid the Gestapo and, within a few days, she could join her husband in Turkey thanks to the twice weekly diplomatic courier flight from Berlin to Istanbul which touched down in Sofia.[14]

Within weeks Elliott had, with London's permission, arranged the Vermehrens' defection. It is not clear that London imagined the defection would have quite the spectacular impact it did but it was a vital priority at that time to disrupt the enemy's intelligence machine in the run-up to D-Day. SIS, Philby included, was playing a major role in operations which had the specific aim of disrupting 'the fundamental reasoning power of the German supreme command.'

In the event, the Vermehrens' defection gave the SD the ammunition it needed to finally liquidate its rival the Abwehr. Himmler, Bormann and many others played on Hitler's frayed temper and the scene was set for the personal exchange that would seal the Abwehr's fate. As news of the Vermehren's defection was played up by the Allies, who falsely claimed, not only that Vermehren was the lynchpin of the Abwehr in Istanbul, but also that he had brought code-books with him, Hitler's fury knew no bounds. He summoned Canaris to his final meeting with him. Hitler's anger was no doubt also fuelled by the fact that part of him appeared still to have entertained the thought of some possible deal through von Papen and the Abwehr with the West. If this indeed was the case, the Vermehrens' defection illuminated more vividly than a flash of lightning on a dark night that the Abwehr was no longer thinking of the chance of any rapprochement and that on the contrary the crew was abandoning ship.

According to one account of this meeting, Hitler accused Canaris of his service disintegrating. Canaris calmly replied that it was 'hardly surprising given that Germany was losing the war.' [15] This was not what Hitler had wanted to hear. Dismissing the admiral, he resolved to subordinate the Abwehr to Himmler.

Barely two weeks later, on 18 February, he issued a decree setting up Heydrich's old dream of a unified German intelligence service under Himmler and Kaltenbrunner's control. The ghost of Heydrich, who two years earlier had struggled in vain to achieve such an end, might have been present that day.

But it was too late. Canaris was neither arrested nor accused of treason. He was simply retired. With his mothballing, however, the service he had built up with such determination over nine years quite literally fell to bits. Hundreds of officers who knew every inch of their territory and sections applied for active postings, even to the Eastern Front. On the Western Front, the experience of Herman Giskes, the Abwehr counter-intelligence chief, who had trapped so many of the SOE agents in Holland with Philby's help, was typical. Giskes resigned rather than take orders from the Himmler, Kaltenbrunner, Schellenberg trio.

As Gilles Perrault has written, 'Giskes' work and outlook were unmistakeably formed by the personality of Canaris who was to his men an example, a chief and a symbol. Even if the admiral sometimes exasperated them by his excessive scruples, they knew it was him they had to thank for being able to keep their hands clean from the mire and blood in which Germany was foundering.' [16]

Schellenberg was intelligent enough to realise that with Canaris' dismissal, he was taking over a ship whose crew had either deserted or were no longer capable of serving effectively. SD officers with the haziest notions of military intelligence procedures and techniques took over positions where networks of agents, painstakingly built up over years, were 'burnt' in weeks. As the intelligence war reached its climax ahead of the Normandy landings, the Abwehr was literally *hors de combat*.

Canaris was banished to Lauenstein castle for four months but at the end of June he was given what Trevor-Roper called an 'acceptable sinecure' as chief of the Special Office for Economic Warfare, at Eiche near Potsdam. He was a shell of his former self. The years of tension and perpetual movement had sapped his physical strength, while the double game he had played with Hitler had dissipated large parts of his mental energy.

However, shortly before the Allies landed in Western Europe, he made one last recorded attempt to use his contact with Menzies to bring about some compromise agreement. According to one source in US intelligence, Canaris was the source of much detailed information on the German order of battle ahead of D-Day.[17] If this was the case, once again Canaris was reacting like a British agent under enemy control. His journey from mere 'ally' to enemy 'asset' was to all practical intent over. 659 was now hindering the German war effort in every way possible in spite of the casualties it might inflict on his own servicemen.

In May 1944, he visited Paris, where, if some sources are to be believed, he asked a young SIS agent by name of Keun to deliver a message to Menzies.[18] In reply, he received a letter from Menzies shortly afterwards, delivered to him at an SIS station housed in the Lazarite convent on the Rue de la Santé. Though the risks of such a meeting-place were obvious to all parties, both the mother superior and several other eyewitnesses confirm Canaris' presence.

The letter's contents remained secret but the courier who delivered it noted that when Canaris had finished reading Menzies' letter, he turned 'white and gave a little gasp. "This is the finish for Germany ..."' Canaris put the letter in one of his inside pockets and the two men sat for a short while without saying a word until Canaris repeated: 'Finis Germaniae'.[19]

Canaris' visit to Paris may have been prompted by his being aware of the conspiracy that was now forming around the young Catholic idealist Claus von Stauffenberg. He was sceptical of it bringing any results. Expiation was running its course. It was too late now, after the lost opportunities of 1943, to produce positive results from Hitler's overthrow. Alone in his villa (he had evacuated his family to Bavaria), Canaris studied Russian with a Baltic friend, Baron Kaulbars. But as the events of 20 July soon showed, he was by no means out of the loop.

On 20 July Stauffenberg, carrying a time bomb made once again of British components, went to Hitler's headquarters at Rastenburg in East Prussia. This time the conspirators' bomb went off. Had the meeting not been transferred at the last minute from its original underground location to an outside hut, it would certainly have killed Hitler wherever it had been placed. But the flimsy walls above ground were blown out by the blast and Hitler escaped.

Stauffenberg, after flying to Berlin, rang Canaris, who recognised Stauffenberg's voice. On hearing that 'the Führer was dead', Canaris replied in the best tradition of the spy chief avoiding a compromising call on an intercepted line: 'Dead? Mein Gott! Who did it? The Russians?' [20]

A few hours later the phone rang again, this time carrying the news that the conspiracy had failed. Canaris immediately went to his office and dictated a congratulatory telegram from his office and staff to 'his beloved Führer'. It fooled no one, but it showed that Canaris was on his mettle, stimulated by the danger and ready for the battle of wits which was about to begin.

Three days later a black Mercedes with SS markings drew up outside Canaris' house. Schellenberg stepped out of the car with a warrant for the admiral's arrest.

'I thought it might be you,' Canaris laconically observed.

As Canaris accompanied Schellenberg to the car he took his arm and said 'Promise me just one thing. That you will arrange in three days for me to have a personal interview with Himmler.' Canaris knew full well that only Himmler's ambition to replace Hitler and seek contacts with the West stood between him and a firing squad.

Schellenberg drove Canaris to Fürstenberg after offering the admiral a chance to escape. But the admiral said he was 'sure of his own case' and would rely on Schellenberg's promise to arrange a meeting with Himmler.

At Fürstenberg prison Canaris found himself with dozens of generals and senior officers implicated in the plot. Many of these would be executed in the coming days, but Canaris bore a charmed life. There is no record of his meeting with Himmler, but Schellenberg makes the convincing point that the meeting must have taken place otherwise Canaris would certainly have been executed long before he met his fate.[21]

As Himmler well knew, the foreign contacts which Canaris possessed were clues to how he and Schellenberg and even Kaltenbrunner might survive. Throughout the late summer and autumn, Himmler worked on peace overtures, again contacting Dulles in Berne. The British, sensing the wedge to be exploited between Himmler and Hitler, reacted with characteristic imagination and ruthlessness. RAF planes dropped blocks of Deutsches Reich stamps with a portrait of Himmler rather than Hitler onto the bemused Austrian peasants beyond Bad Ischl and other parts of the German Reich.[22]

Undaunted, Himmler even persuaded the imprisoned Goerdeler to get in touch with the Zionist leader Weizmann to put proposals from Hitler to Churchill. These involved resurrecting the old terms brought by Hess for an Anglo–German alliance against the Soviet Union. As a sign of good faith, Himmler in the *ratissage* following the 20 July plot, rounded up and shot 'all those Germans who were attempting to reach a settlement with Russia.'[23]

As a colleague of Canaris' noted: 'I am convinced that Himmler kept Canaris alive because he had avenues of communication with the British which Himmler himself coveted.'[24] Himmler's peace overtures were directed mostly towards London.[25]

The 'value' Himmler placed on Canaris even survived the devastating discovery of extracts of his diaries, secreted in a metal box in the cellar at Zossen. The metal box had belonged to Colonel Schrader, a close confidant of Canaris', who had committed suicide in the hours after the failed 20 July putsch.

With the diaries were Hitler's medical records, including a negative assessment of his mental health by a doctor who had examined him after his gassing in the First War. More damaging were reports on German atrocities compiled by Dohnanyi and other members of the Abwehr; reports on Bonhoeffer's conversations in Sweden and Switzerland with British agents and reports on the conversations with the British through the Vatican.

Walther Huppenkothen, the Gestapo commisioner, needed three weeks to sift through the material, sending a copy to Hitler and 'through Martin Bormann to Himmler'.[26] Hitler ordered the discovery of the documents to be kept secret, reserving, as Huppenkothen noted, 'the right to decide what the sequel to this affair would be.' Here was enough evidence to 'hang the lot of them' but Hitler, now acquainted with the full extent of the treason against him, wanted more details and the interrogators were set to work.

Canaris, along with Oster, Mueller and countless other former members of the military *'Prominenz'* were kept in the Gestapo headquarters in the Prinz Albrechtstrasse. Discipline was not so strict as to prevent all human contact, though the prisoners were manacled and Canaris, along with his fellow inmates, was forced to scrub the floors like a sailor on the deck of a ship, much to the amusement of his SS jailers.

But Canaris appears to have been resigned to his fate. No doubt supported by his Christian outlook, he almost seemed to relish 'notching up another cross' of ill-treatment. He played a relentless war of wits with his interrogators, who did not resort to torture, and fenced brilliantly with them, exposing all their intellectual weaknesses.

He also developed an amusing technique of prising information from the guards by asking supposedly foolish questions such as 'I suppose we have pushed the Russians back over the Vistula?' These were invariably answered with a realistic assessment of where the Russian army was at this stage. The ease with which he affected stupidity (always a useful weapon in a spy chief's armoury) astounded those who knew him. He could mislead the interrogators with secondary plots, camouflage the truth and apologetically offer the occasional half-admission of some totally irrelevant fault in order to throw his interrogators off the scent.

In this way he kept secret the names of many who would otherwise have ended up in prison with him, notably Lahousen and Leverkuen, to name but two. Other prisoners did not possess the same moral, intellectual and nervous resources. Oster was confounded by irrefutable evidence. Others were broken by physical torture.

1945 saw little respite in the interrogations despite the approaching armies. Events took a more ominous turn in February. By now, Hitler, already aware that Himmler might be planning to use the surviving conspirators to help broker a peace, decided there was little point in pursuing such option and began burning Himmler's bridges. On 2 February, Goerdeler was hanged in Berlin. The same day the People's Court passed the death sentence on Klaus Bonhoeffer, brother of Dietrich Bonhoeffer, and Hans John, the brother of Otto John. The day after, there was a colossal air raid on Berlin, the most formidable of the war to date: the People's Court was in ruins and the Gestapo prison badly damaged. The decision was taken to evacuate the prisoners to Buchenwald and Flossenberg in the Palatinate.

There Canaris was put into cell 22. In cell 21 was Captain Lunding, Canaris' former opposite number in Denmark, as head of intelligence. Lunding later recalled that though the admiral, whom he recognised at once, was pale, his bearing was still soldierly, though he wore only a grey suit and fur-lined overcoat. The two spy chiefs rapidly communicated with each other using an alphabetical code, which produced the following pattern:

	1	2	3	4	5
1	A	F	L	Q	V
2	B	G	M	R	W
3	C	H	N	S	X
4	D	I	O	T	Y
5	E	K	P	U	Z

The first tap in each call indicated the group, the second gave the letter of the alphabet. Lunding conversed regularly with Canaris and had the distinct impression that the admiral still believed he might be saved. There was still no conclusive evidence.

On 17 March, Kaltenbrunner himself came to interrogate the admiral. The Austrian, whose hands always reminded Canaris of some medieval murderer's, conversed for several hours with Canaris in the courtyard of the prison. No details exist of the conversation. Kaltenbrunner, who must have realised he had no future as the Allied armies approached, would at this stage of the war have sought some information which could save his neck. If he wanted Canaris to give him a name or a contact on the British side who might help him, the admiral was unmoved. After Kaltenbrunner's departure, the interrogators began more physical forms of interrogation.[27]

On 1 and 2 April, Lunding received messages about these from the admiral though Canaris appeared not to complain. Three days later, Hitler was shown another discovery from a safe in Zossen: the complete five volumes of Canaris' diaries. These listed in detail all of Canaris' contacts with the British and his consistent attempts since 1938 to come to an understanding with London.

Here was the evidence, if Hitler had ever needed it, of the 'great conspiracy' to which he could ascribe the destruction of the Third Reich. Kaltenbrunner was ordered to 'proceed with the immediate liquidation' of the conspirators.[28]

Forty-eight hours later Huppenkothen arrived to order a summary trial. With SS Judge Thorbeck presiding, the accused, including Canaris, were led into the 'court', and after reading the accusations and hearing Canaris' simple plea of 'Not Guilty', sentence of death by hanging was passed. There was no defence lawyer present and no examination of the evidence. One final interrogation took place. After which, Lunding received the message from the next door cell: 'That will have been the last ... I think ... Badly treated ... Nose broken.'

Then Lunding received the last message:

'I die for my Fatherland. I have a clean conscience. I only did my duty for my country when I tried to oppose the criminal folly of Hitler leading Germany to destruction. Look after my wife and daughters.' [29] *

At dawn the following day Canaris, Oster, Karl Bonhoeffer and several others were led out and hanged. At a trial after the war of one of the SS executioners at Flossenberg, it emerged that the SS had kept Canaris until the end and then hanged him 'twice', the first time just sufficiently to give 'him a taste of death'.[30]

Josef Mueller, Canaris' Vatican emissary, sat in his cell awaiting his turn, but all that happened was that his cell began to fill with the burnt fragments of the bodies executed that day. The ashes of the corpses being burnt in the nearby yard floated relentlessly through the bars of his cell, settling down all round him.

That evening the rumble of artillery could be heard. In less than ten days the camp would be liberated, but perhaps inevitably, those who had

---

*After the war, two Spanish diplomats would escort Canaris' widow and daughters to Switzerland and from there to a new life in Spain as the guests of General Franco. They swore never to talk about the admiral or the Abwehr during their lifetime.

striven for an understanding with the Allies would now at the moment of their victory be consumed. On 16 April Ewald von Kleist, whose letter from Churchill had been discovered by the Gestapo in his desk, was hanged in Berlin. Even the modest Elser, the clock-maker, who had tried to kill Hitler in the Brauhaus, was executed at this time. The loose ends of the British–German intelligence connection were rapidly being dispatched. Somehow Mueller survived, but his links had principally been with the Vatican.

The Russians arrested Canaris' secretary, Fraulein Schwarte, and plied her with questions about Canaris' missing diary. Schrader's widow, who had been entrusted with a copy of it, said she had burned it on the Lüneburg Heath after the events of 20 July. The diary was the admiral's legacy and would have revealed many details of his attempts to secure an understanding. Many of them would no doubt have embarrassed the victors as much as it would have shocked the vanquished.

According to Colvin, a British naval intelligence officer after the war alluded to the diary [31] being in a Foreign Office file. Other rumours soon spread to suggest it had been spirited away to the Kremlin or Washington, a powerful weapon to be used against the British in those early days of her post-imperial existence.

In any event, no diary was needed to testify that the admiral hanged that spring morning under the harsh lights of arc lamps had, as much as any other German, helped to destroy Nazi Germany and the pagan system it stood for. Alone of the conspirators, Canaris had built the means to take Germany out of the war, had London wanted an accommodation. That no such accommodation occurred cannot be held against the admiral's record.

CONCLUSION

*It is the duty of every sophisticated Intelligence
service to keep open a channel of communication
with the enemy's Intelligence service.*

REINHARD GEHLEN [1]

The enigmatic admiral, whose behaviour puzzled so many both during
and after the war, was in fact remarkably consistent. Though an early
convert to National Socialism as a means of restoring Germany's position
in the world, he was, if not instantly, fairly swiftly disillusioned with it.
He was, like Beck and so many of the other German officers, always to
suffer from the internal contradiction of his military oath, sworn in God's
name, and his opposition to the regime. His loyalty, however, was always
to a higher Germany that could take its place in the ranks of civilised
nations.

Such a Germany was identified even during the war by many eminent
Britons. Keynes, to name but one, recognised in his speech in Cambridge,
at the beginning of the war, to émigré scientists and academics that there
were 'now two Germanies'.

Keynes' subtle intelligence noted: 'This is a war not between nation-
alities and imperialism but between two opposed ways of life and over
what we are to mean by civilisation. Our object in this mad unavoidable

291

struggle is not to conquer Germany but to convert her, to bring her back within the historic fold of Western civilisation of which the institutional foundations are ... the Christian Ethic, the Scientific Spirit and the Rule of Law. It is only on these foundations that the personal life can be led.' [2]

Crucial to the destruction of one Germany – pagan, criminal and vandalistic – and the survival of the other – humanist, Judeo-Christian and civilised – was an 'understanding' with Britain. For this Canaris strove relentlessly in peace and war, taking almost daily tremendous risks. It should not be forgotten, however, that as such an 'understanding' was also high in his master, Hitler's, agenda, he was able to weave his complicated course partly by exploiting that factor. As the leader of the postwar German Federal intelligence service, Reinhard Gehlen, noted, every intelligence service worthy of its salt keeps a channel of communication with the enemy open. In this way the British came to realise that they had in Canaris an 'ally' who embodied the qualities of those members of the elite of German society who desired an understanding with London.

These circumstances gave Canaris a protection denied to modern spy chiefs in today's democracies. It enabled him time and again to allow his conscience rather than political expediency to dictate the agenda. When the officials of the foreign ministry demanded that the Abwehr 'sex up', to use the modern expression, their dossier that would prove beyond any doubt that Belgium and Holland had violated their neutrality and that therefore an invasion was 'justified', Canaris sent them packing. They could not apply the modern weapons of 'an undistinguished conclusion to a distinguished career' or public official disapproval implied by the withholding of some bauble or honour. The concept of the spy chief as an obedient bureaucrat dangling on the end of his political master's string was not generally accepted in those days. It was neither as deeply developed in Nazi Germany as one might have thought or as it was to become in most other countries fifty years later. When ordered to murder Churchill or the French general Giraud, Canaris was able to ensure such offences against the basic ethics of war were frustrated. Political assassination was both in theory and in practice a war crime as far as the Abwehr was concerned and unacceptable to its chief.

That he was able to do this was the consequence of his having built up the Abwehr into an organisation of officers who largely shared his values and outlook and for whom the sharp practice of the Gestapo and SD was compellingly abhorrent. It is one of the unfortunate, but perhaps inevitable, developments of modern times that increasingly, politicians from all parts of the spectrum appear to prefer the more pliant SD model to the more independently-minded Abwehr.

Yet the strength of the latter model is well described by Leverkuen, who noted of the Abwehr that it possessed a confidence that, 'in the ever-changing pattern of events, the right idea would "eventually strike them" ... '

'When a chief finds himself working with men of vision and imagination who are at the same time officers, men bred upon discipline and accustomed both to obey orders and to have their own orders implicitly obeyed, then there is welded a combination of personal and official relationships such as is to be found nowhere else.' [3]

It is not the least testament to the unique qualities of the Abwehr that so vivid a description of the creative energy in an intelligence organisation would be difficult to apply to the grey bureaucracies that embrace so much secret work today.

Canaris' hopes of an alliance with England against Soviet Communism, as we have seen, were not unrealistic. Right up to the end of the war, the Abwehr and British intelligence exchanged material on the Russian threat. The consistency with which distinguished public servants such as Roberts, Wheeler-Bennett and Makins reacted with such extreme and understandable hypersensitivity to peace-feelers emanating from Germany is testimony enough to the plausibility of such moves. Thanks to the incomparable Soviet section of the Abwehr, Canaris was fully aware of the degree of Soviet penetration of the British establishment. Nevertheless, in late 1942 he was prepared to take the risk of meeting his opposite number to discuss the possibility of a compromise peace. As the testimony and documents of the time fulsomely imply, such a peace was closer in 1943 than in 1940, not least because intelligence circles in America strongly supported it. The possibility of Hitler doing a deal with Stalin was Churchill's worst nightmare. That Churchill and Roosevelt might strike a deal with Hitler was Stalin's permanent neurosis and, as these pages show, with reason.

The sequel to the Vermehren's defection underlines vividly the extent to which Philby's activities were primarily directed against any under-standing between London and Berlin taking place.

Billeted in Philby's mother's flat, the Vermehrens furnished Philby with a list of important contacts in the Catholic underground in Germany. These names, which could have formed the backbone of a conservative Christian post-war German political leadership, were liquidated by Philby's colleagues in the KGB. When Allied intelligence officers tried to make contact with them after the war, they found most had disappeared or been murdered.

As Philby later recalled with some passion, and here even his distortions of the truth appear to have been put briefly aside: 'One of the reasons I acted as I did was because the total defeat of Germany was almost a personal matter for me. I had strong feelings about the war and I was directly responsible for the deaths of a considerable number of Germans.'[4]

It was to be Canaris' personal tragedy that these views eventually, after considerable and, still more than half a century beyond the event, secret debate, came to be shared by the war cabinet and Whitehall, for whom 'finishing the war had lower priority than crushing Germany.'[5]

As the influential official Wheeler-Bennett noted with some vitriol in 1943 as the possibilities of peace between Germany and the West were at their most intense: 'At the conclusion of the war we are not going to be liked by any Germans, "good" or "bad". We should not place ourselves in the position of bargaining with any Germans "good" or "bad". This is inherent in the principle of Unconditional Surrender.'[6]

However, even 'unconditional surrender' could, as the case of Italy showed, be conditional and as the intelligence agencies of the West began to get wind of a possible peace deal between Berlin and Moscow, the possibility of a peace with Germany arose for reasons of strategic expediency. The 'Most Secret' telegrams of the end of September 1942, which were reaching London from neutral countries, notably Portugal, clearly reveal the progress of these two separate discussions, mirroring each other with almost perfect symmetry between the autumn of 1942 until the summer of 1944. Most of the peace-feelers led directly or indirectly to Canaris.

It is clear that despite the hopes of stopping the bloodshed which filled the minds of so many, the Allied statesmen were driven primarily by the thought of how to secure a peace that might endure. The experience of the aftermath of the First World War highlighted the need to eliminate German militarism, even if it meant liquidating precisely those families whose scions had been Hitler's most bitter opponents. Moreover, strategic decisions also played their part.

Once Churchill's idea, bruited at Tehran, of an Allied landing in the Adriatic to bid for the Danube and move into central Europe had been rejected by Roosevelt as well as Stalin, it was inevitable that the Red Army would reach Eastern Europe first.

Informal British undertakings to the Soviet Union already in 1941 pointed towards a post-war 'solution' whereby the vacuum left by German influence in central Europe would be replaced by Soviet Russia. While fear of Moscow and the desire to rearm Germany eastwards had been the tacit foundations of Chamberlain's appeasement policy before the war and prevented a deal with the German opposition, now the need to keep Moscow in the war underpinned Churchill's rejection of any accord with the 'good Germans'. Paradoxically in both phases of Anglo-German relations, the Soviet Union was a key determining factor.

Above all, British geo-strategists saw the post-war partition of Germany as the best safeguard against the resurgence of a troubling giant that could again upset the balance of power in Europe. The story of Canaris high-lights more than any other the dazzling possibilities of the Anglo-German relationship and its practical limitations. Those who work to advance this relationship today should heed the lessons to be learnt here.

These calculations, which spelled the doom of Canaris' plans, were of course familiar to him. He knew all too well the thinking of Stalin and Churchill but he felt it his duty as a German and a European to take whatever steps he could to try to save his country from inevitable destruc-tion. He well knew, as his comments to his closest staff confirm, that Germany was facing a process of dissolution without parallel in modern history. As a patriot imbued with a strong moral sense he tried to spare Europe the tragedy of many avoidable months of war, with massive civilian and military casualties. His career nails once and for all the canard that the Germans were only interested in peace once they were losing the war. Long before objective observers could detect any weakening in Germany's military strength, Canaris was working for an understanding with England. Indeed, had his emissary Kleist been taken more seriously by the British government in 1938, there is at least a distinct possibility that the conflict which tore Europe apart might have been avoided altogether.

The failure of Canaris should not distract us from his achievements, which underline, at a time when we hear so much about the importance of team work, the great role the individual can still play in the realm of intelligence.

His intervention materially altered the course of the war. His support for Franco against Hilter at Hendaye was without doubt critical to shoring up Britain's entire position in the Mediterranean in the dark days of 1940. As Goering later ruefully noted to Kirkpatrick, it cost Germany the war.

His consistent and deliberate over-estimation of British forces available to repel invasion after Dunkirk was also a vital factor in the delay and cancellation of operation Sealion.

His commitment to defending certain standards of ethical behaviour permeated everything the Abwehr undertook. He may have occasionally overestimated the mental ability of some of his closest subordinates, but he had confidence in the integrity of those in whom he reposed trust, and here Canaris rarely, if ever, made a mistake. He was not in a position to influence the unique and terrible bestiality of the Holocaust but he did save many Jews from certain deportation to the camps.

The collapse of the Abwehr following Canaris' dismissal and its merger into the SD is a lesson to all intelligence services that if spying is conducted on the lowest ethical plane, the whole organisation quickly becomes contaminated, and both the intelligence officers and their political masters are doomed.

There are other lessons to be learnt from the tragedy of the German Abwehr. No one reading the story of the Abwehr's links with Britain can fail to be impressed by the sure touch of British policy. At every crisis Churchill displayed a firm grasp of the essentials in pursuing a policy which would equip his country with huge reserves of moral strength to play a leading role in Europe, transatlantic relations and the Commonwealth.

With the dismantling of the Berlin Wall in 1989 and the end of the formal post-war arrangements concerning Europe, the challenges Canaris faced may appear remote. But as more recent conflicts have shown, the values of Western civilisation that Canaris espoused remain by no means free from threat in the twenty-first century. The political pressures on the integrity of his service would be instantly recognisable by every modern spy chief whose activities, compared to those of Canaris, must seem at times highly circumscribed. True, they are unlikely to have to pay the high price Canaris paid for following the dictates of his conscience but, at the same time, it would be a rare member of that tiny breed who would not express some faint nod of admiration, if not envy, for the way the little admiral wove his independent path through the thorny maze of the most deadly crisis of modern times.

SOURCE NOTES

Introduction

1 Interview, Sir Stewart Menzies with Anthony Cave Brown, quoted in *The Secret Servant*, p. 6, London 1988

2 This account is taken from Soltikow's memoirs, *Ich war mitten drin*, Vienna 1980. Though a bluff aristocrat with a passion for ladies, Soltikow's account is remarkably dispassionate and convincing.

3 Soltikow, op. cit. p. 428–9

4 See Stafford, *Churchill and Secret Service*, London 1997

5 Soltikow, op. cit. p. 428

6 Cave Brown, op. cit. p. 8

7 Gehlen, *Der Dienst*, p. 119ff, Berg 1971

8 See Leon Papeleux, *Entre Hitler et Franco*, Paris 1977. Also Hans Stille, deposition in the IfZ Munich

9 Stafford, op. cit. p. 203

10 Allfrey, *Man of Arms: Life and Legend of Basil Zaharov*, London 1989

11 Stille, IfZ

12 Kirkpatrick, *The Inner Circle*, p. 195, London 1959

13 Popov, *Spy Counter Spy*, p. 62, London 1957

14 Padfield, *Hess* p. 297, London 1991

15 Cornhill Magazine, Vol XI, March 1950

16 Goebbels, *Diaries 1939-1941*, 21 March 1941, London 1982

17 Philby, quoted by Cave Brown in *Treason in the Blood*, p. 328, New York 1994

18 Author's interview with Vermehren, 12 April 2004

19 See Ingeborg Fleischhauer, *Die Chance des Sonderfriedens*, Siedler 1986; also Paul Leverkuen, *Die Abwehr*, Chapter 7, 1954

20 *Frankfurter Zeitung*, 28 March 1943, quoted by von Hassell in *Diaries*, p. 266, London 1948

21 Schmidt, *Statisten auf der Weltbuehne*, p. 9

22 Gehlen, op. cit. p. 56ff

23 Banfield private papers, Trieste

24 Banfield interview, 4 April 1982

25 See Erlam, *The German Navy*, London 1939

26 Banfield, *The Art of Naval Warfare*, m/s p. 1 Triest 1979

Chapter One

1 Geoffrey Bennett, *Coronel and the Falklands*, p. 177ff, London 1962

2 F.A.Z. Archive

3 Bennett, op. cit. p. 110

4 *Dresden* papers, unpublished, Chile

5 Bennett, op. cit. p. 155

6 op. cit. p. 150

7 op. cit. p. 151

8 Diaries of Captain J. D. Allen, unpublished

9 See MacCormack, *A Life of Ian Fleming*, London 1978

10 Stafford, op. cit. p. 80

11 See Paul von Lettow-Vorbeck, *Heia Safari*, 1921

12 Krause memoirs, unpublished, Chile

Chapter Two

1 Gerd Bucheit, *Der Deutsche Geheimdienst*, p. 17ff, Munich 1966

2 op. cit. p. 17

3 Asquith, *Letters to Venetia Stanley*, p. 26ff, Oxford 1982

4 Heinz Hoehne, *Patriot in Zwielicht*, p. 149, Munich 1976

5 Author interview with HIRM Empress Zita, August 1983
6 Hoehne, op. cit. p. 53
7 W. Gottlieb, *Studies in Secret Diplomacy in World War One*, London 1957
8 David Kelly, *The Ruling Few*, London 1952
9 Allfrey, op. cit. p. 39
10 op. cit. chapter 4
11 Richard Deacon, *A History of the British Secret Service*, p. 218ff, London 1969
12 PRO (FO 372/715 40624 62729)
13 PRO (FO 372/714/44763 50055)
14 ibid
15 FO 372/715/66312, n 129
16 FO 371/2468 80541
17 FO 371/72761 87167 n 141
18 FO 185/1237 749
19 Farago, *The Game of the Foxes*, p. 6, New York 1971; and André Brissaud, *Canaris*, p. 9, London 1973
20 Patrick Beesley, *Room 40*, p. 190, London 1982
21 op. cit. p. 20
22 Hoehne op. cit. p. 19

Chapter Three
1 Theodor Fontane: Unter ein Bildnis Adolf Menzels, Fontane, *Collected Works*, p. 103, Frankfurt 1978
2 Hoehne, op. cit. chapter 1
3 Peter von Gephardt, *Stammbaum der Familie Canaris*, privately printed, Berlin 1938 Canaris papers
4 K. H. Abshagen, *Canaris*, p. 33, Stuttgart 1948
5 See Morgenthau, *Secrets of the Bosporous* 1918
6 Wiedenfeld, *Die Bagdhadbahn*, p. 19 1911
7 P. Rohrbach in *Die Bagdhadbahn*, 1902
8 Gottlieb, op. cit. p. 24
9 Grey, *Twenty Five Years*, p. 20, 1923

Chapter Four
1 Lord Home, *Letters to a Grandson*, p. 18, London 1983
2 U 128 War Diary, 29 November 1918, BAA
3 Hoehne, op. cit. p. 60
4 Allfrey, op. cit. p. xvi
5 Störmer quoted Allfrey, op. cit. p. xvii
6 Hoehne, op. cit. p. 63ff
7 Abshagen, op. cit. pp. 51?7
8 Author interview with Inge Haag, 26 March 2004

9 Philip Noel-Baker, *The Private Manufacture of Armaments*, p. 379ff, London 1936
10 BA/MA OKM/20
11 Kelly, op. cit. chapter 3
12 PRO 5559 HE 396300

Chapter Five
1 Diaries of Captain Thomas Troubridge R.N. 1936-39, IWM
2 Hoehne, op. cit. pp. 137?9
3 Allfrey, op. cit. p. 252
4 Author interview with Inge Haag, 24 March 2004
5 ibid.
6 Hoehne, op. cit. p. 321
7 Troubridge, op. cit.
8 Deacon op. cit. chapter 22; see also Colvin, op. cit. p. 20ff
9 Hoffmann, unpublished diaries, Chile
10 Colvin, op. cit. p. 23
11 ibid.
12 ibid. p. 47ff
13 Colvin, op. cit. p. 26
14 ibid
15 Gerhard Henke, Bericht und Errinerungen eines Ic *Die Nachhut* 15 November 1967
16 Hoehne, op. cit. p. 205ff
17 Oscar Reile, *Geheime Westfront*, p. 47, Munich 1962
18 Leverkuen, op. cit. p. 200
19 Abshagen, op. cit. p. 109
20 See Reinhard Spitzy, *How we Squandered the Reich*, London 1995
21 See Willi Grosse, *Die Juden Stern*, private papers
22 von Hassell, *Diaries*, p. 26, London 1948
23 Lahousen, Allied interrogation KV 2 173, October 1945, IWT and PRO
24 Abshagen, op. cit. pp. 107?123
25 Lahousen, PRO KV 2 173
26 John Wheeler-Bennett, *The Nemesis of Power*, p. 333ff, London 1954

Chapter Six
1 Hilaire Belloc, 'The Salvation of Spain', in *Places*, London 1942
2 Brissaud, op. cit. p. 34

3 Dieckhoff, Series 3, volume 11, p. 9 AA Archives

4 Hoehne, op. cit. p. 223

5 See for example the latest writings of John Keegan

6 Faber du Faur, Series 3, volume 11, p. 11 AA Archives

7 Noel-Baker, op. cit. Craven to Spear, 14 March 1934

8 Hoehne, op. cit. p. 221

9 Colvin, op. cit. p. 35

10 Brissaud, op.cit. p. 43

11 ibid. p 38

12 Peter Kemp, *The Thorns of Memory*, p. 76

13 Brissaud, op. cit. p. 44ff

14 ibid. p. 100

15 Brian Crozier, *Franco*, p. 156, London 1967

16 Merkes, Series 3, volume 11, AA Archives

17 See Stille deposition IfZ

18 Brissaud, op. cit. p. 97

19 ibid. p. 98

20 Hoehne, op. cit. p. 231

21 Cave Brown, *Treason in the Blood*, p. 191ff, New York 1994

22 ibid. p. 189ff

23 Hossbach Memorandum, quoted Brissaud, op. cit. p. 91

Chapter Seven

1 PRO KV2/173

2 ibid. p. 182ff

3 Colvin, op. cit. p. 39

4 Wheeler-Bennett, op. cit. p. 179

5 Hoehne, op. cit. p. 234

6 ibid. p. 234

7 ibid. p. 240

8 Colvin, op. cit. p. 43

9 ibid. p. 41

10 Otto Skorzeny, *Meine Kommando Unternehmen*, p. 90, Munich 1975

11 Colvin, op. cit. p. 43

12 Brissaud, op. cit. p. 106

13 PRO KV2/173

14 PRO KV2/173

15 Colvin, op. cit. p. 46

16 Allfrey, op. cit. p. 253

17 Buchheit, op. cit. p. 191

18 See Hossbach, *Zwischen Wehrmacht und Hitler 1934-38*, p. 186ff, Hannover 1949; for a translation of the Hossbach memorandum see

'Documents on German Foreign Policy 1918-45', Series D I 29-39

19 Colvin, op. cit. p. 45

20 NC/18/1/1026 30 October 1937

21 CAB 23/90 43 (37) 24 November 1937

22 ibid.

23 Orme Sargent, quoted by Lord Home in *Letters to a Grandson*, p. 37, London 1983

24 Allied interrogation of Colonel-General Jodl, October 1945, text in IfZ

25 See G.E.R. Gedye, *Fallen Bastions*, London 1939

26 Karl Bartz, *die Tragödie der Deutschen Abwehrs*, p. 10ff, Salzburg 1955; Colvin, op. cit. p. 50

27 Padfield, *Himmler*, p. 232ff, London 1995

28 Colvin, op. cit. p. 57

29 ibid. p. 60

30 For the bizarre story of Lord Rothermere and Hohenlohe see Martha Shad, *Hitler's Spionin*, Munich 2002

31 Roberts, *The Holy Fox*, p. 203, London 1991

32 Beck, quoted in Hoehne, op. cit. p. 216ff

33 ibid.

34 Schad, op. cit. p. 38

35 Colvin, op. cit. p. 62

36 Wheeler-Bennett, op. ci.t p. 410

37 ibid.

38 Woodward and Butler, Third Series ii 683-9

39 See Kissinger, *Diplomacy*, p. 821, London 1994

40 Spitzy, op. cit. p. 283

41 ibid. p. 284

42 See Donald Cameron Watt essay 'Churchill and Appeasement' in Blake and Louis, Churchill, London 1993, for another misreading of the Kleist visit

43 Partly quoted in Wheeler-Bennett, op. cit. p. 410

44 Roberts, op. cit. p. 308

45 Cameron Watt, op. cit. p. 206

46 Winston Churchill, *The Gathering Storm*, p. 103, London 1948

47 Wheeler-Bennett, op. cit. p. 410

48 Wheeler-Bennett, op. cit.

49 Henderson, *Failure of a Mission*, p. 147ff, London 1940

50 Bloch, *Ribbentrop*, p. 209, London 2003

51 Rothenfels, *The German Opposition to Hitler*, p. 62, Illinois 1948

52 Home, op. ci.t p. 53

53 A.J.P. Taylor, *Origins of the Second World War*, p. 170f, London 1962

54 Rothenfels, op. cit. p. 263

55 Home, op. cit. p. 54
56 ibid.
57 Roberts, op. cit. p. 203
58 See Colvin, Gisevius, Spitz, Vernon Bartlett, David Astor etc.
59 Spitzy, op. cit. p. 246
60 Home, op. cit. p. 63
61 Wheeler-Bennett, p. 422
62 Harold Nicolson, *Diaries*, 20 September 1938, London
63 David Astor, *Balliol Record* 1982
64 Colvin, op. cit. p. 69
65 Weitz, *Hitler's Banker*, p. 237, London 1999

Chapter Eight

1 Lord Halifax, speech at the RIIA, 29 June 1939
2 Hoehne, op. cit. p. 297
3 Home, op. cit. p. 64
4 Hoehne, op. cit. p. 310ff
5 Julian Amery, *Approach March*, p. 70, London 1973
6 Amery Crosby Kemper lecture op. cit.
7 ibid.
8 Leo Amery Diaries, *The Empire at Bay*, p. 396, 13 August 1935, London 1988. Leo Amery had been one of the first British statesmen to visit Hitler. Amery noted 'he (Hitler) did not waste much time on compliments but got on to high politics at once... on this he talked what seemed to me vigorous commonsense... A bigger man on the whole than I had expected... interesting to see how he shapes... if he lasts.'
9 Deacon, op. cit. p. 171
10 Colvin, op. cit. p. 76
11 Farrago, op. cit. p. 15
12 Cave Brown, *The Secret Servant*, p. 177, New York 1987
13 ibid. p. 144
14 private information A.C.L.
15 Frederick Winterbotham, *The Nazi Connection*, p. 164, London 1978
16 ibid. p. 14
17 Spitzy, op. cit. p. 256ff; also Lamb, op. cit. pp. 110-14 and David Marsh, *History of the Bundesbank*, London 1991
18 Lord Halifax, Chatham House speech, op. cit.
19 G. Etherington-Smith interview, 29 January 2004
20 Winterbotham, op. cit. p. 142
21 Padfield, *Hess*, op. cit. p. 118

22 ibid. p. 119
23 Colvin, op. cit. p. 54
24 ibid. p. 82
25 Horace Wilson, 24 July 1939, quoted Lamb, op. cit. p. 110
26 Lewis Namier, *Diplomatic Prelude*, p. 417ff, London 1948
27 Documents on British Foreign Policy FO 371/39178
28 Colvin, op. cit. p. 84
29 Lahousen, PRO KV2/173
30 Johnson, *Germany's Spies and Saboteurs*, p. 12, New York 1995
31 ibid. p. 76
32 Jebb, memo on Beaverbrook, quoted Lamb op. cit. p. 136
33 Trevor Roper Cornhill magazine op cit
34 Inge Haag, interview 26 March 04
35 Neal Ascherson, *Struggles for Poland*, London 1985
36 Hassell, op. cit. p. 73
37 Tatiana Metternich, *Bericht eines ausgewoenlichen Lebens*, p. 178, Vienna 1978
38 Alexander von Stahlberg, *Die verdammte Pflicht*, p. 313ff, Germany 2002
39 Halder, *Diaries*, London 1998
40 Metternich, op. cit. p. 138
41 Colvin, op.cit. p. 89
42 Private information
43 Colvin, op. cit. p 91
44 Josef Garlinski, *The Swiss Corridor*, p. 84, London 1981

Chapter Nine

1 Schmidt, op. cit. pp. 502-3; also Colvin, op. cit. p. 131
2 Hoehne, op. ci.t p. 384
3 ibid. p. 385
4 Colvin, op. cit. p. 108
5 Abshagen, op. cit. pp. 205-11
6 Colvin, op. cit. p. 110
7 Hoehne, op. cit. pp. 263-9
8 Robert Cooper, *The Breaking of Nations*, p. 21, London 2003
9 Owen Chadwick, *Britain and the Vatican in the Second World War*, p. 98ff, London 1986
10 FO 371/24962/72
11 Chadwick, op. ci.t p. 98
12 Hoehne, op. cit. p. 400ff
13 Interview, Lord Amery, 18 September 1993

14 Churchill, *Their Finest Hour*, p. 576, London 1949

15 ibid. p. 310

16 Colvin, op. ci.t p. 118

17 Stafford, op. cit. p. 189

18 Colvin, op. cit. p. 118

19 ibid.

20 Protze, quoted Colvin, op. cit. p. 119

21 Soltikow, op. cit. p. 6

22 Colvin, op. cit. p. 117

23 ibid.

24 Deacon, op. cit. p. 276

25 Werner Emil Hart, deposition 23 June 1953, IfZ

26 Schmidt, op. cit. p. 500

27 Stille, deposition, IfZ

28 Hart, op. cit.

29 ibid.

30 Hart, op. cit.

31 Schmidt, op. cit. p. 501

32 Hart, op. cit.

33 ibid.

34 This school of diplomacy, as the events of March 2003 at the Security Council underlined, regrettably has begun to enjoy something of a revival in certain parts of the 'diplomatic' corps of the Anglo-Saxon nations

35 Schmidt, op. cit. p. 502

36 Stafford, op. cit. p. 202ff

37 WSC to Godfrey, ADM 223/490

38 Stafford, op. cit. p. 203

Chapter Ten

1 Conversation, Julian Amery, 19 Sepember 1993

2 ibid.

3 Amery, *Approach March*, p. 191

4 See Callum Macdonald, *The Killing of Obergrüppen-Führer Reinhard Heydrich*, London 1989

5 Wehrmacht Diary, IfZ

6 Amery, op. cit. p. 172

7 Michael Bloch, *Ribbentrop*, p. 340, London 2003

8 DGFP D/XI no. 325

9 Hart, op. cit.

10 Keitel, quoted by Brissaud, op. cit. p. 218

11 Brissaud, op. cit. p. 232

12 Jodl, quoted by Brissaud, p. 233

13 Cecil Parrott, *Memoirs*, London 1978

14 Amery, op. cit. p. 177

15 von Hassell, op. cit. p. 165

16 Abwehr Diary, IfZ

17 Amery Archive, Churchill College

18 Leo Amery, *Diaries*, 26-27 March 1941

19 D.C. Poole, 'Light on Nazi Foreign Policy', Foreign Affairs XXV, October 1946

20 Hassell, op. cit. p. 162

21 ibid. p. 156

22 Padfield, *Hess*, chapter 30

23 *Nordwestdeutsche Hefte*, 2 January 1947, quoting SS report on 20 July by Obersturmbahnführer Kiesel

24 Harold Nicolson, op. cit. 2 March 1941

25 According to Goredetsky, *Grand Illusion*, London 1995, Churchill was thinking of replacing Eden at the Foreign Office. See also 'Documenti Diplomatici 1940' Volume V, Lequio to Miny

26 Cave Brown, *Treason in the Blood*, op. cit. chapter 8, for Philby's views of circles in London 'still dickering with the Germans'

27 Padfield, *Hess*, op. cit. chapter 8, and Picknett, Prince and Prior, *Double Standards*, London 2003

28 Dragonoff, 13 December 1940, IfZ

29 IfZ 1084153 28 April 1941 1715-1745

30 PRO Prem 3 434/7 Sir A Clark Kerr and Mr Birse

31 Padfield, *Hess*, op. cit. p. 363

32 ibid.

33 von Hassell, op. cit. February 1941 entries

34 IfZ 1084153 28 April 1941 1715-1745

35 IfZ 1085/53

36 Stuart Smith to Tittmann, PRO HW14/10

37 Colvin, op. cit. p. 136

38 Liddell Hart, *The Other Side of the Hill*, p. 174ff, London 1948

39 PRO FO 371 26905/C4161

40 Schweinitz, quoted by Colvin, op. cit. p. 137

41 E. O'Halpin, 'Intelligence and National Security', Volume 17 no 3

42 Weiszäcker, 4 April 1941, IfZ

43 Canaris, quoted by Brissaud, op. cit. p. 241

44 ibid.

45 ibid. p. 245

46 von Hassell, op. cit.4 June

Chapter Eleven

1 Spitzy, op. cit. p. 328

2 Reinicke, quoted by Brissaud, op. ci.t

3 Nicolson, quoted in Gorodetsky, *Stafford Cripps Mission to Moscow*, p. 118ff, Cambridge 1984

4 Milch, *Diaries*, 29 March 1946

5 Macdonald, op. ci.t p. 6; also Hellmut G. Haasis, *Tod in Prag*, Hamburg 2002

6 See *Heydrich Schlusselfigur des Dritten Reiches*, Dusseldorf 1972

7 Pieckenbrock, quoted by Brissaud, op. cit.

8 Johnson, op. cit. chapter 6

9 Macdonald, op. cit. p. 108ff

10 See Gehlen, op. cit.

11 Macdonald, op. cit. p. 109ff

12 Abendschoen, quoted by Brissaud, op. ci. P. 256

13 ibid. p. 257

14 ibid p. 258

15 ibid. p. 264

16 Garlinski, op. cit. p. 88ff

17 private information

18 See chapter 14

19 Deacon, op. cit. p. 282

20 N.E. 14 May 1993

21 ibid.

22 See chapter 7

23 Dusko Popov, *Spy Counter Spy*, London 1957

24 I am indebted to the late Nicholas Elliot for confirming Menzies' authorship of the 'oblique tribute'

25 See chapter 10, p. 216

26 Moravets, quoted by Brissaud, op. cit.

27 ibid.

28 Macdonald, op. cit. p. 155

29 Brissaud, op. cit. p. 272

30 ibid.

31 ibid.

32 ibid. p. 273

33 private information

34 Spitzy, op. cit. p. 328

35 Haasis, op. cit. p 132

Chapter Twelve

1 JA to author, 14 March 1993

2 Cave Brown, *Treason in the Blood*, op. cit. chapter 9

3 private information

4 Cave Brown, op. cit. p. 248

5 Herman Friedhoff, *Requiem for the Resistance*, London 1988

6 Cave Brown, op. cit. p. 248

7 ibid. p. 247

8 Fleischauer, op. cit. p. 56

9 Trevor Roper, *The Philby Affair*, p. 101, 1968

10 See chapter 11

11 Trevor Roper, op. cit. p. 103ff

12 Cave Brown, op. cit. p. 311

13 See chapter 6

14 See McCormack, op. cit.

15 ibid.

16 Sir Alexander Cadogan, *Diaries*, 25 March, PRO FO 800/293-4

17 Deacon, op. cit. p. 274

18 Colvin, op. cit. p. 160ff

19 Hart, op. cit. Ifz

20 Deacon, op. cit. p. 282

21 Cave Brown, *Secret Servant*, op. cit. p. 6ff

22 Colvin, op. cit. p. 147

23 Cave Brown, *Treason in the Blood*, op. cit.

24 Gorodetsky, *Sir Stafford Cripps*, op. cit. p. 286ff

25 Abshagen, op. cit. p. 329

26 Cave Brown, *Secret Servant*, op. cit. p. 452

27 ibid.

28 For a brief outline account see Cave Brown, op. cit.

29 Prem 4/100/8

30 See Deacon, op. cit.

31 NA HW 1/933

32 HW 1/1659 Turkish Ambassador Tokyo to FM Angora 2 May 1943

33 IfZ SD Berichten, November 1942

34 IZMPAA4 Nr 0014 IF 23.3.42

35 Fleischauer, op. cit. chapter 4

36 IfZ SD op. cit. November – August 1943

37 IfZ Spitzy 14 February 1978

38 Fleischauer, op. cit. chapter 4, and IfZ SD Berichten

39 PAA AA 23 January 1943

40 HW1/1659

41 Stahlberg, op. cit. p. 315

42 ibid.

43 Manstein/Fuchs, *Manstein: Soldat im 20ten jahrhundert Militarisch-politische Nachlese*, Munich 1981

44 *Svenska Dagblatt*, 30 April 1943

45 Gorodetsky, op. cit. p. 285

46 Stahlberg, op. cit. pp.320-55

47 IfZ Spitzy papers (Besymin 14 February 1978)

48 NA HWI/1320

49 private information

50 see Skorzeny, op. cit.

51 Brissaud, op. cit. chapter 19

52 see Michael Beschloss, *The Conquerors*, pp. 12–19 New York 2002

Chapter Thirteen

1 Canaris to Lahousen, quoted by Colvin, op. cit. p. 162
2 Colvin, op. cit. p 163
3 ibid.
4 Lamb, op. cit. p. 223
5 Beschloss, op. cit. p. 13ff
6 Lamb, op. cit. p. 222ff
7 Beschloss, op. cit. p. 13
8 Garlinski, op. cit. p. 129
9 Bentinck, quoted by Lamb, op. cit. p. 223
10 Knightley, *The Master Spy*, pp. 105-6
11 Lahousen interrogation, KVetc. op. cit.
12 Spitzy, op. cit. p. 348
13 Spitzy interview with Professor Deutsch, 23 May 1970, IfZ
14 Canaris quoted by Abshagen, Brissaud op. cit.
15 See Colvin, op. cit. p. 161
16 Leverkuen, quoted by Colvin, op. cit. p. 181
17 ibid.
18 OSS dispatch, 24 February 1944, Bern IN-3659
19 von Papen 'Heroes Day Speech', February 1943, quoted by Leverkuen in *German Military Intelligence*, op. cit.
20 ibid. p. 24
21 private information
22 OSS RG 266/108A
23 Leverkuen, op. cit. p. 24ff
24 Lamb, op. cit. p. 224
25 WSC, 14 August 1943, quoted by Lamb
26 K. Sendtner, Die *Deutsche Militäropposition im ersten Kriegsjahr publ.in die Vollmacht des Wissens*, pp. 470-72, Munich 1956. See also Harald Volcke, *Albrecht von Kessel*, pp. 268-78, Freiburg 2001
27 Chadwick, op. cit. p. 256ff
28 ibid.
29 Ciano, *Diaries*, 5th edition, p. 232, 1948
30 Kessel, quoted by Volcke, op. cit. p. 268ff
31 Goebbels, *Diaries*, 26 July 1943
32 Felix Gilbert, *Hitler Directs his War*, Oxford 1950
33 Interview with Karl Wolff, *Die Welt*, 6 March 1972
34 Chadwick, op. cit. p. 275
35 Adolph Berle, Memorandum to Cordell Hull, September 1941, re. conversation with Ralph Stevenson, quoted in the *Guardian* 30 June 1958

Chapter Fourteen

1 Leverkuen, op. cit. p. 209
2 The bomb of British design was thwarted by arctic flying temperatures
3 ADSS 7,439 and 458
4 Lamb, op. cit. p. 252
5 Private information
6 See Colvin, op. cit. pp. 165 ff
7 Deacon, op. cit. p 374
8 See Amé interview, *Corriere della Sera*, 16 April 1980
9 ibid.
10 Amé, quoted by Brissaud, op. cit.
11 see Schellenberg, *Memoiren*, Cologne 1956
12 Cave Brown, *Treason in the Blood*, op. cit. p. 312ff
13 private information
14 Mathias Wegner, *Ein weites Herz*, p. 128ff, Munich
15 Brissaud, op. cit. p. 315ff
16 ibid. p. 318
17 Cave Brown *Bodyguard of Lies*, p. 595, New York 1976
18 ibid. p. 599
19 ibid.
20 Brissaud, op. cit. p. 321
21 Schellenberg, op. cit. p. 204ff
22 Fischerhuette Archiv Toplitzsee Styria Austria
23 Mallet PRO 15 .12. 1944 FO 371/35178; Prem 3/197/1
24 Protze, quoted by Colvin, op. cit.
25 Padfield, p. 58ff, op. cit.
26 Testimony, Walther Huppenkothen, Nuremberg IWT
27 This account is taken mostly from Bartz, op. cit.
28 Mueller quoting Rattenhuber, IfZ
29 Lunding, quoted by Colvin, op. cit. p. 210
30 see IHT 16 October 1950
31 Colvin, op. cit. p. 218

Conclusion

1 Gehlen op. cit.
2 Robert Skidelsky, *John Maynard Keynes*, p. 51, London 1991
3 Leverkuen, op. cit. p. 198
4 Sothebys catalogue of Philby's papers, July 1994
5 Lamb, op. cit. p. 286
6 FO 371/391/37

SELECTED BIBLIOGRAPHY

Private Papers

Amery Papers Churchill College, Cambridge

Banfield Papers Trieste

Cadogan Diaries Churchill College, Cambridge

Canaris Papers Munich

Chamberlain Papers University of Birmingham

German Foreign Ministry Archive IfZ Munich

German Military Archive Freiburg im Breisgau

Hoffmann Archives Chile

National Archives Washington

National Archives Kew

Reinhard Spitzy Correspondence IfZ Munich

SD Berichten IfZ Munich

Stille Deposition IfZ Munich

Troubridge Diaries IWM

Vatican Archives Rome

Vermeheren Archive

Werner Hart Papers IfZ Munich

Published Sources

Abshagen, Karl Heinz, Canaris, Stuttgart 1948

Aid, Matthew M., 'Stella Polaris and the Secret Code Battle in Post-War Europe' in *Intelligence and National Security*, Vol. 17, no. 3, 2002

Allfrey, Anthony, *Man of Arms*, London 1989

Amery, Julian, *Memories of Churchill and How He Would Have Seen the World Today*, London 1994

Amery, Leo, *Diaries*, (ed. John Barnes and David Nicholson), London 1988

Bartz, Karl, *Die Tragödie der Deutschen Abwehr*, Salzburg 1955

Beesly, Patrick, *Room 40*, London 1982

Beesly, Patrick, *Very Special Admiral*, London 1980

Beesly, Patrick, *Very Special Intelligence*, London 1977

Bennett, Geoffrey, *Coronel and the Falklands*, London 1962

Beschloss, Michael, *The Conquerors*, New York 2002

Betts, Richard K., *Paradoxes of Strategic Intelligence*, New York 2003

Bielenberg, Christabel, *The Past is Myself*, London 1968

Blake, Robert and Roger, Louis, *Churchill*, Oxford 1993

Bloch, Michael, *Ribbentrop*, London 2003

Brissaud, André, *Canaris*, Paris 1970

Buchheit, Gert, *Der Deutsche Geheimdienst*, Munich 1966

Burns, Emile, *Karl Liebknecht*, Paris 1934

Cave Brown, Anthony, *Bodyguard of Lies*, New York, 1976

Cave Brown, Anthony, *The Secret Servant*, New York 1987

Cave Brown, Anthony, *Treason in the Blood*, New York 1994

Chadwick, Owen, *Britain and the Vatican in the Second World War*, Oxford 1985

Charmley, John, *Chamberlain and the Lost Peace*, London 1989

Churchill, Winston S., *The Second World War*:

  I: *The Gathering Storm*, London 1948

  II: *Their Finest Hour*, London 1949

  III: *The Grand Alliance*, London 1950

  IV: *The Hinge of Fate*, London 1951

  V: *Closing the Ring*, London 1952

  VI: *Triumph and Tragedy*, London 1954

Colvin, Ian, *Chief of Intelligence*, London 1951

Colvin, Ian, *Flight 777*, London 1957

Colvin, Ian, *The Chamberlain Cabinet*, London 1971

Colvin, Ian, *Vansittart in Office*, London 1965

Cooper, Robert, *The Breaking of Nations*, London 2003

Davidson, Edward and Manning, Dale, *Chronology of World War Two*, London 1999

Deacon, Richard, *A History of the British Secret Service*, London 1969

Farago, Ladislas, *The Game of the Foxes*, New York 1971

Fest, Joachim, *Hitler*, Frankfurt 1973

Gardner, Lloyd C., *Spheres of Influence*, Chicago 1993

Garlinski, Jozef, *The Swiss Corridor*, London 1981

Gehlen, Reinhard, *Der Dienst*, Berg 1971

Gisevius, Hans Bernd, *Bis zum Bitteren Ende*, Darmstadt 1947

Goredetsky, Gabriel, *Sir Stafford Cripps: Mission to Moscow 1940-42*, Cambridge 1984

Gorodetsky, Gabriel, *Grand Illusion: Stalin and the German Invasion of Russsia*, London 1995

Gottlieb, W. W., *Studies in Secret Diplomacy During the First World War*, London 1957

Griffiths, Richard, *Fellow Travellers of the Right*, London 1980

Guasp, Pere Ferrer, *Juan March*, Palma Mallorca 2001

Haasis, Hellmut, *Tod in Prag*, Hamburg 2002

Höhne, Heinz, *Canaris*, Hamburg 1976

Home, Lord, *Letters to a Grandson*, London 1983

Johnson, David, *Germany's Spies and Saboteurs*, New York 1998

Keegan, John, *The Second World War*, London 1989

Kirkpatrick, Ivone, *Inner Circle*, London 1959

Kissinger, Henry, *Diplomacy*, London 1994

Lamb, Richard, *The Ghosts of Peace*, London 1987

Leverkuehn, Paul, *German Military Intelligence*, London 1954

Lewinsohn, Richard, *The Mystery Man of Europe*, Philadelphia 1929

Liddell Hart, B. H., *The Other Side of the Hill*, London 1948

Lukacs, John, *Five Days in London*, London 1999

Masterman, J. C., *The Double-Cross System in the War of 1939-1945*, London 1972

McCormick, Donald, *A Life of Ian Fleming*, London 1978

Metternich, Tatiana, *Tatiana: Five Passports in a Shifting Europe*, London 1976

Montague, Ewen, *The Man Who Never Was*, London 1953

Namier, Lewis, *Diplomatic Prelude*, London 1948

Noel-Baker, Philip, *The Private Manufacture of Armaments*, London 1936

Padfield, Peter, *Hess*, London 1991

Padfield, Peter, *Himmler*, London 1990

Payne Best, Capt. S., *The Venlo Incident*, London 1952

Philby, Kim, *My Silent War*, New York 1968

Picknett, Lynn, Prince, Clive and Prior, Stephen, *Double Standards*, London 2001

Popov, Dushko, *Spy Counter Spy*, London 1974

Ripley, Tim, *German Special Forces in World War II*, London 2004

Roberts, Andrew, *The Holy Fox*, London 1991

Schad, Martha, *Hitlers Spionin*, Munich 2002

Schellenberg, Walter, *Handbook for the Invasion of Britain*, republished London 2000

Schellenberg, Walter, *Memoirs*, London 1956

Schmidt, Paul, *Statist auf Diplomatischer Buhne 1923-1945*, Bonn 1949

Skidelsky, Robert, *John Maynard Keynes*, Volume III, London 2000

Skorzeny, Otto, *Meine Kommando Unternehmen*, Munich 1993

Smith,Michael, *Foley:The Spy Who Saved 10,000 Jews*, London 1999

Spitzy, Reinhard, *How We Squandered the Reich*, London 1997

Stafford, David, *Churchill and Secret Service*, London 1997

Stahlberg, Alexander, *Die Verdammte Pflicht*, Munich 2002

Taylor, A. J. P., *The Origins of the Second World War*, London 1962

Thyssen, Fritz, *I Paid Hitler*, London 1941

Vocke, Harald, *Albrecht von Kessel*, Freiburg 2001

Von Hassell, Ulrich, *The Von Hassell Diaries 1938-1944*, London 1948

Wegner, Matthias, *Ein Weites Herz*, Munich 2003

Weitz, John, *Hitler's Banker*, London 1999

Weizsäcker, Ernst von, *Erinnerungen*, Munich 1950

Wheeler-Bennett, John, *The Nemesis of Power*, London 1954

Wiedemann, Friedrich, *Der Mann der Feldherr Werden*, Kettwig 1964

Winterbotham, Frederick William, *The Nazi Connection*, London 1978

INDEX